T0314985

The Econometric Analysis of Recurrent Events in Macroeconomics and Finance

THE ECONOMETRIC AND TINBERGEN INSTITUTES LECTURES

Series Editors
Herman K. van Dijk and Philip Hans Franses
The Econometric Institute,
Erasmus University Rotterdam

The Econometric and Tinbergen Institutes Lectures series is a joint project of Princeton University Press and the Econometric Institute at Erasmus University Rotterdam. This series collects the lectures of leading researchers which they have given at the Econometric Institute for an audience of academics and students. The lectures are at a high academic level and deal with topics that have important policy implications. The series covers a wide range of topics in econometrics. It is not confined to any one area or sub-discipline. The Econometric Institute is the leading research center in econometrics and management science in the Netherlands. The Institute was founded in 1956 by Jan Tinbergen and Henri Theil, with Theil being its first director. The Institute has received worldwide recognition with an advanced training program for various degrees in econometrics.

Other books in this series include

Anticipating Correlations: A New Paradigm for Risk Management by Robert Engle

Complete and Incomplete Econometric Models by John Geweke

Social Choice with Partial Knowledge of Treatment Response by Charles F. Manski

Yield Curve Modeling and Forecasting: The Dynamic Nelson-Siegel Approach by Francis X. Diebold and Glenn D. Rudebusch

Bayesian Non- and Semi-parametric Methods and Applications by Peter E. Rossi

Bayesian Estimation of DSGE Models by Edward P. Herbst and Frank Schorfheide

The Econometric Analysis of Recurrent Events in Macroeconomics and Finance

Don Harding and Adrian Pagan

Princeton University Press
Princeton and Oxford

press.princeton.edu

Jacket art courtesy of Shutterstock
Jacket design by Rosalind Flower

All Rights Reserved

ISBN: 978-0-691-16708-4
Library of Congress Control Number: 2015958412

British Library Cataloging-in-Publication Data is available

This book has been composed in Kerkis

Printed on acid-free paper. ∞

Typeset by Nova Techset Pvt Ltd, Bangalore, India
Printed in the United States of America

10 9 8 7 6 5 4 3 2 1

Contents

Series Editors' Introduction

The Econometric and Tinbergen Institutes Lectures series deals with topics in econometrics with important policy implications. The lectures cover a wide range of topics and are not confined to any one area or sub-discipline. Leading international scientists in the fields of econometrics in which applications play a major role are invited to give three-day lectures on a topic to which they have contributed significantly.

Recurrent events come in many forms ranging from business and financial cycles to crises, and they occur in almost all economic systems whether they are capitalist or more centrally planned or whether they are developed or less developed. Dating business-cycle features is crucial for accurate forecasting and optimal policy analysis.

The present book written by Don Harding and Adrian Pagan aims and succeeds at such a description. At the most basic level, recurrent events are summarized by binary indicators that are constructed either directly from data or indirectly by models. The book is fully transparent in both analytical and descriptive approaches to these topics. It provides excellent tools for detailed empirical analysis of many business cycle features which users themselves can explore.

All results presented are novel and unquestionably useful for academic researchers as well as professionals in the international banking and government sectors.

The editors of the series are indebted to the Tinbergen Institute for continued support.

Herman K. van Dijk and Philip Hans Franses
Econometric and Tinbergen Institutes
Erasmus School of Economics

Preface

In 1996 we started to discuss a literature that had a long history regarding business cycles. It traced back to work at the National Bureau of Economics Research (NBER), particularly that by Burns and Mitchell (1946). Our interest in the literature came from the fact that one of us had done some previous analysis of this phenomenon, while the other had a colleague—Ernst Boehm—who was part of an international group led by Geoffrey Moore and Victor Zarnovitz which continued to develop and employ Burns and Mitchell's methods of studying macroeconomic movements. We were struck by the fact that although there was a strong interest by practitioners in these turning point-based methods, in academia this was much less true, and the approach had largely been discarded. The reason seemed to reside in a belief that their method was partly judgmental, lacked precision, and could not be formalized and captured in a statistical framework. It seemed to us important to reexamine this contention, and to see whether Burns and Mitchell's work could be given a modern statistical foundation. One thing that convinced us that this was possible was the existence of a computer program that had been developed by Gerhard Bry and Charlotte Boschan (BB) to encapsulate part of Burns and Mitchell's methods in an algorithmic form. Given such a form, it seemed plausible that a statistical framework could be constructed to accompany it.

One problem in progressing further was that the BB algorithm was very complex, owing to the many smoothing operations that were performed on the data. Looking at the code it struck us that despite all the smoothing rounds, the algorithm eventually returned to the original data in its final iterations. This led us to propose a much simpler algorithm for quarterly data that we subsequently called BBQ; one that could be analyzed with mathematical tools much more easily. To be sure there are always costs in such simplification, but we argued that these were compensated for by a greater understanding of what turning point detection involves. Our research over the past 15 years has been focused on extending this analysis so as to handle multiple time series and a variety of other issues, such as predicting recessions.

There have been many applications of BBQ, and a large literature has emerged on its use. For this reason we thought it was time to draw together the material and comment on various strands of the work. The Tinbergen lectures gave us this opportunity. We entitled them as dealing with recurrent events, a much broader topic than cycles, but one that recognizes that turning points can occur in many types of series—asset prices, volatility, interest rates, unemployment rates, and so on—and the methods of analysis are common to them all.

The main aim of the lectures was to provide a framework that could synthesize much of what was in the literature. A key idea was that Burns and Mitchell used what we call prescribed rules for finding turning points. We detail this concept and show that a popular alternative methodology of using a model of the series to locate its turning points can be thought of in this way. In the lectures we also argue for the use of Burns and Mitchell's methods to cast light on the ability of popular models to capture the effects of episodes in history involving expansions and contractions, something that existing techniques do not effectively address. The new methods are highly useful adjuncts to traditional approaches and often provide a novel perspective on questions such as whether we can predict recessions.

The literature analyzing recurrent events is growing rapidly and our lectures could not cover all of the material. Our aim is to provide a broad perspective on the methods rather than a detailed account of specific applications.

Over the years we have given short courses on subsets of the topics covered in these lectures. We thank the International Monetary Fund, Magyar Nemetzi Bank, the Econometric Institute at Erasmus University, and CREATES at Aarhus University, as well as participants of those courses. But ultimately our greatest debt is to the Tinbergen Institute, particularly to Herman van Dijk, for enabling us to pull these lectures together.

We dedicate this book to the memory of Ernst Boehm, who impressed us with his trenchant defense of the Burns and Mitchell method and was generous with his time in explaining the intricacies of the method to colleagues.

The Econometric Analysis of Recurrent Events in Macroeconomics and Finance

Chapter 1

Overview

1.1 Introduction

There are many events that recur. These are evident either directly in time series or through their effects on economic outcomes. Examples would be business and financial cycles, crises, high and low levels of volatility and sentiment, seasonal patterns, floods and droughts, and high and low levels of temperature. These differ in many ways, but a principal one concerns their predictability based on a limited information set that includes only calendar time. Events such as seasonal patterns are highly predictable on the basis of calendar time and are therefore said to be *periodic* events. Of course, even if the event is periodic, its effects on economic outcomes may not be predictable, so we are ascribing predictability to the recurrent event itself. Other events are not strictly predictable but close to it. Thus, on a monthly or quarterly frequency, there are limits on the times that winter and summer can occur, and therefore these are mostly treated as being periodic. This leaves recurrent events such as the business cycle. These cannot be predicted with high probability conditional on just calendar time, leading them to be classified as *nonperiodic*. Such events are the subject of these lectures.

We might ask why there has always been interest in recurrent events such as the contraction and expansion *phases* of the business cycle. By focusing on the phases, one has moved from a comprehensive account of economic outcomes to a concise summary of them. In doing so, we might miss some feature that would be apparent from a detailed examination of the series. Of course this is no different to presenting the mean and variance of a series (and perhaps a measure of skewness) rather than either the series itself or its density function. Any cut of the data may be particularly interesting or informative to us and often becomes a key way of speaking about economic outcomes. In many ways this is true of the business cycle, where a great deal of attention is paid to the possibility and nature of a recession.

Often indicators of the events that are assembled concerning them represent a compression of information, and this can aid communication, just as citing a mean or a variance may suffice when talking about certain outcomes. Humans seem to be in favor of compressing information into manageable forms. It is also the case that in some instances the recurrent events we are looking at represent extreme outcomes, for example, crises, and a great deal of attention gets paid to such extremes owing to the potential for large losses when they occur.

There are three key issues we will need to deal with when discussing recurrent events. These are:

1. The description of the event via a set of statistics.
2. The uses that can be made of these statistics.
3. The possibility of predicting these events, in particular by using information sets that contain more information than just calendar time.

It pays to consider the basic issues involving recurrent events in the context of a simple example, and that is the modus operandi of this overview chapter. In later chapters modifications need to be made to derive more informative descriptions of events than are presented in this chapter, and these lead to additional complexities that need to be dealt with. But many of the fundamental issues are evident in the simple examples we work with here.

1.2 Describing the Events

To summarize the events we will need some *rules* that map the data we observe into a set of indicators that can then be used to construct statistics which describe the recurrent event in a succinct way. Within the literature there are two types of rules—those that are *prescribed* and those that are *model based.* We therefore consider each of these in turn, utilizing some simple examples.

1.2.1 Prescribed Rules

Consider first a *business cycle* in the level of economic activity. A business cycle involves periods of expansions and contractions in the *level* of economic activity.[1] If one viewed a graph of the level of economic activity one would see that a contraction begins when the activity reaches a *peak,* while an expansion begins with a *trough.* These *turning points* then provide a description of the business cycle. By their nature we are led to describe them by locating local maxima and minima in a series.

By far the simplest rule that would locate these features in a series y_t (the log of the level of economic activity Y_t) would be that a peak occurs at t if $y_{t-1} < y_t$ <u>and</u> $y_{t+1} < y_t$, while a trough is signaled if $y_{t-1} > y_t$ <u>and</u> $y_{t+1} > y_t$. Because log is a monotonic operation, the peaks and troughs in Y_t are the same as in y_t. Moreover, instead of using y_t to define a peak, we could use Δy_t, and say that a peak occurs at t if $\Delta y_t > 0$ <u>and</u> $\Delta y_{t+1} < 0$. In this special case an expansion happens in $t+1$ if $\Delta y_{t+1} > 0$, that is, there is positive growth in Y_t at $t+1$. In the same way a contraction at $t+1$ would involve negative growth ($\Delta y_{t+1} < 0$). With such rules there is a one-to-one relationship in the sample path between peaks and troughs and expansions and contractions. This is an example of what we refer to as a *prescribed rule.* It maps data on growth rates into cycle phases and points to the need to consider the nature of the data generating process (DGP) of Δy_t when assessing the likelihood of a peak or trough.

---

[1]That it is about the level of activity is clear from Zarnowitz and Ozyildirium (2006) who say "early studies which defined business cycles as sequences of expansions and contractions in a large array of series representing the levels of total output, employment."

Suppose therefore that Δy_t has the structure

$$\Delta y_t = \mu + \sigma \varepsilon_t, \tag{1.1}$$

where ε_t is normally and independently distributed with expected value of zero and variance of unity. Our abbreviation for this will be $n.i.d.(0, 1)$. Then we would have a recession in t if $\Delta y_t < 0$ and an expansion if $\Delta y_t > 0$. Hence, defining the binary variable S_t as being unity in expansions and zero in contractions, we would have $S_t = 1(\Delta y_t > 0)$, where $1(\cdot)$ has the value unity when $\Delta y_t > 0$, and zero when $\Delta y_t < 0$.[2] The binary variable S_t then summarizes when expansions and contractions occur, and we refer to it as the *cycle* in y_t. Given the model for Δy_t in (1.1) it is clear that

$$
\begin{aligned}
\Pr(S_t = 0) &= \Pr[\Delta y_t < 0] \\
&= \Pr\left[\varepsilon_t < -\frac{\mu}{\sigma}\right] \\
&= \Phi\left(-\frac{\mu}{\sigma}\right),
\end{aligned}
$$

where Φ is the c.d.f. of an $N(0, 1)$ random variable. Consequently, the probability of a recession will depend on the mean growth rate (μ) of Δy_t and its volatility σ.

In the foregoing, a cycle is a binary series which shows when contractions and expansions occur. Thus there is no continuous variable y_t' that is a "cycle," although we might try to construct such a series from y_t so that it had the same peaks and troughs as in y_t. In that instance y_t' would generally be called a *coincident indicator*. Of course it may not be possible to find a y_t' that has this property, and often coincident indicators are constructed so that their turning points are as close as possible to those in y_t, leading to the need to define some metric for measuring "closeness."

Occasionally, interest focuses not on (say) peaks and troughs in the level of the series but on whether variables such as confidence or volatility exceed a particular level. For

---

[2]As Δy_t is continuous in (1.1) we don't need to be concerned about how to deal with $\Delta y_t = 0$. If one is working with data where $\Pr(\Delta y_t = 0) > 0$ then we could define S_t as unity if $\Delta y_t \leq 0$.

example, Bloom (2009) and Caggiano et al. (2014) construct a dummy variable that takes the value 1 when a measure of financial market volatility (v_t) exceeds a critical level. The specific rule employed by the latter is $\xi_t = 1\,(v_t > 1.65\sigma)$, where σ is the standard deviation of v_t. It is clear that this also involves the construction of a binary random variable (ξ_t) based on an underlying variable v_t through a rule, after which ξ_t can be analyzed or used. As stated, ξ_t would be an "exceedance" measure, and these are very popular in studies involving financial contagion.

In history there have been many ways to describe recurrent events in some succinct way. In Chapter 2 we look at three key ways of describing the "ups and downs" of an economy. These involve oscillations, fluctuations, and cycles. Each has a different way of describing the phenomenon being investigated and summarizing it. These vary depending on the frequency of the data one is working with. Moreover, often many series rather than a single one are used to describe the recurrent pattern. This raises some extra compression issues which will be examined in Chapter 3, leaving Chapter 2 to engage in a comparative study of the relationships between oscillations, fluctuations, and cycles.

1.2.2 Model-Based Rules

It is clear that the turning points in y_t found using any prescribed rule will depend on the nature of Δy_t. For this reason it is probably not surprising that a literature has evolved in which a model is assumed for Δy_t that depends in some way on *regimes*. When there are just two regimes, they can be represented by a binary variable ξ_t. To capture the flavor of these models, assume there that are just two regimes, with the model for Δy_t being a mixture of two normals

$$\Delta y_t = \xi_t N(\mu_1, \sigma^2) + (1 - \xi_t)N(\mu_0, \sigma^2). \qquad (1.2)$$

Thus the first regime has a growth rate of μ_0 while the second is μ_1. Then when $\xi_t = 1$ is realized Δy_t would be drawn from an $N(\mu_1, \sigma^2)$ density, whereas if $\xi_t = 0$ is realized, Δy_t would be drawn from an $N(\mu_0, \sigma^2)$ density. In comparison with the model (1.1) where Δy_t is $N(\mu, \sigma^2)$, the *switching model* (1.2) is non-normal with fatter tails.

We might then ask what the probability of observing $\xi_t = 0$ would be given a *realization* of y_t equal to y_t^*? As Hamilton (2011) notes we would have the following probabilities for this model.

$$\Pr(\xi_t = 0, \Delta y_t) = N(\mu_0, \sigma^2) \Pr(\xi_t = 0) \tag{1.3}$$

$$\Pr(\xi_t = 0|\Delta y_t) = \frac{\Pr(\xi_t = 0, \Delta y_t)}{\Pr(\xi_t = 0, \Delta y_t) + \Pr(\xi_t = 1, \Delta y_t)} \tag{1.4}$$

Now, given an unconditional probability of π_0 for the event $\xi_t = 0$, the numerator of (1.4) would be $N(\mu_0, \sigma^2)\pi_0$, while the denominator will be the density for Δy_t. The latter is the following combination of normals:

$$N(\mu_0, \sigma^2)\pi_0 + N(\mu_1, \sigma^2)(1 - \pi_0). \tag{1.5}$$

Once the values for the parameters in each regime are specified, as well as the unconditional probability for $\xi_t = 0$, we can describe what the densities would be at a value for Δy_t of Δy_t^*, and so can compute a value for $\Pr(\xi_t = 0|\Delta y_t)$ from (1.4). In the event that $\mu_0 = \mu_1$, $\Pr(\xi_t = 0|\Delta y_t = \Delta y_t^*)$ would be .5.

Adding on a restriction that $\mu_1 > \mu_0$ would mean that the regimes could be characterized as involving low and high growth rates. Moreover, if one had observed a large positive value for Δy_t^*, it would most likely indicate that $\xi_t = 1$ had been realized at t, whereas negative values would imply that $\xi_t = 0$. Now while this indicates which growth regime might hold, it doesn't describe whether one is an expansion or a recession at time t. To produce the requisite mapping between regimes and business cycle phases researchers need to *define a new binary variable* ζ_t taking the value unity in expansions and zero in contractions. A rule that does this is to set $\zeta_t = 1$ if $\Pr(\xi_t = 1|\Delta y_t^*)$ exceeds some prescribed value c—say $c = .5$. Thus the indicator of expansions and contractions would be $\zeta_t = 1[\Pr(\xi_t = 1|\Delta y_t^*) - c]$ making it clear that although it is tempting to think of the regime variables ξ_t as expansions and contractions (and often this is the loose terminology that is adopted), it is ζ_t that capture those phases and not ξ_t. As we will see in a number of chapters, the realizations of ξ_t and ζ_t can be very different, so it is easy to make mistakes by conflating them.

This regime-switching model is interesting. The parameters to be estimated are μ_j, σ^2, and π_0. This means four parameters, so we need to use four moments of Δy_t to estimate them, that is, more than just the mean and variance are required. One always needs to ask about how many moments are needed for estimation of the parameters of any regime-switching model and what would they be? It is also clear that this model produces a *rule* for determining what ζ_t is. It takes data on Δy_t (Δy_t^*) and elicits a decision about whether ζ_t is unity or zero by computing $\Pr(\xi_t = 1 | \Delta y_t = \Delta y_t^*)$ and then comparing it to the value of c. Because the probability, and hence the rule, comes from a model of Δy_t, we refer to it as a *model-based rule*. It is clear from the simple example that the rule is a nonlinear function of the data and depends on more than the sign of Δy_t^*, all that was used by the prescribed rule when defining S_t. Thus there may be differences between the S_t coming from prescribed rules and the ζ_t coming from model-based rules, and a section of Chapter 4 looks at this.

An estimation problem occurs with this model. From (1.5) the log likelihood for realizations $\{\Delta y_t^*\}_{t=1}^T$ will be

$$L = \sum_{t=1}^{T} \log[\phi_{0t}\pi_0 + \phi_{1t}(1 - \pi_0)],$$

where $\phi_{jt} = \frac{1}{\sqrt{2\pi}\sigma} \exp(-\frac{1}{2\sigma^2}(\Delta y_t^* - \mu_j)^2)$. First, the likelihood is unbounded. As Kiefer (1978) notes this can be shown by setting $\mu_1 = \Delta y_1^*$ (say) and then letting $\sigma_1^2 \to 0$. This means one has to look for interior values of the parameters that set the first-order conditions to zero, that is, to find a local rather than global maxima for L. Second, consider setting $\mu_0 = 1, \mu_1 = 2, \pi_0 = .4, \pi_1 = 1 - \pi_0 = .6, \sigma = 1$, and using these to evaluate the likelihood. By inspection of the last, switching the parameter values for the regimes to $\mu_1 = 1, \mu_0 = 2$, $\pi_0 = .6, \pi_1 = .4, \sigma = 1$ will produce exactly the same value of the likelihood, that is, there are multiple maxima in L. This is what is referred to as the "labeling problem," since the regimes can be interchanged without changing the likelihood, leading to multiple maxima in L. Because such a phenomenon can create numerical problems, some way of avoiding it is desirable. One way is to to impose a constraint such as $\mu_1 > \mu_0$, since we can then rule out the interchange of parameters between regimes. Doing so, regime 1 is always the high-growth regime and regime 0 is the low-growth one. In practice one often sees researchers who use model-based rules deciding which is the high-growth and which is the low-growth regime *after* estimation is performed, that is, if $\hat{\mu}_1 > \hat{\mu}_0$ it is assumed that the high-growth regime is characterized by a mean $\hat{\mu}_1$. Of course this does not solve the multiple maxima problem. Moreover, in the event that there are more parameters in the model which are regime dependent, for example, suppose that volatility takes different values of σ_0^2 and σ_1^2 in the regimes, ex post classification must be problematic, unless one knows what the relative volatilities are in each regime. This is where it becomes very important to state prior information, and it points to a Bayesian approach when this information is good.

We return to the theme above in Chapter 4. Chapter 4 will also look at many extensions of the switching regression model, mostly under the soubriquet of Markov switching. One question that will repeatedly occur in the extensions is whether the corresponding models have too many parameters to estimate. In the foregoing example there are four parameters, and so four moments of Δy_t are needed for estimation. But in some extensions there are huge number of parameters and, with just a single series Δy_t, it is hard to believe that one can estimate them precisely. Chapters 4 and 6 will use some examples from the literature to show that this is an issue, at least when y_t is a scalar. It will emerge that all the issues with the switching regression model in its simplest context will recur. The danger is that with the greater complexity of the models being formulated and estimated, these issues sometimes get lost, so it is worth seeing them in the simplest environment.

1.2.3 Differences between Prescribed and Model-Based Rules

There are two broad ways of describing recurrent events. Prescribed rules work directly with the data. The only decision that had to be made with the version above was how to define a turning point in y_t. In contrast, model-based rules require a model for Δy_t, as this is used to construct the rules. Both work with Δy_t, even though it is the behavior of y_t that is under investigation. Although a turning point is a relatively simple concept to define, one might ask whether the model adopted for Δy_t when formulating model-based rules is a correct description of Δy_t. Suppose it failed to fit the data using standard diagnostic tests? Would we use it then? There seems no answer to this query, since ideally we want to judge the model by its ability to replicate the recurrent patterns. But because we don't directly observe these, they need to be measured in some way. If there was a set of measures that were widely agreed on, and for U.S. business cycles these are the National Bureau of Economic Research (NBER) dates, it seems to make sense to compare the latter with ζ_t when judging the adequacy of the model. In countries where such external measures are not available, it often happens that a comparison is made between the S_t constructed from a prescribed rule and the ζ_t from a model. In that instance one wonders why one fitted a model. The only arguments advanced seem to be that there is an advantage to having an equation for generating the ζ_t, and it is implied that this is not available when the S_t from prescribed rules are used. We argue in this book that there is no such advantage. It is generally possible to work out an approximation that captures some of the main features of the DGP of S_t associated with recurrent events, at least when discussing items like cycles. When one turns to recurrent events involving high and low values of some variable, it is often hard to find a satisfactory prescribed rule that would produce a useful classification. In those instances regime-based models might be useful for giving one adequate rules for defining "high" and "low." Whether they do so is an empirical question.

1.3 Using the Event Indicators ("States")

Once a description is available of when the recurrent events occur, it is natural to inquire into questions concerning how long they persist, the size of their effects, and whether the probability of occurrence depends on some observable variables. These questions are augmented when there are recurrent events in multiple series, for example, one often wants to ask whether the events are synchronized. Chapter 5 makes a start on the agenda of measuring recurrent event features through concepts such as duration, amplitude, and variability of the events. As well as defining and measuring these with some statistics, we need to pay attention to the distributional properties of the latter. We examine the work that has been done on this and suggest some extensions. Chapter 7 uses the measures of Chapter 5 to look at cycles in a range of series and answer some questions that have often driven the literature, for example, on the asymmetric nature of the business cycle.

Often questions are asked either about what would explain the recurrent events or their influence on economic outcomes. An example of the former would be whether the probability of a recession has changed over time or whether it depends on economic and political institutions. To answer the latter, interest might be in whether recessions lead to higher or lower volatility in stock prices. Once either S_t (or ζ_t) are available, it is possible to set about examining these questions. To look at the first set we could "regress" S_t or ζ_t against some variables x_t, while the latter would require a regression of x_t against S_t (or ζ_t).

To answer whether such regressions make sense, it is necessary to know what the statistical properties of S_t and ζ_t are, that is, the main features of their DGPs. Some of their properties clearly originate from the nature of Δy_t. In the models of (1.1) and (1.2), Δy_t is an identically and independently distributed (i.i.d.) process, and therefore both S_t and ζ_t are independently distributed (i.d.). To investigate the impact of some x_t on S_t and ζ_t we would therefore need to allow Δy_t to depend on x_t in some way. Starting with the model

(1.1) used when discussing the prescribed rule $S_t = 1(\Delta y_t > 0)$, assume that $\Delta y_t = \mu + x_t'\beta + \sigma\varepsilon_t$, where ε_t is $n.i.d.(0, 1)$. Then

$$\Pr(S_t = 0|x_t) = \Pr(\Delta y_t < 0|x_t)$$
$$= \Pr(\mu + x_t'\beta + \sigma\varepsilon_t < 0|x_t)$$
$$= \Phi\left(-\frac{\mu + x_t'\beta}{\sigma}\right).$$

This can be recognized as the probit functional form. Moreover, because S_t is independently distributed, $\frac{\mu}{\sigma}$ and $\frac{\beta}{\sigma}$ can be estimated using probit model software. Just as for the probit model only the ratio of parameters can be identified. In Chapter 8 we examine whether this equivalence holds for other types of prescribed rules. In general the answer will be in the negative, since Chapter 2 shows that S_t will not be independently distributed, and so the implications of that fact need to be canvassed. In the case where S_t is i.i.d., using these indicators as either a regressor or a regressand is straightforward. But when S_t has some serial correlation, it is necessary to make adjustments to deal with that fact, and these are described in various points in Chapters 5–8.

The situation is less clear for model-based rules yielding ζ_t. Because the ζ_t are constructed using a model, the simple augmentation of (1.2) to allow for an influence of the x_t on ζ_t would be

$$\Delta y_t = \xi_t N(\mu_1, \sigma^2) + (1 - \xi_t)N(\mu_0, \sigma^2) + x_t'\beta. \quad (1.6)$$

This would mean that a new set of event indicators ζ_t, ζ_t', would be implied, and the mapping between ζ_t' and x_t would be unlikely to be normal. So the two-stage approach used with S_t—first determine S_t, and then investigate the relationship between S_t and x_t—doesn't really apply when model-based rules are used. One needs to describe how x_t affects Δy_t, and after this model is fitted, one can determine the relationship between ζ_t' and x_t. There are a number of ways x_t could affect Δy_t when regime-switching models are involved. One is just through the simple augmentation used in (1.6) where the influence of x_t on Δy_t does not depend on which regime holds at a point in time, but it would also be possible to allow either the regime means (μ_j) or the probability function for ξ_t to depend on x_t. All of these alternatives have been used and will be mentioned in Chapter 4.

1.4 Prediction of Recurrent Events

In the analysis of the preceding subsection we looked at items like $\Pr(S_t = 0|x_t)$. This shows how the probability of *being in a recession at* t varies with x_t. That event needs to be distinguished from the probability of *going into a recession at* t, that is, of encountering a peak in y_t. Often the literature has not made this distinction clear. Below we will point out why it is important, and Chapter 9 will examine it in more detail.

The comment above draws attention to two issues. One relates to the information available when making a prediction. We might be interested in predicting what cycle phase the economy is at $t + 1$ using information Ω_t available at time t. Such information could either be a set of observed variables x_t or even S_t and its history, including the elapsed time since the event last occurred (duration). The distinction between calendar time and duration of the event is of some importance. This book is focused on events that are unpredictable based only on calendar time, so that conditioning on a particular month, quarter, or year yields no information about the event. Nevertheless, there is the possibility that the events could be predictable based on other quantities, such as the time spent in a phase. The popular phrase "at this stage of the business cycle" expresses the idea that the beginning and end of events such as recessions could be predictable based on elapsed duration. But other variables have often been proposed as ways of predicting events such as recessions and turning points.

As seen in Chapter 2 whether S_t is known, and also what part of its history is known, will depend on the rules being used. In the simple prescribed rule dealt with in Section 1.2, once Δy_t is known so is S_t. Hence, in that context it would make sense to assume that the information available was x_t and S_t. Of course S_{t+j} will depend on x_{t+j} so some assumption will also be needed about the nature of x_t. In our examples above, Δy_t was *i.i.d.* so we would need to also have x_t being *i.i.d.* Then, because in that case S_t is independent of $S_{t-k}(k > 0)$, we must have $E(S_{t+j}|\Omega_t) = \mu_S = E(S_{t+j})$, and so one would use the unconditional mean as the best predictor.

As mentioned earlier an alternative item to forecast which has a long history in macroeconomics is whether there is a *turning point* at t. To examine this it is necessary to describe a turning point. We therefore define two binary variables $\wedge_t$ and $\vee_t$, where $\wedge_t$ takes the value unity if a peak occurs at t, and zero otherwise, while $\vee_t$ indicates a trough. Then $\wedge_t = S_t(1 - S_{t+1})$ and $\vee_t = S_{t+1}(1 - S_t)$. Thus

$$\Pr(\wedge_t = 1|\Omega_t) = E(\wedge_t|\Omega_t)$$

$$= E(S_t(1 - S_{t+1})|\Omega_t).$$

When the S_t are independently distributed $E(S_t(1 - S_{t+1})|\Omega_t) = \mu_S(1 - \mu_S)$. Hence $\Pr(\wedge_t = 1|\Omega_t) \leq (1 - \mu_S) = \Pr(S_{t+1} = 0|\Omega_t)$, so that there may be a high probability of being in a recession at $t + 1$ (given x_t), but a low probability of predicting that one will move into a recession (encounter a peak) at time t. If a different set of rules is used and/or Δy_t is not independently distributed, the prediction problem is much more complex and is analyzed in Chapter 9.

1.5 Conclusion

The chapter has introduced many of the concepts and methods that will occupy us in the remainder of the book. A key element is that turning points in a series y_t are defined by a set of rules. Sometimes these rules are prescribed and sometimes they are based on a model for Δy_t. It is not true to say, as Diebold and Rudebusch (1996, 69) do, that "Yet it is only within a regime-switching framework that the concept of a turning point has intrinsic meaning." A turning point gets its meaning from the rules that are applied to locate it. A second item of concern that was bought up in this opening chapter was connected to this, namely, that there has been a confusion between the regimes present in many nonlinear models and the phases of the recurrent events that are isolated with a set of rules. Mixing the two different ideas is something that will lead to many difficulties in later chapters.

Chapter 2

Methods for Describing Oscillations, Fluctuations, and Cycles in Univariate Series

2.1 Introduction

Suppose a single series is used to represent aggregate economic activity. Then there have been a number of approaches to describing the ups and downs of the macroeconomy. One of these has treated the events in a periodic way, as is done in many physical sciences, and this is the study of *oscillations*. The other is that used in Burns and Mitchell (1946), which followed areas such as meteorology in determining the *dates of turning points in economic activity* and used these to define *cycles*. The final view involves the idea of *fluctuations*, that is, the macroeconomy does not evolve in a smooth way but fluctuates around some long-run trend.

We can formalize these three approaches as follows.

1. *Oscillations* refer to the fact that peaks and troughs occur in a regular fashion. As such a pattern can be produced with difference and differential equations it seemed natural to describe the oscillations with those devices.
2. *Cycles* refer to the fact that the ups and downs in economic activity can be seen in a graph as a set of local peaks and troughs. Then the cycle can be summarized by finding exactly where these *turning points* occurred.

3. *Fluctuations* come from the observation that a series showing ups and downs can be said to exhibit volatility. Developments in statistics led to a time series being viewed as realizations of a random variable which could be described by its moments. For fluctuations the specific moment chosen was the variance.

In the following sections we discuss these approaches and their interrelationships in more detail.

2.2 Types of Movements in Real and Financial Series

2.2.1 Oscillations

Oscillations (periodic cycles) are often called the "rocking horse cycle" after Frisch's (1933) famous description. As had been realized for many years if one used an AR(2)

$$z_t = \beta_1 z_{t-1} + \beta_2 z_{t-2} \qquad (2.1)$$

to represent economic activity, complex roots in the polynomial $B(L) = (1 - \beta_1 L - \beta_2 L^2) = 0$ would result in oscillations. But these either died out (if the roots were less than one) or exploded. Frisch's insight was that "up and down" movements could be produced that didn't die out simply by adding on to (2.1) a term $\sigma \varepsilon_t$, where ε_t was an $i.i.d.(0, 1)$ stochastic process, since then the oscillations were continuously being subject to unpredictable shocks. Nevertheless, the shocks were ignored when describing what the oscillation in z_t was—the roots of the polynomial $B(L)$ were taken to capture the latter.

Eventually, however, shocks began to be more fully integrated into the measuring apparatus. It was observed that the AR(2) process with shocks could be summarized via a spectrum $f(\omega)$, where ω was a frequency measured in radians. Moreover, since $var(z_t) = \int f(\omega) d\omega$, the contribution of the oscillation with a frequency ω to the variance of z_t was measured by the spectrum. It followed that the dominant oscillation would be found by locating where the spectrum had its peak. Then, rather than look at the roots of the polynomial $B(L)$, attention shifted to where the peak in the spectrum was. The "roots" view of oscillations is still quite widespread, for example, in programs such as TRAMO-SEATS (see Kaiser and Maravall 2001) and in books such as Arnold (2002); the latter is constantly trying to find models that generate complex roots. In contrast Burnside (1998, 519) expounds the "spectral" approach saying" it is straightforward to determine from the spectrum of a series whether a significant portion of its variation arises from cycles with interesting periodicity."

Now it is possible that one might have the situation where the AR(2) process has both complex roots in $B(L)$ and a peak in the spectrum, and there seems no reason for these to occur at the same frequency. To explore the relationship between the roots and spectral approaches to oscillations we look at the spectral density of an AR(2).[1] Since this is

$$\tilde{f}(\omega) = \frac{1}{\beta_1^2 + 2(\cos\omega)\beta_1\beta_2 - 2(\cos\omega)\beta_1 + \beta_2^2 - 2(\cos 2\omega)\beta_2 + 1},$$

a necessary condition for a local peak in the spectral density is that $\tilde{f}'(\omega) = 0$, which requires that[2]

$$\left| \frac{\beta_1(\beta_2 - 1)}{4\beta_2} \right| < 1. \tag{2.2}$$

Then the presence of complex roots implies an oscillation of $\frac{2\pi}{arcos[\frac{\beta_1}{2\sqrt{-\beta_2}}]}$ periods, while the spectral approach yields a period of $\frac{1}{2\pi} arcos[\frac{\beta_1(1-\beta_2)}{4\beta_2}]$.

It is instructive to illustrate the differences between the roots and spectral approaches with Figure 2.1. This has the AR parameter β_1 on the horizontal axis and β_2 on the vertical axis. In the interior of the triangle the AR(2) is stationary, while on the boundary it has a unit root. Points below the solid curve satisfy the inequality $\beta_1^2 + 4\beta_2 < 0$ and correspond to oscillations associated with complex roots in $B(L)$. The frequencies that correspond to a peak in the spectrum are below the dashed line in the figure. It is clear that the two frequencies need not coincide; although one needs complex

---

[1]The spectral density is the spectrum normalized by the variance of the process.

[2]The sufficient condition requires that $\tilde{f}''(\omega) < 0$.

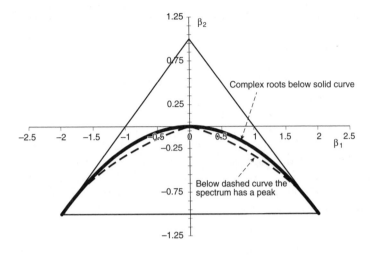

Figure 2.1: Dynamics of an AR(2).

roots to produce a peak in the spectrum, one can have the former without the latter. Although the two lines are close, they can translate into widely differing periods of oscillation. To illustrate this consider the AR(2) process with $\beta_1 = 1.4, \beta_2 = -.57$. Then the roots of $B(L) = 0$ imply an oscillation of 16 periods while the peak in the spectral density of z_t occurs at 23.4 periods. Given such a wide difference, it is natural to ask how does one choose which oscillation best describes z_t? We return to this issue in Section 2.6.

The AR(2) is a standard way of introducing an oscillation, but there are other descriptions of economic activity that are now widely used which also aim to capture them, for example, the *local linear trend plus cycle* model in Harvey and Jaeger (1993) that is embodied in the STAMP program. Here the "cycle" is an oscillatory process of the form $z_t = \psi_t$, where ψ_t follows

$$\begin{bmatrix} \psi_t \\ \psi_t^* \end{bmatrix} = \rho \begin{bmatrix} \cos\omega & \sin\omega \\ -\sin\omega & \cos\omega \end{bmatrix} \begin{bmatrix} \psi_{t-1} \\ \psi_{t-1}^* \end{bmatrix} + \begin{bmatrix} \kappa_t \\ \kappa_t^* \end{bmatrix}. \qquad (2.3)$$

In (2.3), $0 \leq \rho \leq 1$ imposes stationarity on z_t, ω is the frequency in radians of the oscillation, and κ_t, κ_t^* are mutually independent $n.i.d$ $N(0, \sigma_\kappa^2)$ random variables. It may be shown that ψ_t will be a process of the form

$$\psi_t = \frac{(1 - \rho \cos \lambda L)\kappa_t + \rho \sin \lambda L \kappa_t^*}{1 - 2\rho \cos \lambda L + \rho^2 L^2}. \tag{2.4}$$

The numerator in (2.4) is an MA(1) process, whereas the denominator is an $AR(2)$, thereby making ψ_t an $ARMA(2, 1)$ process. Focusing on the AR(2) part, one can see that the roots are $\frac{\cos \lambda \pm \sqrt{\cos^2 \lambda - 1}}{\rho}$. Therefore, since $0 \leq \cos^2 \lambda < 1$, they are complex. Thus (2.4) *imposes* oscillations on a series, and this raises the issue of whether such a restriction is correct. Certainly there is nothing that says that economic data should follow an AR process with complex roots. Effectively, the model is being *designed* to produce such behavior rather than *discover* it. This conflict between model design and discovery recurs in the literature.

Finally we need to ask how one would describe oscillatory behavior in the event that the level of economic activity z_t is not a stationary process. Early treatments assumed that $z_t - a - bt$ was an oscillatory process, where the term $a + bt$ captured any nonstationarity with a deterministic trend. But the emergence of integrated processes suggested that this was not a complete answer. A number of proposals have therefore been made to capture any "unit root" character in z_t. One has been to assume that the oscillations apply to the growth rates Δz_t. Another has decomposed z_t into permanent (z_t^P) and transitory (z_t^T) components, that is, $z_t = z_t^P + z_t^T$, with the transitory components made an oscillatory process. The specification of the permanent component also varies, but a common one has $\Delta z_t^P = \mu_z + \varepsilon_t$, where ε_t is $i.i.d.(0, \sigma_\varepsilon^2)$ and μ_z captures any deterministic trend in z_t. Finally, there has been one suggestion where there are "complex unit roots"—Bierens (2001)—where it was proposed that the $AR(2)$ process be given the form

$$z_t = 2 \cos(\varphi)z_{t-1} - z_{t-1} + a + \sigma \varepsilon_t. \tag{2.5}$$

2.2.2 Cycles

Measurement of the business cycle is inextricably linked with the name of Wesley Mitchell and the NBER. Central to it was a conference organized by the latter in 1922 on what was meant by cycles—see Clements (1923). Mitchell had already written on the business cycle (in his 1913 book) but now extensively developed his ideas on the subject in Mitchell (1927). This program culminated in his landmark book with Burns in 1946. These works set out and illustrated the principles that are used in business cycle measurement to this day.

The famous definition of a business cycle given by Burns and Mitchell has often been cited: "Business Cycles are a type of fluctuation found in the aggregate economic activity of nations... a cycle consists of expansions occurring at about the same time in many economic activities, followed by similarly general... contractions." The quotation has three key elements to it—a business cycle occurs in aggregate economic activity, it has phases of expansions and contractions, and these occur in many economic activities. Each of these elements arises whenever we set out to measure a business cycle, and the trio tells us that three choices need to be made. These are

1. What types of series are to be used to measure aggregate economic activity?
2. How many series are to be used?
3. How is history to be segmented into periods of expansions and contractions?

The answers to these questions have produced a voluminous literature over the past half century.

To answer the first question, one can observe that Burns and Mitchell were quite clear that if a single series was to be used as representative of aggregate economic activity, then it would be GDP. Early in their book they said (72) that "Aggregate (economic) activity can be given a definite meaning and made conceptually measurable by identifying it with gross national product," but at the time they were performing their research, "Unfortunately, no satisfactory series of any of these types is available by months or quarters for periods approximating those we seek to cover" (73). Thus, from Burns and Mitchell's perspective, GDP had disadvantages. It either wasn't available over the period of history they were examining or it was not available at the periodicity that they favored.

The latter was monthly, as they wished to record the months in which phases began and ended. Hence, this led them to use many types of series to measure the business cycle, examples being bank clearings, orders for locomotives, and pig iron production. A recent statement in the same vein is available from the Business Cycle Dating Committee of the NBER in "The NBER's Recession Dating Procedure" (available at http://www.nber.org/cycles/recessions.html). When dating the 2001 recession, they said that "The Committee views real GDP as the single best measure of aggregate economic activity. In determining whether a recession has occurred and in identifying the approximate dates of the peak and the trough, the committee therefore places considerable weight on the estimates of real GDP." But they emphasize that they take account also of movements in employment and income. Thus the stance to be taken on the number of series that should be used will depend a great deal on what one wishes to use the information for. If one is happy to use a quarterly measure of aggregate economic activity, it is very difficult to argue that one should use any series other than GDP, as it is designed to be the best measure of aggregate activity.

The cycle in the *level* of aggregate economic activity was often referred to by the NBER researchers as the *classical cycle*. In many ways dating a cycle is an inherently visual activity and accounts for the extensive use often made of charts by Burns and Mitchell and the NBER Business Cycle Dating Committee. Often close inspection of graphs and a knowledge of history are useful for suggesting reasons that what might initially look like a turning point should not qualify as such. Some of these—seasonal patterns, the impact of wars and strikes—need to be removed before the series are examined, and often considerable adjustments are applied to the raw series before turning point analysis begins. Even after these tasks have been performed, there are other reasons for thinking that what seems like a turning point might not be so. Perhaps the most important of these comes from the idea that a phase has to persist for some time, and therefore some turning points would be eliminated if the phases were too short. All in all, in practice the task of dating turning points can involve a number of "rounds" of smoothing of data followed by checks to see if the resulting set of candidate turning points agree with prior conceptions of phase length, and so on. One also needs to ensure that the type of turning point alternates, that is, the peak which signifies the end of an expansion should be followed by a trough which terminated a contraction. The final set of dates selected for turning points therefore often reflects considerable amounts of judgment.

It was natural that interest would arise in the possibility of automating turning point selection. The first attempt at this was Bry and Boschan (1971), who effectively produced an expert system to replicate the decisions that had been made by Burns and Mitchell concerning the turning points in a given set of series. They developed a computer program that involved the same sort of steps applied by Burns and Mitchell. It incorporated various smoothing and outlier detection rules along with algorithms that enforced judgments about minimum phase and cycle length and amplitudes, and methods to ensure that turning points alternated. Because the procedure was implemented in FORTRAN, specific numerical values had to be assigned to tests involving phase length, and the rule adopted was that phases must be at least 5 months in duration, while a complete cycle must last 15 months. This computer program is widely used in the industry involved with business cycle measurement as a starting point for the determination of a set of final turning points. It is probably rarely the case that the dates for turning points established with it are used without some modification, although the extent of this will depend on exactly why one wants to establish the dates of turning points. For academic work, interest is mainly concentrated on the *average* characteristics of the business cycle, so the precise determination of dates is much less important than it is for policy makers and economic historians. For academic users it might be expected that automated dating methods could be popular.

Of course we have assumed that it is easy to measure the *level* of economic activity. Even if we took this to be GDP, there are a number of ways of measuring that variable—from the production, expenditure, and income sides.[3] So we need to turn these three measures into a single one. Moreover, if dates at a monthly frequency are required, GDP is rarely available, and so one may want to study a variety of measures and combine them in some way. Compressing much of this information into a single measure of activity is a challenging task.

Leaving aside such compression issues until later, we begin with the idea that this has already been done and so just a single series on the level of economic activity is available. We may still want to adjust this series to match more closely what it is desired to study. Suppose this is welfare. Then some adjustment to the series on economic activity might need to be made to account for changing population and (maybe) demographic characteristics. Even if one ignored welfare issues, different decision makers will be interested in various measures of activity. Thus a monetary policy maker might want to measure the part of economic activity that they can influence. Since the long-run outcomes in an economy are largely determined by demographic and productivity movements, the monetary authority may wish to construct measures of activity that net these out. In contrast, an economic planner might view their task as affecting demographic and productivity movements, so they would not want to perform any such adjustment. Both types of decision makers would presumably like their judgments to be unclouded by the normal seasonal movements in economies, as these can rarely be counteracted.

2.2.3 Fluctuations

Rather than focus on recurrent events as revealed in oscillations and cycles, there has been a modern tendency to capture the ups and downs of the economy via a summary of the second moments of the variable describing economic activity.

---

[3]As the NBER Dating Committee point out the income and product measures of GDP showed different behavior in the 2001 and 2007–2009 recessions.

Blanchard and Fischer (1989) is an early statement of this approach. They say,

> The first systematic time series study of business cycles was that of Burns and Mitchell (1946). Their approach was to treat each cycle as a separate episode...starting at a trough and going from trough to peak through an expansion and from peak to trough through a contraction...Most macroeconometricians, however, have abandoned the Burns-Mitchell methodology. This is because the approach is partly judgemental and the statistics it generates do not have well-defined statistical properties. ...Much of the recent work has proceeded, instead, under the assumption that variables follow linear stochastic processes with constant coefficients. (1989, 7)

Prima facie this mixes up the issue of description of cycles with what is a good model for representing activity. Regarding the first, although it is true that the location of peaks and troughs is partly due to judgment (just as is the selection of a model for activity) this does not prohibit the analysis of the S_t that summarize cycles with standard statistical methods. Indeed, this book is about providing a secure statistical foundation for the analysis of turning point information.

Regarding the second point the model selected to describe activity (Y_t) had to recognize that data pointed to the log of the latter (y_t) as being a non-stationary series, so it made no sense to summarize its ups and downs through a variance. Some operation needed to be performed on the y_t to render it covariance stationary. An early way to do this was to assume that $y_t = a + \beta t + z_t$, where z_t was stationary, that is, activity was stationary around a deterministic trend. One could then compute the variance of z_t. However, once one adopted the perspective that y_t contained a unit root, then so must z_t, that is, there was a *stochastic trend* present in both y_t and z_t as well as the deterministic trend in y_t. This led Blanchard and Fischer (1989) to say, "We then think of trends as that part of output which is due to permanent shocks. . . . That part of output that comes from transitory shocks can be thought of as the cycle." This led to a huge literature on how to remove both stochastic and deterministic permanent components from y_t, so as to produce a series y_t' whose variance could be computed.

It is unfortunate that this transitory component was referred to as a "cycle." It certainly has turning points, and they are the cycle, not y'_t itself. In fact turning points in y'_t would correspond to those of the NBER's *growth cycle*, provided that the way of removing the permanent component was that adopted by the NBER.[4]

Why would one use y'_t rather than y_t when studying "ups and downs?" In a sense this position was a long-standing product of the idea that a series was composed of trend plus cycle plus seasonal, plus irregular components, and the task was to filter out trend, seasonal and irregular factors so that one could study the cycle. Such a decomposition is rarely used today by most official statistical agencies. They remove only the seasonal and irregular components by filtering operations. What is left is often labeled "trend/cycle" or just trend.

From an economic perspective, if one thinks of the models today that presumably correspond to Blanchard and Fischer's "linear stochastic processes with constant coefficients," these would be dynamic stochastic general equilibrium (DSGE) models. They arose out of real business cycle (RBC) models. In the latter the central feature was that technology variation gave rise to the ups and downs in activity, that is, led to the business cycle. Those DSGE models used in central banks differ from RBC models in having technology follow a unit root process, and this provides the stochastic trend in y_t. Accordingly, removing the stochastic trend from y_t removes the major factor that RBC modelers thought was driving the business cycle. In brief, ups and downs in y_t are as much a product of supply-side forces as demand, and this points

---

[4]The NBER used a method called phase averaging to remove permanent components rather than any of the popular filters such as Hodrick-Prescott, (1997), Band-pass, and so on. Because every one of these is different, there is no unique growth cycle, so the fact that there are different growth cycle turning points should not be surprising. To emphasize the problem with defining a cycle as a transitory component of y_t, suppose Δy_t was white noise and the Beveridge-Nelson method was used to remove the permanent component. Then the permanent component is y_t, that is, according to the Blanchard-Fischer definition there would be no cycle. Countries like Australia have no serial correlation in GDP growth, so they fit this description. Yet it is clear that they do have turning points in the level of GDP.

to the need to study the level of activity y_t. Of course we may want to know what the relative contributions of the supply and demand-side factors are to the movements in y_t, but that can be done provided there is a model for Δy_t that explains the impact of these. Trying to filter out the permanent component using some arbitrary filter such as Hodrick-Prescott fails to recognize the fact that this filter would almost never correspond to that implied by a DSGE model with permanent shocks, as the latter is invariably given by a Beveridge- Nelson formula. Perhaps another reason there was an increasing emphasis on y_t' rather than y_t was the idea that one couldn't analyze turning points in a nonstationary series. But as Chapter 1 already indicates, this is wrong. The turning points in y_t are found by examining the stationary process Δy_t.

2.3   Prescribed Rules for Dating Business Cycles

We are interested in constructing a pair of binary variables $(\wedge_t, \vee_t)$ from y_t that take the value unity when a peak or trough occurs at date t and zero otherwise. From these a binary variable S_t can then be constructed that summarizes which state (phase) of the cycle holds at time t. For business cycles $S_t = 1$ will be taken to mean an expansion holds at t, while $S_t = 0$ will signal a contraction. A first complication is that often the user of these binary variables is not the producer. Instead the researcher may just be provided with $(\wedge_t, \vee_t)$ and not the y_t used to construct them; this is the case with NBER business cycle dates. In other cases the user will have some knowledge of the y_t that turning points have been constructed from, but rarely full knowledge.

   To understand the nature of the $\wedge_t, \vee_t$, and S_t, we therefore need to have some idea of the transformations that convert y_t into these binary variables. Although it may not be known precisely how this is done, in most instances enough information is available to enable an approximation to the main features of the DGPs of $\wedge_t, \vee_t$, and S_t. It is worth thinking of the conversion process from y_t to $\wedge_t, \vee_t$ as involving three stages, following which the conversion of $\wedge_t, \vee_t$, into S_t invokes a fourth stage. We can then see how the nature (DGP) of $\wedge_t, \vee_t$ changes at each stage, and how that impacts the evolution of S_t. This is done in the subsequent subsections.

2.3.1 Automated Business Cycle Dating Methods: First Stage

In the literature a variety of rules have been employed. The three most popular are discussed in the following three subsections, followed by a brief account of some others that have appeared in the literature.

The Calculus Rule for Dating Cycles. Chapter 1 introduced a simple method for locating turning points, and it might be called the *calculus rule*. This said that a *peak* in a series y_t occurs at time t if $\Delta y_t > 0$ and $\Delta y_{t+1} < 0$. The reason for the name is the result in calculus that identifies a maximum with a change in sign of the first derivative from being positive to negative. A *trough* (or local minimum) can be found using the outcomes $\Delta y_t < 0$ and $\Delta y_{t+1} > 0$. In this special case the states S_t are defined as $S_t = 1(\Delta y_t > 0)$, so that S_t depends only on contemporaneous information. This rule has been popular for defining turning points in economic activity when y_t is yearly data—see Cashin and McDermott (2002) and Neftci (1984).

The Two Quarters Rule for Dating Business Cycles. The rule that two quarters of negative growth initiates the transition from an expansion to a recession is often cited in the media. This rule is different from the other rules considered here because it requires knowledge of both the current state and the future evolution of y_t when defining what constitutes a local peak or trough. Extended symmetrically so that the beginning of an expansion is signaled when there are two successive quarters of positive growth produces the "two-quarters rule":

$$\wedge_t = 1(\Delta y_{t+1} < 0, \Delta y_{t+2} < 0)S_t \qquad (2.6)$$

$$\vee_t = 1(\Delta y_{t+1} > 0, \Delta y_{t+2} > 0)(1 - S_t). \qquad (2.7)$$

In (2.6) we see that a peak occurs at time t ($\wedge_t = 1$) if the growth rates at $t+1$ and $t+2$ are negative *and* $S_t = 1$, that is, an expansion held at time t. A similar interpretation can be given to (2.7). Although the NBER Dating Committee has been quite explicit that they do not define a recession in this way one still sees it used in academic work, for example, Mazurek and Mielcová (2013, 185) who state that "A recession itself is defined by GDP declining for at least two consecutive quarters from the preceding period."

The Bry-Boschan and BBQ Rules for Dating Business Cycles. Common usage of the word "recession" identifies it with a *sustained* decline in the *level* of economic activity. This suggests that the calculus rule may identify too many turning points, with the consequence that expansion and contraction phases may last only a single period. Visualizing a peak in a series leads one to the idea that a local peak in y_t occurs at time t if y_t exceeds values y_s for $t - k < s < t$ and $t + k > s > t$, where k delineates some symmetric window in time around t. One can define a trough in a similar way. By making k large enough, we also capture the idea that the level of activity has declined (or increased) in a *sustained way*. Of course the window in time (k) over which this test is applied needs to be limited when performing the test. This simple idea is the basis of the NBER procedures summarized in the Bry and Boschan (1971) dating algorithm. In that program, designed for the analysis of monthly data, $k = 5$ months. In the event that the analysis is being conducted with quarterly data, we will set $k = 2$ quarters as an analog. Much of our discussion will revolve around the quarterly case, but one can make the appropriate substitutions if monthly data are being examined for turning points.[5]

We refer to this quarterly rule as the simple BBQ rule.[6] In the two quarters case it is defined using the $\wedge_t$ and $\vee_t$ as

$$\wedge_t = 1(y_{t-2}, y_{t-1} < y_t > y_{t+1}, y_{t+2}) \qquad (2.8)$$

$$\vee_t = 1(y_{t-2}, y_{t-1} > y_t < y_{t+1}, y_{t+2}), \qquad (2.9)$$

---

[5]If data are yearly $k = 1$ is the natural choice.

[6]BBQ stands for a quarterly (Q) variant of the Bry and Boschan (BB) approach.

Table 2.1: Application of the Calculus and Simple BBQ Rules to the Logarithm of U.S. GDP 1979/3 to 1982/4

Date	y_t	Calculus			Simple BBQ		
		$\wedge_t$	$\vee_t$	S_t	$\wedge_t$	$\vee_t$	S_t
Sept 1979	15.68532	0	0	1	0	0	1
Dec 1979	15.68791	0	0	1	0	0	1
Mar 1980	15.69114	1	0	1	1	0	1
Jun 1980	15.67065	0	0	0	0	0	0
Sept 1980	15.66913	0	1	0	0	1	0
Dec 1980	15.68749	0	0	1	0	0	1
Mar 1981	15.70798	1	0	1	0	0	1
Jun 1981	15.70065	0	1	0	0	0	1
Sept 1981	15.71206	1	0	1	1	0	1
Dec 1981	15.70032	0	0	0	0	0	0
Mar 1982	15.68345	0	1	1	0	1	0
June 1982	15.68889	1	0	1	0	0	1
Sept 1982	15.68528	0	1	0	0	0	1
Dec 1982	15.68625	0	0	1	0	0	1

which can be expressed as[7]

$$\wedge_t = 1(\Delta y_t > 0, \Delta_2 y_t > 0, \Delta y_{t+1} < 0, \Delta_2 y_{t+2} < 0) \quad (2.10)$$

$$\vee_t = 1(\Delta y_t < 0, \Delta_2 y_t < 0, \Delta y_{t+1} > 0, \Delta_2 y_{t+2} > 0). \quad (2.11)$$

Application of the calculus rule introduced in Chapter 1 is made to the logarithm of US GDP over the period of the double-dip recession, September quarter 1979 to December quarter 1983. This is illustrated in Table 2.1, where the first column is the date and the second is the logarithm of U.S. GDP (y_t). The third and fourth columns of Table 2.1 mark the peaks ($\wedge_t$) and troughs ($\vee_t$) located with the calculus rule, while the fifth column gives the corresponding state S_t. The sixth and seventh columns give the simple BBQ peaks and troughs defined by equations (2.8) and (2.9), respectively. It is evident that every simple BBQ turning point is also a

---

[7]Where $\Delta_2 y_t = y_t - y_{t-2}$.

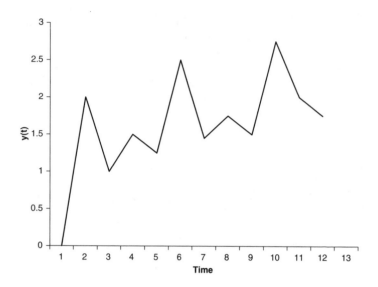

Figure 2.2: Example of Multiple Local BBQ Peaks.

calculus rule turning point, but the converse is not true. For example, March 1981 is a calculus peak and June 1981 is a calculus trough, but neither are BBQ turning points. For the peak this comes about because the September quarter 1981 level of GDP exceeds that for March 1981, thereby violating equation (2.8). In relation to the troughs, GDP in December 1980 and December 1981 is lower than in June 1981, violating equation (2.9).

The simple definition of local peaks and troughs with $k > 1$ raises the complication that peaks and troughs are no longer assured to alternate, and this may lead to multiple peaks (or troughs) that are "adjacent" to each other. Figure 2.2 shows the case of multiple adjacent local peaks that would be identified with the simple BBQ rule and $k = 2$. Notice that with $k = 2$ the simple BBQ rule in equations (2.8) and (2.9) would find no local troughs over the range of observations shown in the figure. Hence the rule needs to be supplemented with procedures to select one of the adjacent turning points. How this is done is discussed in the next section with second-stage rules.

It is worth noting that the presence of multiple "adjacent" turning points can modify the formulae relating S_t, $\wedge_t$ and $\vee_t$ given in Chapter 1. For example, if S_t is constructed via

$$S_{t+1} = (1 - \wedge_t) S_t + \vee_t (1 - S_t), \qquad (2.12)$$

then in the Figure 2.2 only the first of the multiple peaks or troughs would be selected, and it would no longer be the case that $\wedge_t = S_t(1 - S_{t+1})$ and $\vee_t = S_{t+1}(1 - S_t)$. These relations would only hold for the first of the multiple adjacent turning points.

The program implementing the Bry-Boschan (BB) procedure involves a good deal of smoothing of the data and elimination of outliers. Because quarterly data are generally much smoother than monthly data, BBQ does not employ any smoothing, although this could be done prior to the determination of turning points. There will be times when the quarterly series will reflect unusual movements. Examples would be bringing forward expenditures on goods and services if a tax on these is introduced. Others would be the impact of droughts, floods, and severe winters. These are generally best handled via an adjustment to the series y_t through dummy variables before the determination of turning points. Programs implementing both the BB and BBQ algorithms have been widely used to determine turning points in activity in many countries as well as many series.

Other Rules for Dating Business Cycles. Fair (1993) proposed two definitions of a recession. The first was that it occurred at t if there were at least two consecutive quarters of negative growth in real GDP over the next five quarters, while the second was that there were at least two quarters of negative growth in real GDP over the next five quarters. The first definition had widespread use in the analysis of macroeconometric models during the 1960s and 1970s. More recently Anderson and Vahid (2001) have used the second.

2.3.2 Second Stage Rules for Constructing Turning Points: Censoring

The second stage in constructing the $\wedge_t$ and $\vee_t$ from y_t involves enforcing certain requirements relating to minimum distances between turning points. We refer to such constraints as *censoring*. The procedures used by the NBER and Centre for Economic Policy Research (London) (CEPR) business cycle dating committees when dating U.S. and European business cycles automatically impose alternation of turning points. In terms of other rules, both the calculus rule and the two-quarter rules do the same. In their basic form for finding local maxima and minima, the BB and simple BBQ algorithms do not automatically impose alternation in the local peaks and troughs. Accordingly, both need subroutines that enforce alternation. These subroutines start with the local peaks and troughs and then iteratively eliminate the lowest of multiple adjacent peaks and the highest of multiple adjacent troughs. This continues until the algorithm converges on to a set of turning points that alternate. As such the set of alternating turning points are akin to fixed points. The properties of these subroutines have not been studied in detail. What is known is that this form of censoring can be important in Monte Carlo simulations, and care has to be taken to ensure that it is properly applied when dating cycles with simulated data. In this book we have used an extensively rewritten version of the program employed in Harding and Pagan (2002) in an attempt to ensure that the alternation is performed accurately—the rewritten version will be called modified BBQ (MBBQ) and derives from work by James Engel. MATLAB and GAUSS versions of it (as well as an EXCEL form) are available at http://www.ncer.edu.au/data/.[8]

There is a need for further censoring in that it is known that a standard requirement of the NBER when dating business

---

[8]The method used in MBBQ essentially stays in an existing phase until criteria have been satisfied that would signal a change. Artis et al. (2004) have a similar approach. These algorithms tend to be much more computationally efficient than the original BB and BBQ algorithms. It should be noted that code implementing the equivalent of MBBQ is available in a number of computer packages such as Stata and in languages such as R. Furthermore it needs to be said that despite its name, MBBQ can be applied to monthly and yearly data. However, it should be emphasized that MBBQ does not engage in the extensive smoothing operations for turning point identification that was in the first BB program.

cycles is to ensure that completed phases have a duration of at least two quarters. This requirement is evident in the NBER business cycle data, where there is no completed phase with duration of less than two quarters.[9] By default this seems to have been used around the world by others when dating the business cycle. The exact censoring restrictions imposed in the BB algorithm were that contraction and expansion phases of a business cycle must have a minimum duration of 5 months while a completed cycle must have a minimum duration of 15 months. We emulate this in MBBQ with quarterly data by imposing two-quarter and five-quarter minima to the phase lengths and complete cycle duration, respectively.[10] Obviously one could impose other censoring restrictions involving the magnitude of the decline in output, and it seems likely that most users would in fact implicitly impose such a restriction.

Clearly the process above means that a first set of turning points is identified from local peaks and troughs. After this, a new set is produced by ensuring that peaks and troughs alternate. Finally there are further operations to ensure that minimum phase duration and minimum cycle length hold. To avoid confusion between these different sets of peaks and troughs it is often useful to have some way of distinguishing them. This will be done by defining $(\wedge_t, \vee_t)$ as the local turning points, that is, those established using the simple rules in equations (2.8) and (2.9), and then indexing the turning points with a superscript i to produce $\left(\wedge_t^i, \vee_t^i\right)$ under various constraints. Accordingly, $i = a$ would indicate that the turning points have been forced to alternate; $i = p$ means, in addition, that they have a minimum phase duration imposed; and finally, $i = c$ augments the $i = p$ case with a minimum cycle length. In this book we use this convention where the context does not make it evident which concept of a turning point is being used. In many later chapters however we just use $(\wedge_t, \vee_t)$

---

[9]It is also the case that no NBER completed phase has duration less than 17 months.

[10]For yearly data it would make sense to have a minimum phase of one year and a minimum complete cycle of two years.

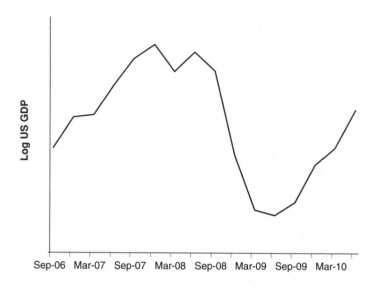

Figure 2.3: The 2007–2010 U.S. Business Cycle.

to mean turning points found with MBBQ rather than making explicit the appropriate superscript c.

Starting from an initial set of turning points, the BB and MBBQ algorithms contain subroutines that involve iterations which converge on a final set of turning points that simultaneously alternate and satisfy the minimum phase and cycle restrictions. In doing so the algorithms identify the features of the data that are apparent to the human eye. In Figure 2.2 this involved the moderately complex task of selecting the highest of the three adjacent local peaks, whereas in Figure 2.3, which shows the log of U.S. GDP over the quarters 2007/1–2010/1, the algorithm has a simple task. MBBQ marks out the fourth quarter of 2007 as a peak in the business cycle, since it has GDP being larger than for any of the two quarters before or after it. Notice that while 2008/1 was a quarter of negative growth, this was not true of 2008/2, so we are not defining a recession as two periods of negative growth. The graph also indicates that the recession clearly terminates in the second quarter of 2008. The contraction phase is six quarters long, while the expansion starting in 2008/3 must be at least two

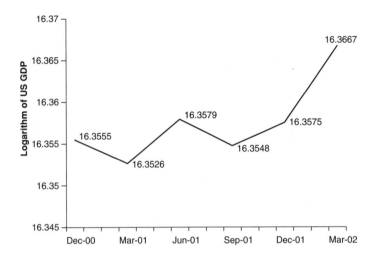

Figure 2.4: The 2001 NBER Recession.

quarters long, thereby ensuring the phase and complete cycle length restrictions are satisfied by the chosen dates for turning points.

The 2001 NBER recession, described in figure 2.4, provides a helpful illustration of how censoring rules in BBQ and BB determine turning points. The *simple BBQ* rule would place a peak at June 2001 because U.S. GDP is higher at that date than in any of the two quarters preceding and following it.[11] But for the following reasons, the simple peak at June 2001 is censored out by MBBQ and BB. Consider September 2001. It is not a simple BBQ trough because March quarter 2001 GDP is lower than September quarter 2001 GDP. However, GDP in March 2002 is higher than in June 2001 so that if a peak were left at June 2001, the next BBQ turning point would not be until the peak at December 2007. Hence this would yield two adjacent peaks with no legitimate trough in between them. This reasoning serves to illustrate the complexity of censoring decisions which MBBQ has to implement.

---

[11]This is a close decision. Based on the March quarter 2015 vintage of data shown in the figure, the log of U.S. GDP is 16.3579 in June 2001 and 16.3575 in December 2001.

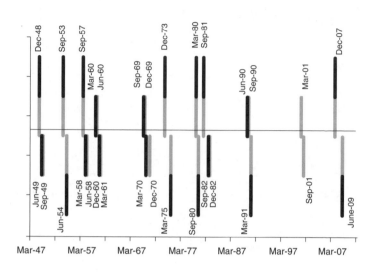

● BBQ ALGORITHM   ▪ NBER

Figure 2.5: Comparison of NBER and BBQ U.S. Cycle Dates.

One should think about these algorithms in the same way that we think about Taylor rules for monetary policy. It is not that a Taylor rule reproduces the actual decisions made by the Fed about the Federal Funds rate, but that it is a good enough approximation to be a useful tool for summarizing their decisions. Thus, to assess the utility of the algorithm, we might compare the business cycle turning points established by applying the algorithm to quarterly U.S. GDP data with what decisions were actually made about the turning points in economic activity by the NBER committee.[12] Harding and Pagan (2002) found that there was a good correspondence between the decisions of the NBER committee and the dates established with BBQ. An updated version of that comparison using MBBQ and applied to U.S. GDP can be seen in Figure 2.5.[13]

---

[12]In this instance the turning point dates remain the same whether the censoring rules are applied or not.

[13]Note MBBQ is here applied to the December quarter 2014 vintage of U.S. GDP data.

In the update it is the case that MBBQ does not flag a recession in 2001 because of the pattern of GDP growth during 2001 seen in Figure 2.4. As the figure shows, although there are periods of negative growth there are also positive growth outcomes, so that there is never any t where $y_t > \{y_{t+1}, y_{t+2}\}$.

2.3.3 Third Stage for Constructing Turning Points: Judgment

Although there are exceptions, in many instances the turning points researchers are presented with involve modification of the turning points that one would get from the two stages above. This modification stems from the application of expert judgement or what has often been called the "narrative approach."[14] It should be emphasized that there is no doubt that the two stages above are inputs into the final decision. Because of this, the lessons learned from the analysis are important when working with the final turning points. In particular, the nature of the processes for $\wedge_t$ and $\vee_t$ established in stages one and two is likely to carry over to the final turning points that have been modified by judgment.

2.3.4 Fourth Stage: Constructing S_t

Provided the turning points alternate the binary states can be constructed from the turning points via

$$S_{t+1} = \left(1 - \wedge_t^i\right) S_t + \vee_t^i (1 - S_t) \qquad i = (a, p, c). \quad (2.13)$$

The properties of the S_t are then inherited from the turning points. The convention used here is that the peak is the last period of an expansion phase and the trough is the last period of the recession phase. To appreciate the need for such a convention, we note that the NBER does not produce a binary variable to record expansion and recession phases. In part this may be because the NBER Dating Committee has said in its Frequently Asked Questions that "December 2007 is

---

[14]When business cycle dating first began, a key source for deciding on final dates was Thorp (1926). In much work on crises, the data are taken from Reinhart and Rogoff (2014) which involves judgment.

both the month when the recession began and the month when the expansion ended. Similarly, June 2009 is both the month when the recession ended and the month when the expansion began." This stance is strictly inconsistent with representing expansions and recessions by a binary variable as the statement just cited would require that the number one equals zero. For this reason a convention such as ours is needed.

It is also useful to note that

$$S_{t+1}(1 - S_t) = \vee_t^i (1 - S_t) \tag{2.14}$$

and

$$(1 - S_{t+1}) S_t = \wedge_t^i S_t. \tag{2.15}$$

Thus, if one is given the S_t, and then uses the transformations (2.14) and (2.15) to obtain the peaks and troughs, one is obtaining the product of the censored troughs and peaks with $1 - S_t$ and S_t.

2.4 Prescribed Rules for Dating Other Types of Real Cycles: Medium-Term and Acceleration Cycles

There are other types of cycles in real variables which have been the object of interest. One of these arose from the situation where the data showed only increasing economic activity, that is, there are no ups and downs. When the NBER researchers came to study Germany and Japan in the 1950s and 1960s, there was no evidence of any turning points in the level of the series that they used to measure economic activity. China would be a good recent example. They therefore decided that they would remove a component from the series and study turning points in what was left— see Mintz (1969). The resulting cycle they named the *growth cycle*. Because the series whose turning points are being studied involves a subtraction operation, it has sometimes been called a *deviations cycle,* since one is looking at turning points in a series that represents a deviation from the level of activity. Generally, the quantity that is subtracted off represents the permanent level of output, and therefore there are as many growth cycles as there are definitions of a permanent component, something we have already remarked on. This should not be confused with a cycle that could exist in a series on *growth rates*, that is, one might study turning points in the growth rates of activity. Harding (2004) called this the "acceleration cycle" as it aims to find periods of time when growth is accelerating and when it is decelerating. He produced a chronology for the euro area to 1998 and Darne and Ferrara (2011) have updated the chronology.

Often researchers do not seem to clearly define what they are looking at when they are referring to a cycle. Thus Comin and Gertler (2006) have looked at "medium-term business cycles." In terms of the definition above, this is a growth cycle that differs from others solely by how the permanent component of activity is measured. Mostly the latter has involved measuring the contribution to activity of oscillations with a long period. Typically such filters used to construct the permanent component retain oscillations that have periodicity of greater than eight years. In contrast, Comin and Gertler set the upper bound to 50 rather than 8 years.[15] What is odd about their medium-term cycles is why a deviation is involved. The motivation for considering such cycles is that "Over the postwar period many industrialized countries have tended to oscillate between periods of robust growth and relative stagnation. The U.S. economy, for example, experienced sustained high-output growth during the early to late 1960s. From the early 1970s to the early 1980s however, output growth was low on average. Since the mid-1990s, there has been for the most part, a return to strong growth" (p. 523) This seems to point to a cycle in growth rates measured at a frequency that is much longer than a quarter. To capture this effect it would seem sensible to define the growth rate as $\varphi_t = z_t - z_{t-k}$, where $k = 20$ or 40, that is, growth is measured over five or ten years. Then a medium-term cycle would be seen in the turning points of φ_t.

---

[15]In fact many papers also filter out short oscillations when constructing the series on which cycle analysis is to be performed, typically anything less than two years. Comin and Gertler allow for oscillations of two quarters. It seems odd to call this a business cycle in that using widely accepted NBER rules a complete business cycle will always be at least 15 months long.

2.5 Prescribed Rules for Dating Financial Cycles

All the methods that we have discussed in connection with business cycles appear in the determination of financial cycles. By "financial cycles" we mean cycles in series such as equity prices, housing prices, and credit. In this literature there are sometimes just two phases and these are often given names such as bull and bear markets (equity), hot and cold markets (IPOs and real estate), and easy and tight (credit). In other cases the generic description might be of crisis and noncrisis although this has the extra implication of some extreme event.

The calculus rule for forming S_t is represented in the early warning systems literature in the form

$$S_t = 1 \left(\left[\sum_{j=1}^{n} ((\Delta \ln z_{jt} - \mu_j)/\sigma_j) - k > 0 \right] \right),$$

where z_{jt} are series such as the log of the exchange rate and foreign reserves, μ_j and σ_j are their means and standard deviations, and k is a predefined constant. Here the S_t are generally labeled as indicators of financial crises.

The two-periods rule has sometimes found favor. Thus Lunde and Timmermann (2004) and Ibbotson and Jaffee (1975) used variants of this nonparametric rule for finding bull and bear periods in stock prices and hot and cold markets for IPOs respectively. The latter defined a hot market as being signaled by whether excess returns, and their changes for two periods, exceed the median values. Eichengreen et al. (1995) and Classens et al. (2011) employ rules of this type to establish the location of crises in time.

Finally, the MBBQ rule has been applied to quarterly financial data on equity prices, housing prices, and credit by Claessens et al. (2011). They apply the rule to data from 21 advanced industrial economies over 1960/1–2007/4. Pagan and Sussounov (2003) and Bordo and Wheelock (2006, 2007) use BBQ, although the former set $k = 8$, since the higher volatility of monthly asset prices means one generally wants a longer period of decline before one would be confident about the emergence of a bear market. They also applied a constraint that a bear market could last for less than four months if the decline in equity prices was more than 20% over the period. Largely this was to capture the 1987 bear market. Christiano et al. (2011) also provide turning points in real equity prices. It is not entirely clear from their paper how this was done, but the graphs they present suggest that it is based on the Bry-Boschan philosophy.

The minimum phase constraint is evident in many data series on S_t with financial series. For example, it is noticeable that for the S_t representing financial crises, there appears to be a minimum duration of time spent in each of the two states, and this is greater than a single period. This seems likely to be the outcome of imposing the belief just described that states should persist for some time if they are to be of interest to decision makers.

2.6 Relations between Cycles and Oscillations

What is the relation between cycles and oscillations? We need to discuss this separately for the cases where z_t is stationary and when it is nonstationary. Consequently, the next two subsections examine this question.

2.6.1 Cycles and Oscillations in Stationary Series

Let us return to the basic AR(2) with $\beta_1 = 1.4$ and $\beta_2 = -.57$ but without a shock. Then the complex roots point to an oscillation in z_t of 16.4 periods. What happens if we look for a cycle in z_t using MBBQ? We generate a series of observations on z_t stating from nonzero values for z_0 and z_{-1}. Passing this data through MBBQ, we find that cycles are 16 periods long. This should not be surprising. Because z_t follows a sine wave, the peaks and troughs always occur the same distance apart, and a program to detect turning points will find them at the correct spacing. Now let us add on a shock ε_t with a variance of unity to this AR(2) process. The process for z_t now has a spectral density with a peak corresponding to an oscillation of 23.4 periods. The period of oscillation is invariant to the

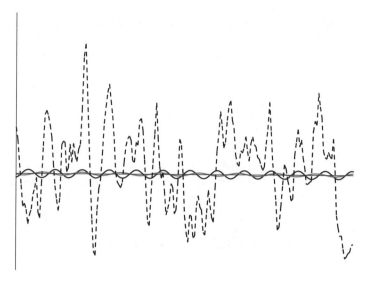

— Band pass filtered 16 period oscillations
- - Band pass filtered 23 period oscillations
— Simulated Ar(2) with complex roots and spectral peak

Figure 2.6: Data, 16-Period and 23-Period Oscillations for the Simulated AR(2) Process with Complex Roots and a Spectral Peak.

variance of ε_t. It is also the case that cycles found with MBBQ have turning points that are also invariant to $var(\varepsilon_t)$, since rescaling of z_t does not affect their location. Treating z_t as a quarterly process, after simulating 1600 observations on it, we find that the MBBQ cycle would be (on average) 11.3 quarters long, which contrasts with the oscillations predicted by either the complex roots or the spectral peak. To examine this further, we extract 16- and 23-quarter oscillations from the simulated data (using a Band pass filter) and these are plotted in Figure 2.6 along with the raw data. It is clear why the cycle length differs from the oscillations as there are far more turning points than either the roots or spectral density oscillations suggest. Neither oscillation captures the simulated data very well.

What would happen if we changed β_1 and β_2 so that there are complex roots but no spectral peak? Setting $\beta_1 = 1.4$,

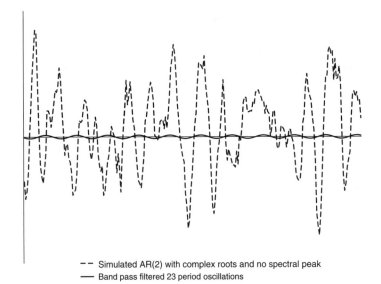

- - Simulated AR(2) with complex roots and no spectral peak
— Band pass filtered 23 period oscillations

Figure 2.7: Data and 23-Period Oscillation for the Simulated AR(2) Process with Complex Roots but No Spectral Peak.

$\beta_2 = -.53$ eliminates a spectral peak but leaves complex roots. With the changed parameter there is now an oscillation period of 22.6 quarters. Simulating data from the process and applying MBBQ gives a cycle average of 11.8 quarters. Unlike the large shift in the period of oscillation due to the parameter changes, the difference in the MBBQ-defined cycle length is likely to be just due to sampling fluctuations. Again Figure 2.7 plots the simulated data along with a 23-quarter oscillation. It is clear that the oscillations don't match the turning points very well and explain little of the variation in the series.[16]

Now let us change the AR parameters to $\beta_1 = 1.4$ and $\beta_2 = -.49$. Because $\beta_1^2 + 4\beta_2 = 0$, there are no complex roots and

---

[16]This is also true for other processes. Thus, using the Harvey-Jaeger model for z_t in (2.3), and the parameter values they give from fitting such a model to U.S. GNP, one finds that the 22-period oscillation their model predicts explains a tiny fraction of the "ups and downs" in the simulated series.

also no peaks in the spectral density. So very small changes in the magnitude of β_2 have led to very large changes in whether there are oscillations. In contrast the MBBQ-defined cycle length from the simulated data is 11.7 quarters, which departs little from what was found with the previous two sets of parameter values.

This shows that there is little connection between oscillations and cycle length. In many ways this is an old result—Sargent (1979, 240) simulated data from an AR(1) process and observed, "This illustrates how stochastic difference equations can generate processes that 'look like' they have business cycles even if their spectra do not have peaks."

2.6.2 Cycles and Oscillations in Nonstationary Series

To consider the differences that arise when there is nonstationarity in z_t, assume that Δz_t is now an AR(2) with no shocks and parameters equal to $\beta_1 = 1.4, \beta_2 = -.57$. This gives an oscillation of 16 periods in Δz_t. It also gives an oscillation of the same length in z_t. The reason is clear—turning points in z_t occur when Δz_t cuts the zero axis and, because Δz_t is following a sine curve, this must be the same distance apart as peaks and troughs in Δz_t. Note that the turning points in z_t are shifted from those in Δz_t—the latter occur when $\Delta^2 z_t$ is greater or less than zero, whereas those of z_t require Δz_t to be greater or less than zero.

When shocks are added, the situation changes. Now there is a spectral peak with 23-quarter oscillations. Simulating data on z_t and applying MBBQ produces an average cycle of duration 16 periods. Unlike the 16-period oscillation, this is just an average and the individual cycles have a range of durations. Because there is a unit root in the process for z_t the variance of z_t given some z_0 rises over time, so when a band-pass filter of 16 periods is extracted it accounts for very little of z_t, just as happened in the stationary case. It is interesting to observe that when $\beta_1 = 1.4, \beta_2 = -.49$ and there are no oscillations signaled by roots or spectral peaks, the simulated data have an average cycle of 23.5 quarters.

Finally, as we observed in Chapter 1, whether one gets a turning point depends on the mean of Δz_t in relation to the standard deviation of the shocks. Oscillations do not depend on either of these quantities. Thus, using the process

$$\Delta z_t = .008 + 1.4(z_{t-1} - .008) - .57(z_{t-2} - .008) + .003e_t,$$

it is found that the average duration of a cycle dated by turning points in z_t would be around 28.5 quarters, and this will change depending on the mean and standard deviation of the shocks. It is also the case that unlike all simulations to date, the phases are now of very different lengths. Contractions with this process would be 4.5 quarters and expansions 24. In all the previous simulations phases are close to having identical durations.

It is worth returning to the Bierens model of "complex unit roots" in (2.5). Data were simulated from it with φ set to produce an oscillation of 21 periods. Applying MBBQ to this data also produces a cycle of duration 21 periods. Thus, if the data is generated by a Bierens-type model, dating it using MBBQ would produce a cycle with duration that equaled that from the model. It is interesting then to observe that when estimating Bierens's model with U.S. data on GDP from 1947/1 to 2013/3 (after removing a deterministic trend) a value of φ is found implying an oscillation of 35 quarters. In contrast, MBBQ applied to the same data yields a cycle duration of just 13 quarters. This suggests that Bierens's model is not a good representation of the ups and downs in U.S. GDP.

2.7 The Nature of S_t and Its Modeling

To date we have said nothing about the nature of S_t, that is, what its data-generating process (DGP) is. As will be seen, the latter depends on the rule used to perform the dating as well as the nature of the Δy_t process. Understanding what determines the DGP of S_t will be important for engaging in empirical work with it, and this theme comes up a number of times in later chapters. Accordingly, we need to spend some time looking at the DGP in a variety of cases. It should be emphasized that the S_t have been *constructed* from data by using some rule and so although they are binary random variables, they are not like those occurring in microeconometrics. Instead they exhibit dependence in time and are best thought of as restricted Markov chains.

2.7.1 The Calculus Rule

Suppose that Δy_t is a Gaussian covariance stationary process and the calculus rule is employed. In this instance, Kedem (1980, 34) sets out the relation between the autocorrelations of the Δy_t and $S(t)$ processes. Letting $\rho_{\Delta y}(k) = corr(\Delta y_t, \Delta y_{t-k})$, and $\rho_S(k) = corr(S_t, S_{t-k})$, he determines that

$$\rho_S(k) = \frac{2}{\pi} \arcsin\left(\rho_{\Delta y}(k)\right). \qquad (2.16)$$

Thus $corr(S_t, S_{t-k}) = 0$ only if $corr(\Delta y_t, \Delta y_{t-k}) = 0$. Notice that the order of the S_t process changes with the degree of serial correlation in the Δy_t series. If the series is non-Gaussian, as would be true of those involving financial variables, there may be serial correlation in S_t, even if there is none in Δy_t. Thus series such as stock returns—which have little serial correlation—could nevertheless have quite large amounts in $sgn(\Delta y_t)$, that is in the process $1(\Delta y_t > 0)$. This arises owing to the presence of generalized autoregressive conditional heteroskedasticity (GARCH) in the returns.

Because the calculus rule was $S_t = 1(\Delta y_t > 0)$ when the underlying process for Δy_t is

$$\Delta y_t = x_t'\theta + \varepsilon_t, \qquad (2.17)$$

where x_t is assumed to be strictly exogenous (and so can be conditioned on) and ε_t is $n.i.d.(0, 1)$, then $S_t = 1(x_t'\theta + \varepsilon_t > 0)$ is a static probit model. Thus we could clearly capture the relation between S_t and the single index $z_t = x_t'\theta$ using such a model because $\Pr(S_t = 1|x_t'\theta, S_{t-1}) = \Phi(x_t'\theta)$.

2.7.2 Two-Quarters Rule

The "two-quarters rule" for peaks and troughs is given in equations (2.6) and (2.7). Since the two-quarters rule automatically produces turning points that alternate, S_t can be written as a recursion involving S_{t-1}, $\wedge_{t-1}$ and $\vee_{t-1}$, namely,

$$S_t = S_{t-1} - S_{t-1} \wedge_{t-1} +(1 - S_{t-1}) \vee_{t-1}. \qquad (2.18)$$

This implies that S_t evolves according to

$$S_t = [1 - \mathbf{1}(\Delta y_t < 0, \Delta y_{t+1} < 0)] S_{t-1}$$
$$+\mathbf{1}(\Delta y_t > 0, \Delta y_{t+1} > 0)(1 - S_{t-1}). \qquad (2.19)$$

Lagging the recursion (2.19) one period shows that S_{t-1} is a function of $\Delta y_{t-1}, \Delta y_t$, and S_{t-2}. By continued lagging of (2.19) and then substitution back into the recursion, S_t is found to be a nonlinear function of Δy_{t+1}, Δy_t, and the entire past history of Δy_t. So in this case S_t follows a nonlinear dynamic relation. Consequently, even if the DGP for Δy_t is (2.17), the relationship between S_t cannot be captured through a single index $z_t = x_t'\theta$. A comparison of this example with the calculus rule illustrates how the DGP of S_t is determined by the interaction between the dating algorithm and the DGP of Δy_t.

2.7.3 The MBBQ Rule

Using the calculus and two-quarters rules, much can be said, from first principles, about the nature of the DGP of S_t. In large measure this is because both rules automatically produce turning points that alternate and because they involve no minimum phase or cycle censoring. In contrast, the MBBQ rule involves both of these things, with the result that the DGP of S_t may never be precisely known. Nevertheless, some features can be found when simple approximations for S_t are used, and these can be useful for empirical work.

In the case of the simple BBQ rules, a peak is signaled at t when y_t is greater than $y_{t\pm k}$ $(k = 1, 2)$ and a trough when y_t is less than $y_{t\pm k}$ $(k = 1, 2)$. This can be expressed in terms of the binary indicators $\wedge_t$ and $\vee_t$ as

$$\wedge_t = 1(\{\Delta y_t > 0, \Delta_2 y_t > 0, \Delta y_{t+1} < 0, \Delta_2 y_{t+2} < 0\})$$

$$\vee_t = 1(\{\Delta y_t < 0, \Delta_2 y_t < 0, \Delta y_{t+1} > 0, \Delta_2 y_{t+2} > 0\}).$$

Now when using the MBBQ rule, there are further restrictions. One of these will be that phases must last for at least two periods. This enforces some constraints on the evolution of S_t. To illustrate that, suppose we fit a regression based on the form

$$E(S_t|S_{t-1}, S_{t-2}) = a_0 + a_1 S_{t-1} + a_2 S_{t-2} + a_3 S_{t-1} S_{t-2}.$$
(2.20)

An observed pattern $S_{t-1} = 1, S_{t-2} = 1$ (expansion) is compatible with S_t being either 1 or 0. But the pattern $S_{t-1} = 0, S_{t-2} = 1$ can only result in $S_t = 0$, since it would be impossible for S_{t-1} to be a contraction, as $(1, 0, 1)$ would mean a contraction lasting only a single period. Similarly $S_{t-1} = 1, S_{t-2} = 0$ must be followed by $S_t = 1$. Hence, imposing these constraints on (2.20), means that

$$a_0 + a_2 = 0$$
(2.21)

$$a_0 + a_1 = 1.$$
(2.22)

To see that these restrictions hold for MBBQ-like rules, we take the quarterly S_t consistent with the NBER turning point data for 1959/1 to 1995/2. Running the OLS regression in (2.20) of S_t on a constant, S_{t-1}, S_{t-2}, and $S_{t-1}S_{t-2}$ we get (Newey-West heteroskedasticity and autocorrelation consistent (HAC) t-ratios in brackets for window width of four periods)

$$S_t = \underset{(3.8)}{0.4} + \underset{(5.6)}{0.6S_{t-1}} - \underset{(-3.8)}{0.4S_{t-2}} + \underset{(3.1)}{0.35S_{t-1}S_{t-2}} + \eta_t.$$
(2.23)

It is clear that the expected restrictions eventuate and *these are simply due to the phase length restrictions* and do not come from the nature of the data Δy_t.

To formalize the MBBQ rules, which ensure that the states alternate and impose a minimum duration of two quarters to be spent in each state, Harding (2010a) establishes that the

S_t follow the following recursion (for quarterly data).[17]

$$S_t = S_{t-1}(1 - S_{t-2}) + S_{t-1}S_{t-2}(1 - \wedge^p_{t-1})$$
$$+(1 - S_{t-1})(1 - S_{t-2})\vee^p_{t-1} \tag{2.24}$$

By comparing (2.24) with (2.18) it can be seen that the dependence in S_t has lengthened to be at least of second order.

Further censoring to ensure that completed cycles have a minimum duration of five quarters can be dealt with by defining minimum cycle censored turning points $\wedge^c_{t-1}$. These must have the feature that when a peak is placed at $t-1$, the result is a complete cycle with duration of four quarters and the recursion will be[18]

$$\wedge^c_{t-1} = \wedge^p_{t-1}[1 - S_{t-1}S_{t-2}(1 - S_{t-3})(1 - S_{t-4})S_{t-5}]. \tag{2.25}$$

A comparable equation to (2.25) can be obtained for troughs, namely,

$$\vee^c_{t-1} = \vee^p_{t-1}[1 - (1 - S_{t-1})(1 - S_{t-2})S_{t-3}S_{t-4}(1 - S_{t-5})].$$

Thus, with minimum phase duration of two quarters, and a minimum completed cycle of five quarters, S_t evolves according to

$$S_t = S_{t-1} - S_{t-1}S_{t-2}\wedge^c_{t-1} + (1 - S_{t-1})(1 - S_{t-2})\vee^c_{t-1},$$

so it is now a fifth-order process.

In general the DGP of S_t requires knowledge of the DGP of Δy_t, as well as the rules used to define local peaks, alternation, and minimum phase lengths. Therefore it is quite a difficult task to precisely describe this DGP. However, what we can say is that the DGP of S_t from MBBQ-type rules would be expected to be at least of fifth order. If the states relate to monthly data, then there are different minimum phase and cycle restrictions.

---

[17]Following our earlier definition the superscript p indicates that the turning points have been censored to ensure that not only do they alternate, they also have phases with minimum duration of two quarters.

[18]Complete cycle durations of less than four quarters are ruled out by the requirement that completed phases have a minimum duration of two quarters combined with the requirement that phases alternate.

These can be imposed in a manner comparable to that shown above for quarterly data.

In the presentation we have focused on the backward-looking aspect of how censoring affects the nature of S_t, and provided a simplified exposition of how the latter is determined. It is also the case that censoring has a forward-looking component. This ensures that locating a turning point at date t would not result in a short phase or cycle in the future. This forward-looking component leads to alternating turning points in effect being defined as fixed points: the iterative procedures used in the dating algorithms serve the purpose of finding these fixed points. Analysis and mathematical representation of these aspects of censoring algorithms is the subject of ongoing research that may help to better understand the precise nature of the binary states S_t.

2.8 Conclusion

This chapter has investigated the three ways that economic researchers have approached the task of describing the ups and downs in the macroeconomy—oscillations, fluctuations, and cycles. It has contrasted the methods based on their mode of operation. This book will take a cycle perspective, that is, there will be an emphasis on locating turning points in the *levels* of economic activity, stock prices, interest rates, and credit. Although this was perhaps the earliest approach, and it still forms the basis of a good deal of empirical work by agencies engaged in policy analysis, it has languished in academia due to a perception that it cannot be given a sound statistical framework. As this book shows, that is a misperception. Turning points can be represented and analyzed in the same way as any time series. To be sure, there are difficulties, owing to the fact that the representation involves binary time series which, because they are constructed in some way from an underlying continuous process, are rarely likely to be independently distributed. This means that they need to be treated carefully, and the book aims to elaborate on the complications for applied work that is caused by the nature of the binary time series.

Chapter 3

Constructing Reference Cycles with Multivariate Information

3.1 Introduction

In many instances there may be more than one measure of economic activity, financial assets, and so on, and we would wish to combine these in some way to provide a single account of any recurrent event—such as a cycle—present in the series. This task involves compression of the information in the individual series into a single representative that is often called the common or reference cycle. Most published reference cycles in economic activity, equity prices, and so on, almost certainly utilize a number of series. Thus the NBER Dating Committee is known to use more than just one measure of the level of activity when deciding on the turning points in the U.S. business cycle.

There are many arguments for using more than a single series to capture the business cycle. GDP has the advantage that it incorporates many sectoral output series, but it does weight these in a particular way. Moreover it has the disadvantage of only being available on a quarterly basis, and in many countries it is not easy to get a long historical record at the desired frequency. Therefore, if it is accepted that a number of series will be used, the first question that arises is how one is to come up with a single business cycle measure when each of the series would generally have different turning points? This is the issue of *aggregation of turning points*. Methods to deal with this differ not by the number of series that are adopted but in how one *uses* them. In the first stage the series $y_{jt} = \ln Y_{jt}$, $j = 1, \ldots, n$ are examined to find either their phase states or turning points. This process leads to *specific cycle* indexes represented by either the phases—through S_{jt}—or turning points $(\wedge_{jt}, \vee_{jt})$. Subsequently, the S_{jt} or $\wedge_{jt}, \vee_{jt}$ are combined to produce a single set of representative phases—S_t^a—or turning points—$(\wedge_{jt}^a, \vee_{jt}^a)$. These constitute the *reference cycle*. Accordingly, Section 3.2 sets out rules that take the S_{jt} and combine them together to get S_t^a. In contrast, Section 3.3 uses as inputs the turning points in y_{jt} and aggregates those to define turning points in the reference cycle. Finally, Section 3.4 combines the series y_{jt} themselves to give y_t^a, after which the cycle in y_t^a is found, that is, this method finds *turning points in an aggregate*.

3.2 Determining the Reference Cycle via Phases

3.2.1 Diffusion Indexes to Determine the Phases

As mentioned in Chapter 1 when the calculus rule was used for locating turning points, it is often best to first determine the states of expansion and contraction S_t, after which turning points can be derived. The construction of *diffusion indexes* proceeds in this way. Consider the changes $\Delta y_{jt+1} = y_{jt+1} - y_{jt}$. Suppose we have n^+ of the Δy_{jt+1} series that are positive and n^- that are negative. Then, if $\frac{n^-}{n} > .5$, a recession is said to be present in $t + 1$, that is, there is a peak at t.[1] This approach is used by a number of agencies around the world for finding when recessions and expansions are operative, for example, the South African Reserve Bank and the Japanese ESRI (provided at http://www.esri.cao.go.jp/en/stat/di/di2e.html). The latter mentions that turning points were also found with Bry-Boschan methods, although there seems to have been some smoothing of the series before they are used to locate the states. The South Africans use

---

[1] In practice the rule is a little more complex to allow for $\Delta y_{jt} = 0$. In this case different weights are assigned to $\Delta y_{jt} > 0, \Delta y_{jt} = 0$, and $\Delta y_{jt} < 0$. These numbers are then summed for each series and compared to $\frac{n}{2}$. One also needs to allow for the fact that with series such as interest rates the difference in levels (not the logs) would be employed. In addition, series such as the unemployment change would be multiplied by the negative of unity before using them in the test.

186 series—see Bosch and Ruch (2012). In the United States the Conference Board also works with diffusion indexes, although with a relatively small number of monthly series. They mention that there are two variants of the method that might be applied. One is that described above, which is referred to as a *one monthly index*. There is also a *six-monthly index*, which works with the signs of $y_{jt+6} - y_{jt}$. Here the turning points are located by reference to the phase one was in at $t + 4$. This is obviously closer to the Bry-Boschan approach as it requires the growth rate to be positive or negative for a minimum amount of time.

3.2.2 Constructing a Reference Cycle by Common Phases

Krolzig and Toro (KT) (2004) proposed that a reference cycle be found by first finding what phases the n series are in at time t. Once these were available they used the rule that a recession (or an expansion) in aggregate economic activity occurred at t if the percentage of the series that are in that phase at t exceeds .5. It is worth seeing how this method performs when a a small number of series are selected to represent economic activity. When dating the December 2007 peak the NBER Business Cycle Dating Committee mention looking at five series—quarterly GDP and four monthly series on real personal income less transfers, real manufacturing and wholesale-retail trade ("sales"), industrial production, and nonfarm employment. A very long series of data is available on industrial production and employment, but the other two are only available from 1959.1.[2] The phases in each of the monthly series are found by dating with MBBQ, and then a simple rule is used that if at least two series are in the same phase at t, this is the phase of the reference cycle at that point in time. After the reference cycle phases have been established one can construct the turning points. Table 3.1 gives these as well as those provided by the NBER.

The KT procedure seems quite good at replicating the NBER turning points, although there are a few cases where

---

[2]It should be noted that in this book we refer to monthly dates with a period and quarters with a back slash (/). Thus 1959.1 is January 1959 while 1959/1 would be the first quarter of 1959.

Table 3.1: Comparison of U.S. Business Cycle Turning Points:
Krolzig-Toro Method and NBER

Turning point	Krolzig-Torro	NBER
peak	1960.4	1960.4
trough	1961.1	1961.2
peak	1970.3	1969.12
trough	1970.11	1970.11
peak	1974.7	1973.11
trough	1975.3	1975.3
peak	1979.6	1980.1
trough	1980.7	1980.7
peak	1981.1	1981.7
trough	1982.12	1982.11
peak	1990.7	1990.7
trough	1991.3	1991.3
peak	2001.2	2001.3
trough	2001.11	2001.9
peak	2008.8	2007.12
trough	2009.6	2009.6

there are relatively large discrepancies. One example of this
is the difference in location of the peak before the last U.S.
recession—2008.8 (KT) and 2007.12 (NBER). An advantage of
the KT rule is that it is very simple to apply, and this makes it
appealing when performing automated dating of the reference
cycle in the presence of many series.

3.3 Combining Specific Cycle Turning Points to Get the Reference Cycle

3.3.1 Harding and Pagan's (2006) Algorithm

The idea behind this strategy is to say that a turning point in
aggregate economic activity occurs at t if the turning points of
the individual series *cluster around* the point t. The problem

then is to decide on what clustering means, that is, how to find a central tendency for these specific cycle turning points which can be used as the reference cycle turning point. How one proceeds to do that depends partly on the information available about where the turning point might be. Harding and Pagan (2006) gave a relatively simple algorithm to find the central tendency, and we now describe its essence.

Consider a point in time t as a candidate for the reference cycle turning point. The turning points of the jth series that are closest to t will lie at (say) t_j^P (for peaks) and t_j^T (for troughs). Taking peaks as an example, we then measure the absolute distance between the closest peak in the jth series—which occurs at t_j^P—and t, calling it $\tau_{jt}^P = |t_j^P - t|$. At any t this gives a vector of n values which need to be summarized in a single value. One might use the mean of τ_{jt}^P, but Harding and Pagan adopted the median as the central tendency measure. Let this be τ_t^P. Then, if the series τ_t^P has a local minimum at t^* that would be taken as a peak for the reference cycle, that is, since τ_t^P has its smallest value at $t = t^*$ this would be the time around which the peaks of the individual series cluster. In practice there may not be a single t^*—the minimum value may occur at a range of values for t. There is less chance of this for large n. However, when ties occur, some rule has to be applied to break them. One criterion would be to choose between potential t^* values by using the value of $\sum_{j=1}^{n}(\tau_{jt}^P)^2$ at those points, that is, a smaller value of this dispersion index might be taken to indicate that the turning points are more closely clustered. There are obviously other criteria that might be adopted.

The method originated from a perusal of the NBER procedures as documented by Geoffrey Moore but was formalized by studying the spreadsheets used by Boehm and Moore (1984) when obtaining an NBER-like reference cycle for Australia. The algorithm seemed to be able to produce quite a good replication of the reference cycle published by the NBER and also the equivalent set of information for Australia. The first of these replications appeared in Harding and Pagan (2006), and we update it here. It uses the same four monthly series as those adopted in the previous section when discussing the Krolzig and Toro approach. Table 3.2 shows the turning points in the four series. It is clear that there is an extra set

Table 3.2: Comparison of Harding-Pagan Algorithm's and NBER
Dating of the Reference Cycle

	Ind prod	Emp	Sales	Income	HPA	NBER
peak	1960.1	1960.4	1960.1		1960.1	1960.4
trough	1961.2	1961.2	1961.1		1961.2	1961.2
peak	1967.1					
trough	1967.7					
peak	1969.10	1970.3	1969.10		1969.10	1969.12
trough	1970.11	1970.11	1970.11		1970.11	1970.11
peak	1973.11	1974.10	1973.11	1973.11	1973.11	1973.11
trough	1975.3	1975.3	1975.3	1975.4	1975.3	1975.3
peak	1979.6		1979.3	1979.12	1979.6	1980.1
trough	1980.7		1980.7	1980.7	1980.7	1980.7
peak	1981.7	1981.7	1981.8	1981.8	1981.7	1981.7
trough	1982.12	1982.11			1982.11	1982.11
peak	1984.7					
trough	1985.12					
peak	1990.9	1990.6	1990.8	1990.7	1990.7	1990.7
trough	1991.3	1991.5	1991.1	1991.12	1991.4	1991.3
peak	2000.6	2001.2	2000.9	2001.3	2001.2	2001.3
trough	2001.11	2003.8	2001.9	2003.2	2001.10	2001.9
peak			2002.8			
trough			2003.2			
peak	2007.12	2008.1	2007.10	2008.3	2007.12	2007.12
trough	2009.6	2010.3	2009.6	2010.2	2009.6	2009.6

of turning points in sales and industrial production but at
different times. Since they only occur in a single series, we
would ignore them when constructing a reference cycle, that
is, we would not locate a turning point in the aggregate cycle
if there is just a turning point in only a single series.

Now there are some problems that can arise when applying
the Harding and Pagan algorithm (HPA) in this context. One of
these comes from the fact that there are just four series y_{jt}. So
what is the median of the four τ_{jt} found from MBBQ? We adopt
the convention that the median is the second value among the

four numbers ordered from lowest to highest. A second issue comes from the fact that there may be ties, namely, because τ_t is an integer it may have the same local minimum value for a number of time points t, and if it does, there will be no unique outcome for t^*. Suppose we found that τ_t had the same local minimum at t_1 and t_2. Then, as mentioned earlier, one might choose between t_1 and t_2 as the value for t^* by using that time point for which $\sum_{j=1}^{4} \tau_{jt}^2$ is lowest, that is, chose t_1 if $\sum_{j=1}^{4} \tau_{jt_1}^2 < \sum_{j=1}^{4} \tau_{jt_2}^2$. This supplementary criterion would seem to accord with the notion of achieving a tighter clustering. However, even utilizing this extra test is not always enough to get a unique set of turning points for the reference cycle.

We illustrate these points with three cases.

1. Take the case of MBBQ troughs at 2009.6, 2010.3, 2009.6, and 2010.2 in the four series. Selecting $t = 2009.6$ as a trial date for the reference cycle trough we would get $\tau_{jt} = [0\ 9\ 0\ 8]$, which gives the median value (τ_t^T) of 0 and so $t^* = 2009.6$. Experimentation with other possible values for t^* shows that $t^* = 2009.6$ is unique. One implication of this example is that when there are just four series, and there are two or three turning points at the same t, then that date will be selected as a reference cycle turning point.

2. For the candidate peaks in 2000/2001 we have 2001.2 producing $\tau_{jt} = [8\ 0\ 5\ 1]$ while 2001.3 will be $\tau_{jt} = [9\ 1\ 6\ 0]$. Hence, there is no discrimination based on the median values for τ_{jt} since this will be unity in both cases. But $\sum_{j=1}^{4} \tau_{jt}^2$ is less for 2001.2 and so it is selected as the reference cycle peak.

3. There are a number of cases where ties cannot be broken. A first example involves the peaks in 2007.12, 2008.1, 2007.10, and 2008.3. Here we find that when $t = 2007.11$, τ_{jt} would be $[1\ 2\ 1\ 4]$; when $t = 2007.12$, it is $[0\ 1\ 2\ 3]$; and finally, when $t = 2008.1$, τ_{jt} will be $[1\ 0\ 3\ 2]$. Clearly two of these candidates for t^*—2007.12 and 2008.1—have the same median of unity. Looking at $\sum_{j=1}^{4} \tau_{jt}^2$ for these two dates we find the same value, and so one cannot break the tie with that criterion. Consequently, we have just chosen

2007.12 as the peak. Similar cases are the peaks in 1981, where there are two series which have one date for the peak while the other two series have a different date. In this instance, we have just taken 1981.7 as the reference cycle peak. Finally, one cannot differentiate between 1990.7 and 1990.8 as peaks. One might need to resort to quantitative measures based on the amplitudes of the cycles to break these ties, and it is here that judgment clearly plays a role.

A perusal of the results shows that the HPA reference cycle gives a good match with the NBER results. The exception is that relating to the end of the 1970s. It is interesting that MBBQ dates the peak in quarterly GDP as being in the first quarter of 1980 and, since the Business Cycle Dating Committee mentioned that this was a fifth series they looked at, it may explain why they chose 1980.1 as the peak rather than the 1979.6 of HPA. It is notable that HPA provides a much better match to the turning points of the last recession (as defined by the NBER) than that of the Krolzig-Toro approach. Furthermore, there are a number of other cases where the HPA correspondence is closer.

3.3.2 Stock and Watson's (2010) Algorithm

Stock and Watson (2010) considered the case where many series are available and one is looking to establish where a reference cycle turning point should be placed in an interval (called by them an *episode*), given that it is known that there is a turning point within it. With this constraint any episode k will have turning points in the jth series at dates t_{kj}^P (if a peak) and t_{kj}^T (if a trough). They then formulate equations for each episode of the form (using the peak for illustration) $t_{kj}^P = a_k + \beta_{jk} + \varepsilon_{kt}$. Here a_k is designed to measure the date of the reference cycle peak within the kth episode, while β_{jk} will be the lead or lag of the individual series peaks relative to the reference cycle peak. To see what this means let $\beta_{jk} = 0$ and apply OLS to the relation. Then $\hat{a}_k$ would be the mean of the peaks found in the kth episode and this would be taken as the reference cycle peak. Harding and Pagan's algorithm works in much the same way except it uses the median and does not need the idea of an episode. Of course if Stock and Watson used a least absolute deviations (LAD) estimator of a_k this would produce the median. Given the similarity to Harding and Pagan's algorithm, it seems odd that there is no discussion by them about ties, but it may be that this is less of a concern owing to the large number of series they employ (270), and the fact that the series may be either leading or lagging indicators of aggregate activity rather than coincident. The role of the parameter β_{jk} is to deal with that latter feature. In Harding and Pagan's approach it is effectively assumed that the series being dated have been chosen to be coincident indicators, and they recommend testing for this in advance by checking how synchronized the cycles are. One would not use series with this method unless they were highly synchronized. Methods for examining the degree of synchronization are discussed in Chapter 6.

Stock and Watson treat the data t^P_{kj} as panel data, and this enables them to compute some standard errors for a_k and β_{jk}. They refer to their strategy as "date and aggregate." There are complications since the asymptotic theory assumes that the series have been randomly selected, whereas there may be substantial correlation between them. Accordingly, they suggest some stratified sampling methods to account for this. Of course, the main issue is how to select the episodes. In Stock and Watson (2014) "heat maps" are presented which show what the magnitude of Δy_{jt} are in terms of colors, and they say that these maps "suggest that the disaggregated series would also be useful for ascertaining whether a turning point has occurred." However, they follow that with "but we do not pursue that. Henceforth, we focus on data by episode, where an episode is defined to be the NBER turning point date $\pm$ 12 months" (372). In some ways the use of the magnitudes of Δy_{jt} points to a heat map providing some of the same information about turning points found with diffusion indexes.

The method works quite well. They do highlight some cases where their method fails to closely replicate the dates chosen by the NBER. Thus they find peaks at January 1960 and October 1969 instead of the April 1960 and December 1969 dates given by the NBER. It is interesting that Harding and

Pagan's method, which uses just the four monthly series the NBER Dating Committee focus on, also produces the same dates for peaks as Stock and Watson find.

3.4 Finding Turning Points by Series Aggregation

In this method the individual series y_{jt} that were used to construct the S_{jt} are weighted together to form some aggregate, and then the turning points in the latter series are taken to be those of the reference cycle. In some cases it is obvious what the weights should be. For example if we were dating the euro area business cycle with GDP then y_{jt} would most likely be the GDP of the jth country in the euro area, and so it would seem reasonable to weight the y_{jt} with their share in euro area GDP. In cases such as the four monthly indicators of U.S. economic activity used in preceding sections there is no obvious way to choose weights, as the series are very disparate. For this reason weights have been selected either by parametric or nonparametric estimation procedures.

Parametric methods work with some form of principal component analysis, either in a static or dynamic form. Stock and Watson (1991) pioneered the idea of using principal components and the method they used in Stock and Watson (1999) has subsequently been adopted in forming the Federal Reserve Bank of Chicago's National Activity Index (CFNAI).[3] A dynamic version of this that combines the y_{jt} and their lags in a nonparametric way was developed by Forni et al. (2001).

A useful way of thinking about both parametric and nonparametric approaches is via factor models. A common factor representing aggregate economic activity is taken to drive all the y_{jt} and the issue is how to extract it.[4] The format connecting the common factor and series is generally assumed to be of the form

$$\frac{\Delta \log Y_{jt} - \mu_j}{\sigma_j} = \gamma_j \Delta f_t + v_{jt}, \qquad (3.1)$$

---

[3]See http://www.chicagofed.org/webpages/publications/cfnai/index.cfm.

[4]There may be more than one common factor, but these can be aggregated to make a single one after they have been isolated.

where Δf_t is the common factor and there are $j = 1, \ldots, n$ series. Static and dynamic principal components are known to span the space of factors and so could be used to reconstruct Δf_t. With a parametric approach the system above can be written as $\Delta y_{jt} = a_j + G_j \Delta f_t + u_{jt}$, and the factor Δf_t can be extracted once a_j and G_j are estimated. To do this some parametric statistical model is needed to describe the evolution of the factor. Thus Stock and Watson have Δf_t following an $AR(2)$ with a standardization of $\Delta \ln Y_{jt}$ by σ_j. As we discuss in the next chapter, Chauvet (1998), Chauvet and Piger (2003), Krolzig and Toro (2004), and Artis et al. (2004) use Markov switching models for the Δf_t. Thereafter, some method for finding turning points in f_t is employed, and this produces the reference cycle.

One advantage of finding a reference cycle through a weighting scheme is that the resulting series f_t or y_t^a can be regarded as a *coincident index*. It is a continuous variable rather than a discrete process as the S_t^a would be. There is no certainty that the turning points in either f_t or y_t^a would match those in the NBER reference cycle unless the weights were chosen with a criterion that reflected such an objective.

3.5 Conclusion

The chapter has looked at how recurrent events might be dated by using a number of series rather than a single one. There is no one method to do this, but in many cases, the procedures come up with rather similar results. Much depends on how one wants to use the dating information. If it is for judging models or evaluating some macroeconomic propositions, then the ability to automate the selection process easily would be a paramount consideration. Alternatively, if it was desired to establish a definitive dating of cycles in activity or financial series, then it is probably the case that a variety of methods would be used with some judgment applied when determining the weight given to each. Further work is needed on how the methods perform when faced with simulations from estimated models rather than using actual data, as their effectiveness is unclear in such a changed environment.

Chapter 4

Model-Based Rules for Describing Recurrent Events

4.1 Introduction

The prescribed rules for cycles detailed in the preceding two chapters seem relatively simple to apply and have had widespread use. As mentioned in Chapter 1, an alternative approach to describing recurrent events involves using a model that incorporates different regimes. Some mechanism is then given for determining how the regimes come about at any point in time, and the information provided about the regimes is then used to date the recurrent events. If this approach is adopted, the major question arising concerns the nature of the regime switching model. In Chapter 1 the model had regimes being chosen randomly according to some unobserved exogenous process. Perhaps the most common extension of this involves allowing the probability that a particular regime occurs to depend on what regime was present in the preceding period of time. This leads to the class of Markov switching (MS) processes.

There are many variants of MS models and Sections 4.2.1–4.2.6 discuss them in the context where there is only a single series in which the recurrent event is observed. These sections look at the ability of MS models to date recurrent events, principally the business cycle, as this has been the major application to date. A major issue arising in this context was foreshadowed in Chapter 1 and pertains to the estimation and validation of MS models. Another relates to whether the model-based rules need to be adapted to reflect the censoring of phases as these were a key feature of prescribed rules. There are also issues of interpretation. These arise because the latent variables distinguishing the regimes are often invalidly equated with the recurrent events. The subsections of Section 4.2 deal with all these issues in the context of some simple MS models, as well as reviewing more complicated MS models that have been proposed.

An alternative approach is to make the regimes depend on an observable rather than an unobservable variable. This leads to the class of what can broadly be designated as threshold models in which an unobserved variable exceeding some threshold ensures that a different regime holds. There have been suggestions along these lines, for example, van Dijk and Franses (1999) tried to determine business cycle phases that way. Diebold and Rudebusch (1996, 69) say, "Although threshold models are of interest, models with latent states as opposed to observed states may be more appropriate for business cycle modelling." Although there can be little doubt that the MS approach to regimes has dominated research on applications to this topic, Section 4.2.7 briefly looks at a threshold case where the regimes strictly depend on some observed variable. Finally, Section 4.3 considers using more than one series to describe the recurrent events and deals with some of the questions that arise in that context.

4.2 Model-Based Rules for Dating Cycles with Univariate Series

4.2.1 Two Simple Models for Dating Recurrent Events through a Regime Perspective

An alternative way of formulating a turning point rule is to base it on the output of some model for Δy_t. By far the most popular variant of these have been regime-switching models. Following from Chapter 1 a simple version would be

$$\Delta y_t = \mu_t + \sigma \varepsilon_t \tag{4.1}$$

$$\mu_t = \mu_1 \xi_t + (1 - \xi_t)\mu_0, \tag{4.2}$$

where ξ_t is a binary random variable and ε_t is $n.i.d(0, 1)$. Taking ξ_t to be independently distributed with $\Pr(\xi_t = j) = p_{jj}$ was the model presented in Chapter 1 and, following the EViews8 description, it might be termed a simple switching (SS) model. A different model allows ξ_t to follow a first-order Markov process with transition probabilities $p_{ij} = \Pr(\xi_t = j | \xi_{t-1} = i)$, and this is the hidden layer Markov chain introduced into econometrics by Hamilton (1989). This variant is often given the shortened descriptor of an MS model.

Now the dating rule employed to find the recurrent states involves comparing $\Pr(\xi_t = 1 | F_t)$ (where F_t is some observed data on the past and/or future history of Δy_t), with a critical threshold value c. This comparison produces a new binary random variable of the form $\zeta_t = 1([\Pr(\xi_t = 1 | F_t) - c > 0])$. This binary variable ζ_t describes the recurrent event. Thus, when $\zeta_t = 1$, we would see an expansion/bull market/crisis, and so on, at time t, and this occurs if $\Pr(\xi_t = 1 | F_t) > c$. Otherwise ζ_t would be zero. Accordingly, it should be clear that *the ζ_t corresponds to the recurrent events* signaled by the model-based rule; ξ_t *are not the recurrent events*.

The choice of c is mostly decided outside of the model. Hamilton (1989) originally proposed $c = .5$, and this has been used quite a bit, although values down to $c = .33$ have been adopted. One has to be careful with choosing low values for c, as seen from the fact that the unconditional probability of a recession is $.15$ (based on NBER dates). Accordingly, if a value for c of around $.15$ was used, fitting any model would be quite unnecessary. There have been at least two suggestions for making c depend on the data. First, Candelon et al. (2012) considered a range of methods to determine an optimal c, balancing the Type I and Type II errors which would occur for any given value of c. Of these methods the favored one was to choose c to minimize the ratio of false to true positive outcomes. Clearly such a criterion relies on the fact that we have already established a "true" set of recurrent states outside of the model, and so it raises the same issues as would arise when setting thresholds for prescribed rules based on the past history of Δy_t. Second, Chauvet and Morais (2010, 12) proposed that "a peak (trough) is called if the probability of recession increases (decreases) beyond its mean plus one standard deviation." When dating business cycle phases, c will then be equal to the sample mean of $\Pr(\xi_t = 0)$ plus 1 standard deviation.

4.2.2 Using an Approximate Linear Model to Understand the MS Model Rule

It is instructive to effect a comparison of the simple prescribed rules used by BBQ for establishing cycle phases with the rule based on an MS model. This requires us to find a simple expression for the "MS rule" that can be compared to the "BBQ rule." Because the MS rule is an unknown nonlinear function of the data, we look at a linear approximation to it. It turns out to be an accurate enough approximation for our purposes— Harding and Pagan (2003) showed this in the context of the model and the data used in Hamilton (1989).

To derive the linear approximation we note that Hamilton (1989, 360) showed that the binary nature of ξ_t means that it can be represented as an AR(1) process

$$\xi_t = (1 - p_{00}) + (p_{11} + p_{00} - 1)\xi_{t-1} + \eta_t, \qquad (4.3)$$

where $E(\eta_t) = 0$ and

$$v_\eta = var(\eta_t) = \frac{(1 - p_{00})p_{11}(1 - p_{11})}{2 - p_{11} - p_{00}} + \frac{(1 - p_{11})p_{00}(1 - p_{00})}{2 - p_{11} - p_{00}}.$$

As he observes, the error term η_t is actually conditionally heteroskedastic, since it depends on ξ_{t-1}. Moreover, it is a discrete random variable. Suppose however η_t is treated as $n.i.d.(0, v_\eta)$. Then (4.1), (4.2), and (4.3) would represent a state space form and the Kalman filter might be applied to compute $\hat{\xi}_{t|t} = E(\xi_t | \Delta y_t, \Delta y_{t-1}, \ldots)$. Moreover, because ξ_t is a binary random variable, $\Pr(\xi_t = 1 | \Delta y_t, \Delta y_{t-1}, \ldots) = \hat{\xi}_{t|t}$. Since the state space form (4.1) and (4.3) is time invariant, the steady-state Kalman filter equations can be used to determine $\hat{\xi}_{t|t}$ recursively as

$$\hat{\xi}_{t|t} = a + b\hat{\xi}_{t-1|t-1} + c\Delta y_t, \qquad (4.4)$$

where a, b are functions of the MS model parameters. Solving (4.4) gives

$$\hat{\xi}_{t|t} = (a + c\Delta y_t) + b(a + c\Delta y_{t-1})$$

$$+b^2(a + c\Delta y_{t-2}) + \ldots \quad (4.5)$$

$$= a + \sum_{j=0}^{T} \delta_j \Delta y_{t-j}, \quad (4.6)$$

and so we would set the *recurrent event state* ζ_t to unity if $a + \sum_{j=0}^{T} \delta_j \Delta y_{t-j} > c$, but otherwise it would be zero. If one forms the smoothed estimate of ξ_t, that is, using all the data and not just the past history, then $\hat{\xi}_{t|T} = a' + \sum_{j=0}^{T} \varphi_{\pm j} \Delta y_{t \pm j}$ involves a weighting of the current, past, and future Δy_t with weights $\varphi_{\pm j}$ that depend on the model parameters. Hamilton actually used the smoothed probabilities for his dating of business cycles, and this has been the most common response in the literature.

By inspection of the rule based on the MS model versus that of BBQ it can be seen that they both use information on growth rate outcomes but in different ways:

1. In BBQ only the set $\{\Delta y_{t-1}, \ldots, \Delta y_{t+2}\}$ is used to make a decision about whether there is a turning point at t, that is, to determine what phase holds at that point. In contrast the MS model approach computes and uses $\Pr(\xi_t = 1|\mathcal{F}_t)$, where $\mathcal{F}_t$ generally uses either *all* the growth rate data over a complete sample (smoothed estimate) or only the information up to Δy_t (filtered estimate).

2. In BBQ only qualitative information on growth rates (signs) are used, whereas the MS parametric model combines growth rates together to form a single index (the $\Pr(\xi_t = 1|\mathcal{F}_t)$) which is then compared to some critical value c.

It is clear that both methods are dating the business cycle. There has always been some confusion in the literature over this point, with scattered comments from users of the MS model that one is dating what was earlier called a growth cycle, seemingly because the model is based on Δy_t.

It is worth using the perspective provided by the analysis above to think about sorting any set of data y_t into "high" and "low" regimes. A rule-based approach would use (4.1) and (4.2) (but with Δy_t replaced by y_t) and decide on high and low regimes based on whether $\Pr(\xi_t = 1|F_t) > c$. Using the state space form approach above this would involve checking if $\sum_{j=0}^{T} \varphi_{\pm j} y_{t \pm j} > c - a'$ (in the smoothed case). Essentially this points to the need to form a centered moving average of y_t as a suitable prescribed rule. The length of the moving average will depend on how rapidly $\varphi_{\pm j}$ goes to zero as j rises. Effectively, this is a prescribed rule and it would require the setting of a threshold $c - a'$. Of course the model based rule has a similar issue in that c has to be set because it is not found from the data.

4.2.3 Estimation and Validation Issues with Regime-Switching Models

Because we are using a model, the question arises of whether there are any problems involved in estimating its parameters, and how one decides what is an adequate fit of it to the data. To begin we look at fitting some MS models to U.S. GDP growth. A variant of the simple MS model given in (4.1) and (4.2) is used. This matches what Hamilton (1989) fitted to U.S. GNP data and has the form

$$\Delta y_t - \mu_t = \sum_{j=1}^{4} \beta_j (\Delta y_{t-j} - \mu_{t-j}) + \sigma \varepsilon_t, \qquad (4.7)$$

where μ_t is governed by (4.2) and ξ_t follows the Markov process.[1] The model is fitted to data over two periods—the original Hamilton period of 1952/2–1984/4 and a longer one

---

[1] This is often referred to as an MS model in the mean (MSM) versus a model in which the MS model drives the intercept (MSI). The difference is that the MSM inroduces lagged ξ_{t-j} into the model through μ_{t-j}.

of 1952/2–2013/1. Over the shorter period this produced parameter estimates of

$$\mu_0 = -.0103, \quad \mu_1 = .0097, \quad \beta_1 = .34, \quad \beta_2 = .09,$$

$$\beta_3 = -.09, \quad \beta_4 = -.16, \quad \sigma = .009, \quad p_{11} = .945,$$

$$p_{00} = .169,$$

while over the longer period they became

$$\mu_0 = -.0123, \quad \mu_1 = .0087, \quad \beta_1 = .40, \quad \beta_2 = .23,$$

$$\beta_3 = -.17, \quad \beta_4 = -.09, \quad \sigma = .007, \quad p_{00} = .338,$$

$$p_{11} = .959.$$

The model parameter estimates look reasonably stable, although the probability of staying in the regime indexed by zero once one has gotten into it has risen.[2]

Because Hamilton (1999) found that a good match to NBER cycle dates was found by using an MS model-based rule, we look at the smoothed estimate of $\Pr(\xi_t = 0)$ from the model fitted to the longer period. This is given in Figure 4.1. It is clear that the model fails to produce a good match to business cycle information. One can see that there are no recessions signaled during the early 1990s and 2000s. Moreover, during the last recession—which the NBER has as beginning in 2007/4—the first period that the probability exceeds .3 is 2008/4, and then the rule would say that the recession only lasts for two quarters. The model works much better for recessions before the 1990s, although even then it is not a good match to the NBER data on the lengths of the 1970s recessions. The NBER has the recession in 1969/1970 as lasting for 4 quarters, while that of the mid-1970s went for 5 quarters. In contrast, the MS model says that the 1970s recession lasted only one period (using virtually any value of c) and during 1973–1976 only

---

[2]Estimation was performed using the MS option under switching regressions in EViews8.

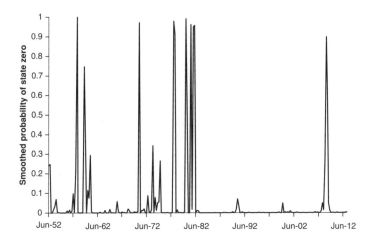

Figure 4.1: Smoothed Probability of Being in State Zero from MS Model Estimated over 1952/2–2013/1.

1973/3 gave a smoothed $\Pr(\xi_t = 0) > .3$.[3] Ahking (2013, 6) comes to the same conclusions as us, saying, "we find very disappointing results when we use the full-sample smoother to determine business cycle turning points for the longer sample period 1948:I–2011:III from the MS model estimated with real GDP. We find the following quarters to have a probability of a recession of greater than 50%: 1949:IV, 1958:I, 1970:IV, 1980:II, 1981:II, 1981:IV–1982:1, and 2008:IV–2009:I. Again, these are not very meaningful turning points." To some extent this seems to be a consequence of the shift from GNP (used by Hamilton) to GDP. Ahking notes that

we are unable to find any meaningful turning points from our MS model estimated with real GDP rather than with real GNP for 1951:I–1984:IV however. For example, there are only four

---

[3]If one used the Chauvet and Morais method of selecting c, one finds that the mean of smoothed $\Pr(\xi_t = 0) = .06$ with standard error of .196, so this would suggest a value of c equal to .256. If this critical value was adopted it would slightly modify our conclusions since 1975/1 had $\Pr(\xi_t = 0) = .265$ and 2008/3 was .269. It should be noted that we have computed $\Pr(\xi_t)$ given all the data but simply refer to it as the smoothed probability rather than writing out the conditioning.

quarters for which the probability of a recession is greater than 50%. They are 1958:I, 1970:IV, 1980:II, and 1981:II. This result is rather surprising since the correlation coefficient between real GDP and real GNP is 0.99 for this sample period, and the correlation coefficient for the growth rates of real GDP and real GNP is 0.94!

One response to this is to argue that a new MS model is needed, and some alternatives will be discussed later. Another is that the poor performance might come from estimation difficulties. When estimating MS models it becomes apparent that the likelihood is ill-defined. Hamilton (1990) noted this and suggested that one should use the EM algorithm to ensure that the likelihood was maximized. The program used in this chapter to compute the parameter estimates was that provided in EViews8. EViews8 tries to get around the local maxima problem by using both a fixed and random set of starting values, and it can be structured to engage in random searches from the final estimated parameter values. Our experience is that it seems to produce higher likelihoods than some other well-known MS programs, such as Perlin (2012). However, there is no doubt that the starting values used in EViews8 can be important in determining whether a maximum to the likelihood is found. Because of this an EM algorithm was also applied when the model in (4.7) was fitted to the shorter and longer data periods. The same conclusions were reached regarding the periods of time spent in recessions as given earlier.[4]

One might well ask why the likelihood is ill-defined. As observed in Chapter 1, an identification issue is exhibited in simple switching models due to a "labeling" problem, and this goes over to MS models, that is, in the simple switching model there were two different sets of values of the parameters which gave identical likelihoods.[5] One can ease the problem by imposing constraints such as $\mu_1 > \mu_0$, but this is unlikely

---

[4]We thank Tom Boot of Erasmus University for providing his MATLAB program that performs ML estimation of MS models using the EM algorithm.

[5]Smith and Summers (2004) was an early description of the impact of this problem in estimating MS models.

to completely resolve it, unless some constraints are placed on the p_{ij}.

A second problem is the autoregressive structure in (4.7). If one thinks about estimating the model parameters when $\beta_j = 0$, then there are just five parameters to estimate, requiring five moments of Δy_t. As seen in the previous subsection ξ_t is an autoregressive process whose parameters depend on the p_{ij}, and so the serial correlations in Δy_t are useful for estimating the transition probabilities. But when an AR model is employed, these are "used up" in estimating β_j. Accordingly, higher order dynamic correlations are needed to perform estimation, and these may not be well defined in smaller samples. To investigate this further we simulated 2000 data points from the MS model with the longer sample parameter values. Then this data was used to fit the model

$$\Delta y_t = \mu + \sum_{j=1}^{4} \beta_j \Delta y_{t-1} + \gamma |\Delta y_{t-1}| + \sigma_t \varepsilon_t, \qquad (4.8)$$

where σ_t followed an ARCH process (GARCH did not seem to be needed). Both γ and the ARCH coefficient were significantly different from zero (t-ratios of 3.09 and 4.5), so that there are enough moment conditions to determine all parameters. However, when only 200 observations of the simulated data were used, the t-ratios became 1.1 and .6. So estimating the MS model with a sample size comparable to most of those coming with quarterly data will mean that is harder to get good estimates.

Increasingly there has been a use of Bayesian methods to estimate the parameters of MS models. Let $L(\theta)$ be the log likelihood and θ the model parameters. Then the mode of the Bayes posterior density is found by maximizing $C = L(\theta) + \log p(\theta)$, where $p(\theta)$ is a prior. Clearly in small samples this will certainly smooth out C. If the prior was dominant then there should be no estimation problems since $\log p(\theta)$ has a well-defined maximum. But if $L(\theta)$ is very badly behaved, then it is not clear that a Bayesian approach will solve the problem, as C will also feature local optima. Indeed, Liu et al. (2011) estimated a DSGE model driven by MS shocks and it was clear that there were local optima to C, so that their algorithms had to be carefully applied to ensure that a maximum was reached.

Of course the methodology employed to get the Bayesian estimates is often not that of maximizing C, followed by the construction of a posterior simulator, but rather the Gibbs sampling approach, which involves conditioning on one set of parameters and then simulating another. Nevertheless, the local optima problems with C now show up as multimodal posteriors—see Liu et al. (2011) for examples—since one is drawing from different densities. This labeling issue has been discussed a good deal in statistics and a number of proposals have been made to deal with it, for example, Frühwirth-Schnatter (2001) and Stephens (2000). Both authors have suggested labelling algorithms to try to reduce the identification problems, but few of these seem to have been applied to empirical work with MS models in economics.

The analysis raises the question of how one validates the fitted MS model. Breunig et al. (2003) argued that a minimal test of an MS model would be to see if it could replicate the sample moments of Δy_t. When there are problems due to an ill-defined likelihood or multimodal posteriors, these may show up in the MS model failing such simple tests. This is particularly true of Bayesian estimates, since the moment conditions defining the mean and variance of Δy_t are not directly used to estimate the parameters. Another measure that has a business cycle flavor would be to compute the fraction of negative Δy_t from the model and the data. The latter measure would be much less interesting if the recurrent event being studied is not cycles but whatever the application is, it should suggest some alternative. There is clearly a need to design the measures to validate MS models according to why one is fitting the models, and so more work is needed on what good measures would be.

Instead of the moment-based measures advocated above the MS model is often validated by two other tests. One is to ask whether there is just a single regime rather than two, in which case $\mu_1 = \mu_0$. There are some technical problems involved in doing such a test, but almost always the MS model is preferred when it is done. As argued in Engel et al. (2005), this could just be because the MS model picks up a

Table 4.1: MS and SS Model Comparisons via Various Criteria

	MS			SS		
	L	AIC	BIC	L	AIC	BIC
Period 1	411.63	−6.15	−5.95	411.59	−6.16	−5.99
Period 2	820.8	−6.65	−6.525	818.6	−6.64	−6.529

few outliers and these dramatically increase the likelihood. Leaving aside such issues, the practice of asking if there is a single state doesn't seem to be quite the right comparison. Instead of an MS model one might have an SS model, that is, there are still two states but they are drawn randomly and not with a Markov structure. The estimated SS model parameters for the two sample periods used above are given below. They are clearly quite close to those from the MS model.

$$\mu_0 = -.0121, \quad \mu_1 = .0093, \quad \beta_1 = .33, \quad \beta_2 = .09,$$
$$\beta_3 = -.08, \quad \beta_4 = -.17, \quad \sigma = .011, \quad p_1 = .958$$

$$\mu_0 = -.013, \quad \mu_1 = .008, \quad \beta_1 = .37, \quad \beta_2 = .23,$$
$$\beta_3 = -.16, \quad \beta_4 = -.10, \quad \sigma = .009, \quad p_0 = .960$$

Table 4.1 compares the two models using a variety of criteria. Because the MS model has an extra parameter, it must have a higher log likelihood. The Akaike information criterion (AIC) and Bayesian information criterion (BIC) criteria make some adjustment for the number of parameters. Based on both AIC and BIC, the SS model is preferred in the first period and, using the BIC, it is also preferred in the second. Even then the differences are not marked and, because the MS model is more complex than an SS one, it is not clear that one would prefer the former. It is worth noting that the implied smoothed $\Pr(\xi_t = 0)$ of SS are similar to those from the MS model, with neither model showing the recessions of the early 1990s or 2000s.

A second validation approach that seems to be used a good deal is to compare the MS-based states ζ_t with the S_t coming from prescribed rules or, in the U.S. business cycle case, from the NBER. What we have with MS rules is a model for Δy_t and a dating rule for isolating when the economy is in certain states. In contrast, the prescribed rules of previous chapters did not specify a model for Δy_t. It is true that the outcomes from prescribed rules will depend on the nature of Δy_t, but there seem to be advantages in separating these two activities. There are also many exercises which require that crises, recessions, and so on be identified by a dating rule that is independent of a particular model, such as an MS one. For example, suppose one wishes to see whether a real business cycle (RBC) model with technology shocks driven by an AR(1) process can produce recessions such as those observed in practice. Then output growth from such a model does not follow an MS process. Are we then to say that no business cycle can be generated by the model? This has to be a doubtful proposition. Consequently, it does not seem productive that one insist on data being represented by a particular statistical model if one is only interested in describing actual cycle outcomes. Sometimes the justification used for the MS strategy is that one needs an MS model to take account of past state information when predicting future states. As we have already noted in Chapter 2 this is incorrect—it is the definition of the state that provides the structure needed to do the prediction.

4.2.4 Interpreting Quantities in the MS Model

As has already been intimated, it is crucial to note that $\zeta_t \neq \xi_t$. ζ_t is directly comparable with the S_t described in Chapter 2. The ζ_t are the recurrent states of interest, not ξ_t, although this does not seem well understood in many MS applications, where one often sees ξ_t described as recession/expansion, bull/bear states, and so on, when they are not that at all. Indeed the properties of ζ_t and ξ_t can be very different. This can be seen in a number of examples. The first of these comes from Maheu and McCurdy (2000) who fitted a MS model with duration dependence in the latent states to a series on U.S.

equity returns (this is the model DDMS-DD in their table 4). Based on the smoothed $\Pr(\xi_t = 1)$ Maheu and McCurdy state that 90% of the time the market is in a bull state. However, if one looked for turning points in the level of equity prices, we find that $\Pr(S_t = 1) = .7$, and so bull markets hold just 70% of the time. A second example involves the 2000 data points that were simulated from the MS model of the preceding subsection. The average duration of time spent in state $\xi_t = 1$ is 33 quarters. By comparison the time spent in the state $\zeta_t = 1$ is 25.9 quarters. It is also worth looking at applying MBBQ to this simulated data so as to produce the prescribed business cycle states S_t. Then the average duration of time spent in $S_t = 1$ is 43.7 quarters. Accordingly, there is a wide range of outcomes for durations depending on which of the three random variables ξ_t, ζ_t, and S_t we look at.

Again, using the simulated data a regression of ζ_t against ξ_t gives (heteroskedastic-consistent standard errors are in parentheses),

$$\zeta_t = .43\zeta_{t-1} + .54\xi_t - .03\xi_{t-1} + .09\xi_{t-2},$$

$$(8.5) \quad (11.9) \quad (-.6) \quad (3.4)$$

with an R^2 of .58. This shows the difference between ζ_t and ξ_t quite clearly. As well, the ζ_t are much more persistent than the ξ_t, with an AR(1) coefficient of .56 versus .2.

The examples help us understand why some of the uses of MS models to determine cycle characteristics can be misleading. In our simplest MS model there were parameters $p_{00}, p_{11}, \sigma, \mu_0$, and μ_1. Then $E(\Delta y_t) = \Pr(\xi_t = 0)\mu_0 + \Pr(\xi_t = 1)\mu_1$, where ξ_t are the latent states, and these probabilities depend upon p_{00} and p_{11}. Hence it is clear that $E(\Delta y_t)$ can be varied by changing μ_0 and μ_1 while keeping p_{00}, p_{11} constant. So p_{00}, p_{11} alone cannot tell us about the average duration of an *expansion and contraction*. It follows that the frequent use of $1/(1 - p_{11})$ and $1/(1 - p_{00})$ as measures of the average duration of expansions and corrections is incorrect. They are valid estimates of the duration of time spent in the states $\xi_t = 1$ and 0, but not of the duration of time spent in either of the other states, that is, $\zeta_t = 1$ (or 0) and $S_t = 1$ (or 0).

In particular, the last depends on the mean growth in each of the regimes as well.

4.2.5 Censoring and the MS Model-Based Recurrent States: Stage 2

The second stage in constructing S_t from y_t involved imposing some constraints on S_t to satisfy certain requirements relating to minimum completed phase lengths. In the case of recessions and expansions, it is known that a standard requirement of the NBER when dating business cycles is for completed phases to have a duration of at least five months. This feature is evident in the published NBER business cycle data. By default this seems to have been used around the world by others when dating the business cycle. Thus the issue naturally arises of how one is to deal with this feature when using model-based rules. Chauvet and Morais (2010), when dating recessions in Brazil using an MS model, say, "We augment this definition with a rule specifying how long a phase must persist before a turning point is identified." Failure to implement such a constraint can lead to odd results. For example, Chen (2005) uses an MS model to find dates for the bull and bear phases of stock markets. For nominal returns, one of the bull markets lasts only a month, and, for real returns, just two months. Siliverstovs (2013) fitted a three-state MS model to Swiss GDP data and reports that there are two "recession regimes" that last for just one quarter. This is clearly unsatisfactory, but it is a common outcome when using MS models to date phases.

4.2.6 More Complex MS Model-Based Rules

As seen, the original simple MS models have not fared well as new data have come in. This has also been the case when data from other countries have been investigated. This has led to extensions of the basic model. These could be classified in three ways.

1. Whether they introduce movements in the μ_j, σ_j of the basic two-regime MS model—perhaps via some different latent variables.

2. Whether they expand the two-regime model to a higher number of regimes.
3. Whether the transition probabilities between regimes are allowed to change in some way.

We look at each of these in turn, illustrating the categories with some models selected from the literature.

Allowing the MS Regime Means to Change. Eo and Kim (2015) fitted a model where the regime means μ_0 and μ_1 change both over time and epochs. Their motivation is the failure, demonstrated above, of the basic MS model to signal recessions in the 1990s and the early 2000s. The model they use has the following structure.

$$\Delta y_t = \delta_t + (1 - \xi_t)\mu_{0\tau} + \xi_t \mu_{1,\tau} + \sigma_{e,t} e_t$$

$$\mu_{0,\tau} = \mu_{0,\tau-1} + \theta_0(\pi_0 \mu_{0,\tau-1} + \pi_1 \mu_{1,\tau-1}) + (1 - \xi_t)^{1/2} \sigma_{\omega,0} \omega_{0,t}$$

$$\mu_{1,\tau} = \mu_{1,\tau-1} + \theta_1(\pi_0 \mu_{0,\tau-1} + \pi_1 \mu_{1,\tau-1}) + \xi_t^{1/2} \sigma_{\omega,1} \omega_{1,t}$$

$$\delta_t = \delta_{t-1} + \sigma_\varepsilon \varepsilon_t$$

$$\ln(\sigma_{e,t}^2) = \ln(\sigma_{e,t-1}^2) + \sigma_\eta \eta_t$$

$$\Pr(\xi_t = 0 | \xi_{t-1} = 0) = q, \Pr(\xi_t = 1 | \xi_{t-1} = 1) = p$$

In this variant, the mean of Δy_t changes over time in two ways. First there is an evolving part (captured by δ_t) and, second, a recursive structure defining epochs τ for each of the conditional means. There are also components to the variance of the growth rate, with the non–MS model shock e_t having an evolving stochastic variance process. Because δ_t has a unit root, it seems likely that Δy_t has the same property, and so simulations from this process are complex and the simulation period cannot be too long, as the process is not stationary. Bayesian estimation methods were used with a sample period of 1947/4–2011/3. It is clear that in generating posterior densities some value needs to be provided for initial conditions of δ_t, and so on. They preset these to

$$\delta_0 = .9, \sigma_\varepsilon^2 = .0004, \sigma_{e,0}^2 = 0, \mu_{0,0} = 1, \mu_{1,1} = -1, \xi_0 = 1,$$

and did not estimate them.[6] Given this, a likelihood can be defined and the remaining parameters can be estimated, producing

$$p = .785, \quad q = .204, \quad \theta_0 = -.2924, \quad \theta_1 = -.1163,$$

$$\sigma_{\omega,0} = \sqrt{.1195}, \quad \sigma_{\omega,1} = \sqrt{.1476}, \quad \sigma_\eta = \sqrt{.0141}.$$

Because the initial conditions are preset, it is possible to simulate the process for Δy_t over a 65-year interval, corresponding to the length of the estimation period.

The estimates they give for the smoothed estimate of $\Pr(\xi_t = 0)$ shows that the probability of being in a recession in the 1990s was virtually 1 while in the early 2000s it was .8. The latter seems to be extraordinarily high given how weak the recession of 2001 was, with GDP growth being both positive and negative in succeeding quarters. One is led to ask about validation of the model. To this end we perform some of the tests suggested by Breunig et al. (2003). Simulating the model produces a mean of Δy_t of 1.23 versus .77 in the data; a standard deviation of 1.74 versus .99 in the data, and the fraction of the sample that has $\Delta y_t < 0$ is .21 versus .152 in data. The latter has a t ratio of -3 and even a robust one of -2.3. So the model seems to produce too many negative growth rates for GDP.

Multiregime Models. Early on in work with MS models, there were suggestions that three rather than two regimes would be needed. In some ways this was driven by the idea that there was a period of fast growth in the early stages of an expansion—Sichel (1994)—but it was also found in GDP growth in a number of European countries—Krolzig and Toro (2004). Adding extra states raises the number of parameters to be estimated and hence the number of moment conditions needed. Some parsimony can be gained by restricting the transition probabilities, for example, the fast growth phase comes after the expansion has started, suggesting a move from a low-growth to fast-growth regime. Given that it would

---

[6]We thank Yunjong Eo for providing the code and these initial values.

be deemed impossible to go from a high-growth regime back to a slow-growth one, this makes for a zero transition probability in describing the movement between those two regimes. Even then there are quite a lot of parameters, and, with just a single series to do the estimation, this will be a challenging task. The labeling problem is of course still present. Thus Frühwirth-Schnatter (1991) comments in connection with a three-state model estimated by Chib (1996) that "although the choice of prior means obviously implies the belief that the first state has the lowest mean and the last state highest mean, the prior does not prevent label switching...rendering the parameter estimates in Chib (1996) somewhat dubious" (205–6). Indeed, there are major differences between Chib's estimates (table 3, 206) and hers, the latter being based on her preferred solution method of "permutation sampling" as a way of dealing with the labeling problem.

It is important to reiterate again here that there is a distinction between the number of latent model regimes and the number of cycle states. They are not the same. A three-regime model can be used to describe data that has only two cycle states—expansions and contractions. The multiple regimes are about the nature of any nonlinear process describing the data. It is of course possible to have more than three cycle states. If so, then there would be additional binary variables that presumably have names like expansion, boom, and recession. Construction of these would mean using some extra criteria to separate (say) expansions into those that are a boom and those that are just normal. With prescribed rules this would be done by defining a boom as an expansion with a very large rise in output, for example, above some threshold value. Analysis of these multiple cycle states proceeds in the same way as for the simple binary case.

It is rare to see more than three-regime models, but Billio et al. (2012) propose a fourth one. They work with the log of monthly industrial production (ip_t) rather than GDP and allow the means and variance to vary with the regimes. There is also a fourth-order AR structure in their MS model. This gives a total of 24 parameters to estimate. It is hard to believe that one has that many useful moments of Δy_t, particularly given the fitting of the fourth-order AR component. Bayesian estimation methods are employed. The data from 1949 to 1959 are used for training purposes and to calibrate priors. So the formal estimation period is 1960–2011. Because there are so many parameters it seems worthwhile testing the match of this model against the data. It should be noted that Billio et al. work with $\Delta_3 ip_t = (1 - L^3) ip_t$, not Δip_t as stated in their paper, so our comparisons are with $\Delta_3 ip_t$. The extensive serial correlation seen in their estimated AR(4) coefficients comes from this transformation. Then the simulated mean of $\Delta_3 ip_t$ is .47 versus .77 in the data, the standard deviation is 3.16 versus 1.76 in the data, and the fraction of negative $\Delta_3 ip_t$ is .35 (.24 in the data).

Allowing the Transition Probabilities to Change. Diebold et al. (1994), Durland and McCurdy (1994), and Filardo (1994) were early papers that allowed the transition probabilities to change over time. The first paper was methodological, showing how one could maximize the likelihood using an expectation-maximization (EM) algorithm, while the other two fitted the models to data. Filardo had the transition probabilities varying with some observed variable, while Durland and McCurdy emphasized duration dependence, that is, the transition probabilities varied according to how long had been spent in a particular regime. Billio and Casarin (2010) allowed the transition probabilities to be stochastic. A study by Iiboshi (2007) involves fitting (by Bayesian methods) a standard MS model with an AR(2) component to the monthly Japanese Coincident index over the period 1982.1–2004.6. A Weibull specification was used to capture the duration dependence. The latter meant the transition probabilities changed as

$$p_{11,t} = \exp\{(\lambda_1 d_1)^{p_1} - [\lambda_1(d_1 + 1)]^{p_1}\}$$
$$p_{00,t} = \exp\{(\lambda_1 d_0)^{p_1} - [\lambda_1(d_0 + 1)]^{p_0}\},$$

where d_j represents the duration of time spent in the jth $(j = 0, 1)$ regime and λ_j, p_j are parameters to be estimated. In the estimated model the probability of staying in regime j declines as d_j grows.

Using the estimated parameters the model was simulated to produce 2000 observations. The standard deviation of Δy_t

from the model is almost 50% higher than in the data, and a robust t-statistic that these are equal is 3.93. This high volatility shows up as producing much more extreme values for Δy_t than in the data, although the fraction of negative growth rates is not significantly different to what it is in the data. It is interesting to look at the variance more closely. To do this an AR(2)-EGARCH(1,1) model was fitted to both the actual and simulated data. This model had the form

$$\Delta y_t = c + \beta_1 \Delta y_{t-1} + \beta \Delta y_{t-2} + \sigma_t \varepsilon_t$$

$$\log(\sigma_t^2) = a + \gamma|\varepsilon_{t-1}| + \delta\varepsilon_{t-1} + \varphi\log(\sigma_{t-1}^2),$$

with estimated parameters of

$$Data: \quad c = .03, \quad \beta_1 = .29, \quad \beta_2 = .23, a = -.61,$$
$$\gamma = .44, \quad \delta = .04, \quad \varphi = -.71$$

$$Model: c = .04, \quad \beta_1 = .06, \quad \beta_2 = .31, \quad a = .09,$$
$$\gamma = -.02, \quad \delta = -.07, \quad \varphi = .74.$$

One can see that these are very different processes, particularly the estimated values of φ. In both data and simulations this parameter has an absolute t-ratio of around 6, so testing if the value from the data is the same as from the model would lead to an emphatic rejection.

4.2.7 Threshold Models for Dating Recurrent Events

As mentioned earlier, it has been proposed that which regime holds at t could depend on some observable variable x_t. Leaving aside any difficulties in fitting threshold models, one that is specific to the dating of recurrent events is that only current information on x_t is used in deciding on a regime. In contrast, as seen in previous chapters and in earlier sections of this one, dating by prescribed or MS model-based rules utilizes data *after* time t when deciding on what phase held at t. Indeed, one could not accurately describe the times at which phases hold *without using future information*. Accordingly there are few papers utilizing only a threshold perspective for dating business cycles—Van Dijk and Franses (1999) is an exception. Most research focuses on the advantages of using latent rather than observed threshold models, and Billio et al. (2013) and Deschamps (2008) represent two examples of this.

Billio et al. fit a self-exciting threshold autoregressive (SETAR) model to the three-monthly growth in industrial production ($\Delta_3 ip_t$) and unemployment. For the first of these series the two regimes are differentiated by whether $x_t = \Delta_3 ip_{t-2}$ falls below .21%. They conclude that dating with the SETAR model fails to reproduce European business cycles (unlike the MS model they also employ). It does seem unlikely that this model would in fact produce a correct dating of recessions, since a recession involves negative growth, not just weak growth.

Deschamps uses a two-regime threshold model where the variable representing economic activity is the monthly seasonally adjusted U.S. unemployment rate U_t. The threshold variable is the yearly change $\Delta_{12} U_{t-1}$. The only evidence he provides in regard to business cycle dating is his figure 3 labelled "transition functions." This shows the probability of going into a regime that is said to capture recession as distinct from one characterizing an expansion. In this figure there is not a good match to the NBER dates for cycle turning points. Moreover, if one used the standard rule that a recession held once this transition probability exceeded .5, then there are four more recessions than actually occurred, including two in 1996 and 2003. So the threshold model doesn't give a good account of the business cycle. It should be said that Deschamps is really more interested in forecasting U_t rather than determining business cycle turning points, and the nonlinear threshold model does seem to provide some gains for this. It should be noted that the papers citing his work just use his threshold model for forecasting various series rather than dating cycles.

4.3 Model-Based Rules for Dating Events with Multivariate Series

Multivariate analysis with model-based rules has proceeded in much the same way as for prescribed rules, except that there is no analog to the method of aggregating the turning points. Instead, the methods get the turning points from some aggregate and the question is therefore how to construct the aggregate. Some analyses compress the multivariate series to a single measure and then fit a model to this quantity to determine the phases, while others work with a multivariate setup.

4.3.1 Factor Models

In Section 3.7 it was suggested that a single factor might be allowed to drive the n series and that this be taken to be an AR process. The equivalent solution here is to allow the factor to follow an MS process. Diebold and Rudebusch (1996), Kim and Nelson (1998), Chauvet (1998), Chauvet and Piger (2003), and Krolzig and Toro (2004) all use Markov switching models for Δf_t. Extraction of the factor provides the information necessary to date the cycle states in the standard way discussed earlier in relation to the use of ξ_t.

4.3.2 Principal Components

Another solution has been to form the first principal component and then fit an MS model to this. After that the phases can be computed from the smoothed $\Pr(\xi_t = 1)$. Instead, one might combine all n series so as to produce a single series using some weights, after which the MS model is fitted to that aggregated data. Probably the most popular choice has been to model a published coincident index as an MS process. The Iiboshi study that we have just looked at is an example of this.

4.3.3 MS-VAR

In this method the n series Δy_t are treated as a vector autoregressive (VAR) with the intercepts shifting according to a single MS model. Hence it has the form

$$\Delta y_t = \mu_0 \xi_t + \mu_1 (1 - \xi_t) + B_1 y_{t-1} + e_t, \qquad (4.9)$$

where μ_j are $n \times 1$ vectors. Krolzig and Toro treated European phases in this way, fitting a VAR(1) to GDP growth in six European countries from 1970/3 to 1995/4, and allowing for a three-regime MS process for the intercepts. When they estimated the model on the countries individually there was little evidence of three regimes, but it became much clearer when multivariate estimation was undertaken. There are a large number of parameters being estimated—the VAR(1) in six series alone requires 36, while the MS(3) process makes for an extra 12 (connected with μ_0 and μ_1) plus the 9 from the transition probabilities. In fact the number of parameters in this application was even greater, as the covariance matrix of the VAR shocks also shifts according to the regimes. Although there are more moments available for estimation now, the number of unknown parameters is so great as to make one wonder if it is possible to get good estimates of the parameters.

It is worth looking at the MS-VAR from a principal components perspective. Suppose that we took the first principal component of Δy_t. It would have the form $PC_t = w'\Delta y_t$ and so

$$PC_t = w'\Delta y_t = (w'\mu_0)\xi_t + (w'\mu_1)(1 - \xi_t) + w'B_1 y_{t-1} + w'e_t,$$
(4.10)

and it is clear that the MS process shows up in PC_t as well as Δy_t. One might fit an MS model to this variable and thereby use the model-based rule associated with MS processes. The major problem is the presence of $w'B_1 y_{t-1}$ in the relation. Unless B_1 is diagonal with the same elements this does not reduce to $G \cdot PC_{t-1}$, and so to get the ML estimates of $(w'\mu_0)$, and so on, one needs to allow for the terms $w'B_1 y_{t-1}$ in the likelihood. Such a complication is not handled by existing computer programs.

A variant of what Krolzig and Toro did is Kaufmann (2010) who makes each series Δy_{jt} follow a univariate AR process rather than a VAR. The intercepts in each series then follow a single MS process. She allows for many series, but these are essentially grouped into just two types—coincident and leading. Each group has the same AR and MS structure, so the analysis is more like a bivariate MS process, such as estimated by Bengoechea et al. (2006). The groupings are made using a multivariate two-state logit model driven by variables such as the correlation with GDP. Now the series used for the model are actually $z_{jt} = \sigma_j^{-1}(\Delta y_{jt} - \mu_j)$ rather than Δy_{jt} and so, with the mean having been subtracted away from the growth rate, the peaks and troughs in the series effectively being examined viz. $(y_t - \gamma t)$, would be those in which a deterministic permanent component is removed, so they are really turning points of a growth cycle (as recognized by Kaufmann).

4.4 Conclusion

The chapter has discussed a particular way of producing rules to summarize the nature of the recurrent events. These rules come from the idea that the data incorporating the recurrent event can be captured by models that specify a number of regimes and then using the information provided by the fitted model to date the recurrent event. Regime-switching models turn out to be quite difficult to estimate, so care needs to be taken to select suitable algorithms when attempting to quantify them. It seems likely that this problem will get worse in a multivariate context, unless the number of regimes is kept quite small, and this was illustrated with an application. We raised the issue of whether it is sensible to rely on a model to provide a dating of the recurrent event, since then the model presumably needs to be a good description of the data. In some instances it might be useful to adopt a regime-switching model to provide a summary of what needs to be explained. It is unclear that this is the case for capturing cycles in series, where there is a long tradition of doing that via observable turning points in the series. However, it may well be an advantage if interest is in a recurrent pattern expressed in terms of whether the series is at a high or low level, as would occur if a series on sentiment was being dated.

Chapter 5

Measuring Recurrent Event Features in Univariate Data

5.1 Introduction

After the recurrent event states S_t have been found, it is desirable to use them to summarize information about features of the events. Quite a few suggestions have emerged about what would be good measures. One of the earliest observations was that upturns in economic activity are much longer than downturns, although this was not so true of financial asset prices. Section 5.2 therefore looks at the factors explaining that feature. After doing so we turn our attention to methods for describing a single phase and, by extension, what the average phase would look like. Section 5.3 begins with a visual representation of a recession, and this leads to the most basic measures involving amplitudes and durations which are studied in Section 5.4. The shape of the phase—that is, the shape of the path between peak and trough for recessions— is studied in Section 5.5. Moving beyond average features, Section 5.6 looks at the diversity of phases. Special features of recoveries such as Friedman's (1973) plucking hypothesis and Eckstein and Sinai's (1986) recovery time are dealt with in Section 5.7. Finally, a question that often comes up is whether the probability of remaining in a phase depends on how long one has been in it. This issue of duration dependence is discussed in Section 5.8.

5.2 The Fraction of Time Spent in Expansions

Historically one of the first observed features of cycles was that the period of time spent in expansions was very different to that for contractions, leading us to ask what determines this feature. Using definitions of conditional probability, and with the location of peaks being described by the binary variable $\wedge_t$ while troughs are $\vee_t$, we have

$$Pr(\wedge_t = 1) = \Pr(S_{t+1} = 0, S_t = 1)$$
$$= \Pr(S_{t+1} = 0|S_t = 1)Pr(S_t = 1) \qquad (5.1)$$
$$Pr(\vee_t = 1) = \Pr(S_{t+1} = 1, S_t = 0)$$
$$= \Pr(S_{t+1} = 1|S_t = 0)Pr(S_t = 0). \qquad (5.2)$$

Making the additional assumption that the random variable S_t is strictly stationary implies that $Pr(S_{t+1} = 1) = Pr(S_t = 1)$. Because the number of peaks and troughs must be the same (in infinite samples),

$$\Pr(\wedge_t = 1) = E(\wedge_t) = E(\vee_t) = \Pr(\vee_t = 1), \qquad (5.3)$$

and by definition $Pr(S_t = 1) = 1 - Pr(S_t = 0)$. Consequently, it follows that there are four unknowns in (5.1) and (5.2). Once two of these are fixed the other two follow. NBER dating rules essentially fix the probabilities of turning points and $Pr(S_t = 1)$, since the latter follows once the turning points are located. Other rules focus on the transition probabilities

$$\Pr(CE) = \Pr(S_{t+1} = 1|S_t = 0)$$
$$\Pr(EC) = \Pr(S_{t+1} = 0|S_t = 1),$$

where $\Pr(CE)$ is the probability of moving from a contraction (C) to an expansion (E), that is, of encountering what was called a contraction terminating sequence in Harding and Pagan (2002) (and there is an analogous definition for $\Pr(EC)$). Because of (5.3) equations (5.1) and (5.2) will imply that

$$\Pr(S_{t+1} = 0|S_t = 1)Pr(S_t = 1) = \Pr(S_{t+1} = 1|S_t = 0)Pr(S_t = 0)$$
$$= \Pr(S_{t+1} = 1|S_t = 0)(1 - \Pr(S_t = 1)),$$

meaning

$$\Pr(EC)\Pr(S_t = 1) = \Pr(CE)(1 - \Pr(S_t = 1)). \qquad (5.4)$$

Rearranging (5.4), $Pr(S_t = 1)$ can be solved for to yield

$$\Pr(S_t = 1) = \frac{\Pr(CE)}{\Pr(EC) + \Pr(CE)}. \qquad (5.5)$$

Now it is clear that $\Pr(S_t = 1)$ depends on the nature of the rule employed to determine turning points as well as on the nature of the series y_t that we are seeking turning points in. It turns out to be quite hard to analytically derive the transition probabilities for many prescribed rules (such as the MBBQ rule), and we will see why later. A rule that is close to it and amenable to analysis is the two-quarters rule. But the simplest rule that yields major insights into the determinants of what fraction of time is spent in expansion—$\Pr(S_t = 1)$—is the calculus rule, in which the phases are defined as $S_t = 1(\Delta y_t > 0)$, that is, when there is a positive growth rate at time t, the economy is an expansion state (E), while a negative one signifies a contraction (C).

Now supposing that $\Delta y_t = \mu + \sigma e_t$, where e_t is $i.i.d.(0, 1)$, the probabilities of a change in phase at time t when employing the calculus rule would be

$$\Pr(EC) : \Pr(S_{t+1} = 0 | S_t = 1) = \Pr(\Delta y_{t+1} < 0 | \Delta y_t > 0)$$

$$\Pr(CE) : \Pr(S_{t+1} = 1 | S_t = 0) = \Pr(\Delta y_{t+1} > 0 | \Delta y_t < 0).$$

In this context $\Pr(EC)$ has the form

$$\Pr(\Delta y_{t+1} < 0 | \Delta y_t > 0) = \Pr(\mu + \sigma e_{t+1} < 0 | \Delta y_t > 0)$$

$$= \Pr\left(e_{t+1} < -\frac{\mu}{\sigma}\right),$$

due to the independence of Δy_t and Δy_{t+1}. Furthermore, when e_t is assumed to be $N(0, 1)$, $\Pr(EC) = \Phi(-\frac{\mu}{\sigma}) = \psi$ and $\Pr(CE) = 1 - \psi$, where Φ is the distribution function of an $N(0, 1)$ random variable. Hence $\Pr(S_t = 1) = \frac{1-\psi}{\psi+1-\psi} = 1 - \psi$. So the period of time spent in the expansion state will become longer as ψ falls. But this depends solely on $\frac{\mu}{\sigma}$—the ratio of long-run growth to the volatility of shocks. As the long-run growth rate rises, or the volatility of growth rates declines,

$\frac{\mu}{\sigma}$ will rise, and so ψ will fall, that is, more time will be spent in expansions (and of course less time in contractions). This makes sense as there is a smaller probability of a negative growth rate being observed.

If we take the special case that $\mu = 0$ then $\Pr(S_t = 1) = \frac{1}{2}$, and so the time spent in expansions and contractions would be equal. If $\mu \neq 0$ the extent to which expansions last longer than recessions is directly measured by

$$\frac{\Pr(S_t = 1)}{\Pr(S_t = 0)} = \frac{1 - \psi}{\psi}.$$

Using data on U.S. GDP growth $\mu = .00836, \sigma = .0102$ so that $\psi = \Phi(-\frac{\mu}{\sigma}) = \Phi(-\frac{.00836}{.0102}) = .2$, making $\frac{\Pr(S_t=1)}{\Pr(S_t=0)} \cong 4$, that is, the U.S. economy would spend four times as long in expansions than in contractions. In fact, using NBER data on S_t, the ratio is more like seven, and that is because the rule to date U.S. recessions is not the calculus rule, so the principles above are qualitative rather than quantitative. Nevertheless, it can be shown that if one used the two quarters rather than the calculus rule, one would find that this ratio also depends on ψ, but in a more complex way—see Harding and Pagan (2002).

5.3   Representing the Features of Phases

A phase can be defined as the time period elapsing after one event up to and including the next event. For example, the recession phase commences in the period after a peak and terminates at the next trough. In many cases interest focuses on obtaining parsimonious summaries of the features of variables over phases defined in this way. The discussion will be assisted by Figure 5.1, which shows a stylized recession phase. There is an equivalent one for expansions. Here the y-axis is y_t (the log of the level of economic activity, Y_t) and the x-axis is time. Thus the graph shows a peak at A and a trough at C. The length of AB is the *duration* of the recession, while the vertical distance between A and C is the *amplitude* of the recession, effectively expressed as a fraction of the peak, since it is the difference $log Y_C - \log Y_A$. Once we know where the turning points are located in time, that is, we have either

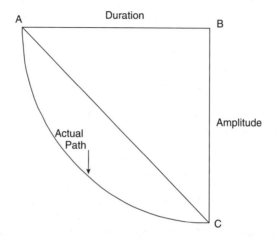

Figure 5.1: Stylized Recession.

S_t (from prescribed rules) or ζ_t (from model-based rules), these measures can be computed. Moreover as they just involve examining some definitions of y_t that the S_t and ζ_t are found from, the methods described below apply equally to business, growth, and growth rate cycles. The rules may differ, but they will always produce some binary variables to describe the recurrent events.

Once we have summary measures of the features of individual phases interest turns to making inference about the average features of phases as well as the variation in those features. These issues are taken up in the following sections.

5.4 Amplitudes and Durations of Phases

Let the turning point dates produce $\hat{K}$ estimated expansions and contractions, with the duration of the *ith* $(i = 1, ..., \hat{K})$ expansion being D_i^E, and that of the contractions being D_i^C. Then, dropping the i subscript, the quantities summarizing average durations of the phases will be

$$\overline{D}^E = \frac{1}{\hat{K}} \sum_{i=1}^{\hat{K}} D_i^E, \overline{D}^C = \frac{1}{\hat{K}} \sum_{i=1}^{\hat{K}} D_i^C.$$

Generally these refer to completed durations, that is, if the expansion (contraction) is still ongoing at the end (beginning) of the sample period it will not be counted when computing the average. Of course the duration of the average cycle will be $\overline{D}^E + \overline{D}^C$.

It is also possible to produce the same measures $\overline{A}^E$ and $\overline{A}^C$ for the amplitudes of the phases. Notice that since the y-axis is the log of output, the amplitude A_i^C will be the difference between the log of output at the trough and at the peak. Provided these changes are not too large, this difference is the percentage change in output over the phase. However, as is well known, such an approximation breaks down for larger changes, and so it is the case that it will only be approximately correct for some expansions, as these tend to run for lengthy periods, and so the change in output across them tends to be large. Since we will mostly be doing comparative analysis the changes in the logs will be reported—readers should bear in mind that an adjustment would be needed to get the exact percentage change if the latter is large.

It is useful to write the expressions above in terms of the S_t. Then, since each completed cycle has a peak, it will be that $\hat{K} = \sum_{t=1}^{T-1}(1 - S_{t+1})S_t$, because the series $(1 - S_{t+1})S_t$ equals unity only when a peak occurs at time t, that is, when $S_t = 1, S_{t+1} = 0$.[1] Consequently, as the total time spent in expansions is $\sum_{t=1}^{T} S_t$ the average duration of an expansion will therefore be

$$\overline{D}^E = \hat{K}^{-1} \sum_{t=1}^{T} S_t.$$

Similarly the average amplitude of expansions will be

$$\hat{A} = \hat{K}^{-1} \sum_{t=1}^{T} S_t \Delta y_t.$$

---

[1]Some difficulties can arise with these formulas due to the possibility of incomplete phases at both ends of the sample. If one used *completed* phases the summation should run from the beginning of the first completed phase until the end of the last one, rather than over $1, ..., T$.

These expressions show that $\overline{D}^E$ is the ratio of two random variables and can be written as

$$\overline{D}^E = \left(\frac{T}{\overline{K}}\right) \frac{1}{T} \sum_{t=1}^{T} S_t.$$

Now although $\frac{T}{\overline{K}}$ will tend to a constant as T increases, in finite samples the distribution of the ratio may well be far from normal, and this was mentioned in Pagan and Sossounov (2003). So some adjustment may be needed if confidence intervals are to be placed around $\bar{D}^E$. A different way of seeing the issue is to write out a moment condition that approximately determines $\overline{D}^E$, namely,

$$\sum_{t=1}^{T-1} [S_t - \bar{D}^E(1 - S_{t+1})S_t] = 0.$$

In turn this could be written as

$$\sum_{t=1}^{T-1} z_t[S_t - x_t\hat{\delta}] = 0, \tag{5.6}$$

where $z_t = 1, x_t = (1 - S_{t+1})S_t$ and $\hat{\delta} = \bar{D}^E$. Consequently,

$$\hat{\delta} = \frac{\sum_{t=1}^{T-1} z_t S_t}{\sum_{t=1}^{T-1} z_t x_t},$$

emphasizing that $\bar{D}^E$ can be thought of as an instrumental variable (IV) estimator. Obviously $\bar{A}^E$ can be handled in the same way.

In the case where we are comparing models to the data it is best to compute confidence intervals for these statistics by simulating from the model, that is, to use a parametric bootstrap. If a model is not available to do this, confidence intervals are often computed in the standard way as $\hat{\delta} \pm \varphi std(\hat{\delta})$, where φ is some chosen critical value, say 1.96 if the distribution of $\hat{\delta}$ is taken to be normal. Using the NBER values of S_t for expansions from 1947/1 to 2010/2 we would find that $\bar{D}^E = 20.36$ and $std(\hat{\delta}) = 5.9$ (using HAC standard errors from the IV regression).[2] Thus the 95% confidence interval would be approximately 8 to 32 quarters.

The method above involves computing a confidence interval by testing if $\delta = \delta^*$ and finding the range for δ^* that would produce an acceptance of the hypothesis $\delta = \delta^*$ at a prespecified confidence level, that is, after setting some value for φ. Now it is known that when $E(z_t x_t)$ is close to zero, that is, there are "weak" instruments, then the IV estimator will rarely be normally distributed and can be biased in small samples. In that instance a more accurate confidence interval is found by using the Anderson and Rubin (1949) approach, which involves testing if $\delta = \delta^*$ using the test statistic

$$AR = std(\delta^*)^{-1} \sum_{t=1}^{T-1} z_t [S_t - \delta^* x_t].$$

Because $\sum_{t=1}^{T-1} z_t [S_t - \hat{\delta} x_t] = 0$ AR can be written as

$$\sum_{t=1}^{T-1} z_t (\hat{\delta} - \delta^*) x_t,$$

with standard deviation of $std(\sum_{t=1}^{T-1} z_t [S_t - \delta^* x_t])$. Applying this to the same NBER data as above would produce a 95% confidence interval of 13–47 quarters. This is a very easy quantity to compute and, given its success in the IV literature, seems the recommended approach.

Camacho, Perez-Quiros, and Saiz (2008) suggest correcting the point estimate $\hat{\delta}$ that one would get from the data. In Kilian (1998) an AR(1) coefficient was bias corrected by simulating data using the fitted AR(1), averaging over the simulated parameter estimates, and then using this average instead of the original point estimate from the data. Therefore it seems worth applying the idea in the context of estimating durations and amplitudes. A first complication is that duration is a parameter in a regression that depends on S_t. However, S_t

---

[2]The summation here runs to $T-1$ as there may not be data for S_{T+1}, for example, if the data set stops at 2010/1. However, attributing a value of unity to S_t for $t = 2010/2$ seems unexceptional when viewed from March 2014 and this is what we do.

is not observed. Instead, it is constructed from data on y_t via some prescribed rule such as in MBBQ. So they suggested that new sets of y_t be constructed by resampling the data on Δy_t. They produce 10,000 samples which we will term $\Delta y_t^{(j)}, j = 1, ..., 10000$. Then the average duration $D^{E(j)}$ can be computed for each simulated sample and averaged to get $\bar{\gamma}$. This value will then be the bias-corrected average duration estimator. As an experiment to assess the performance of this method, they start with an MS model as the DGP and then simulate 10 series on Δy_t from it. Let the kth data set be $\Delta y_t^{(k)}, k = 1..., 10$. It follows that each of these series would produce a value for D^E and a corresponding $\bar{\gamma}$, so one can see what the "aggregate bias correction" would be.

Now the problem is how one is to assess the success of the adjustment. Without an adjustment the average duration was around 52 periods. Their correction reduces it to what they consider to be the true value of 41 quarters. However what they take to be the true value is the duration of time spent in the state $\xi_t = 1$, which is the latent state in the MS model used as the DGP for Δy_t. But as noted in the previous chapter, this is not the duration of time spent in the MBBQ state $S_t = 1$, and that is what is being bias corrected. In fact, simulating many expansions from their MS model shows that the average duration of time spent in the state $S_t = 1$ stays close to 52 quarters, while the average time spent in $\xi_t = 1$ is 41 quarters. So the bias reduction actually *introduces a bias*, since it reduces $\bar{D}^E$ toward 41 quarters, which is not the correct value.

5.5 The Shapes of Phases

Often one is interested in what the shape of an expansion and contraction (bull and bear markets, etc.) look like. There have been many proposals in this regard and we look at some, trying to show the connections.

5.5.1 An Excess of Growth

Figure 5.1 shows that other things might be measured. One of these is the cumulated gain or loss during a phase—the area under the curve which describes the actual path for the log of GDP. This is measured by

$$F = \sum_{j=1}^{D}(y_j - y_0) - \frac{A}{2}.$$

Basically we might think of approximating the area under the curve by summing a series of rectangles of unit length and height $y_j - y_0$. Now we know that this overstates the area because the length on one side of the rectangle is $y_j - y_0$ and, on the other, is $y_{j+1} - y_0$. Hence it is desirable to correct for this by taking away the area of the triangle that has length unity and height $.5(y_{j+1} - y_j)$, that is, $\frac{(y_{j+1} - y_j)}{2}$. Summing over all cycles this latter term is $\frac{A}{2}$.

A useful benchmark for the magnitude of F is the area of the triangle ABC ($AR = \frac{D \times A}{2}$), and we call the difference between the two of them, divided by the triangle area, the *excess area*

$$E = \frac{F - AR}{AR}.$$

This shows how much extra output per period is gained or lost during an expansion or contraction when compared to the situation where the economy expands or contracts at a constant growth rate. It can be computed for both phases (and is best expressed as a percentage), although it is unlikely to be very reliable for contractions, as these are very short. We often think of this as a measure of the *shape* of the phase. It isn't entirely satisfactory for that as it would be possible for E to be zero if the curve initially went below the hypotenuse of the triangle, but then went above it for the remainder of the phase. The absolute value might be a better measure, but we feel that E is quite good at capturing what has been cited historically as an important feature of some business and financial cycles. In the next chapter we discuss the evidence for this feature.

5.5.2 Asymmetry

Within the literature there are other ways of measuring the "shape" of the cycle, often gathered under the heading of "asymmetry." Neftci (1984) was one of the first to deal with this issue. He defined an indicator $I_t = 1(\Delta y_t > 0)$ and then asked whether the runs of $I_t = 1$ were larger than those for $I_t = 0$. He did not formally define an expansion or a contraction but argued that expansions were generally sequences of positive growth while contractions exhibited sequences of negative growth. Accordingly, if there was a greater chance of a run of positive values than negatives that would point to expansions being of longer duration than contractions. To formally test this he *assumed* that I_t followed a second-order Markov process and focused on estimating its transition probabilities $p_{11}^I = \Pr(I_t = 1 | I_{t-1} = 1, I_{t-2} = 1)$ and $p_{00}^I = \Pr(I_t = 0 | I_{t-1} = 0, I_{t-2} = 0)$. Once ML estimates of these were found he tested for asymmetry by testing if $p_{11}^I = p_{00}^I$. For the U.S. unemployment rate this hypothesis was rejected.

Given that a second-order Markov chain would imply the relation

$$I_t = a + bI_{t-1} + cI_{t-2} + dI_{t-1}I_{t-2} + \eta_t, \qquad (5.7)$$

we could test if $p_{11}^I = p_{00}^I$ by testing if $a + b + c + d = 1 - a$, that is, $2a + b + c + d = 1$. Although it is not an efficient estimator, OLS can be applied to (5.7) to provide such a test. Doing so when y_t is the log of U.S. GDP, one gets a t-ratio of 26, so there is a strong rejection of the hypothesis. Replacing I_t with S_t defined by MBBQ and performing the same test would produce a t-ratio of 21, so one gets the same outcome. Of course this should be expected, simply because expansions are long and recessions are short in the presence of trend growth, and there is a much lower probability of a recession progressing to longer durations than for an expansion.

5.5.3 Steepness and Deepness

There is a large literature concerned with shape issues described in phases such as "steepness," "deepness," and "sharpness." Sichel (1993, 225) while looking at asymmetry distinguished between when contractions are "steeper than expansions" and when "troughs are deeper than peaks are tall." He motivated these with graphs of simulated time series. In his steep cycle graph the slope of the expansion was clearly smaller than that of the contraction, while the graph showing a deep cycle had the rise to a peak being greater than the fall to a trough. Just like Neftci, Sichel did not provide definitions of expansions and contractions, arguing that these asymmetric features would be seen in series c_t and Δc_t, where c_t is y_t with a permanent component removed. Specifically, he looked at standard statistical tests of skewness in such series. These involved testing whether the third moments of c_t and Δc_t were zero, giving his tests for deepness and steepness, respectively.

Looking at his test for deepness, it would involve testing if $\tau = E(c_t - E(c_t))^3$ is zero. In testing for steepness, c_t was replaced by Δc_t when computing τ. Sichel estimated the expectations defining the sample moments of c_t. Clements and Krolzig (2003) extended Sichel's analysis by assuming that the process generating c_t was an MS one, which gave a specific form for the expectations. These ultimately involve the MS model transition probabilities, and so the tests for deepness and steepness came down to testing hypotheses about the transition probabilities. For a two-regime MS process of first order, τ would be zero if $p_{10} = p_{01}$. Again these tests are being based on the density of the latent variable ξ_t and don't specifically address the properties of the contractions and expansions ζ_t which would be implied by the model. Moreover, the formulas for the expectations are only valid if the MS model is a correct description of the data. In contrast, Sichel's measures do not utilize a model.

It seems desirable to directly address these issues by being precise about what expansions and contractions are. In terms of our previous discussion, steepness of a phase is naturally measured by the angle of the triangle formed where the hypotenuse intersects the base, and the tan of this is A/D, leading us to advocate $STEEP = A/D$ as a suitable index. In contrast, the "deepness" of a phase is naturally measured by the height of the triangle and, of course, this is just the amplitude A. To measure the average degree of steepness over all (expansion) phases we would have

$$STEEP = \frac{\hat{A}}{\hat{D}} = \frac{\sum_{t=1}^{T} S_t \Delta y_t.}{\sum_{t=1}^{T} S_t}.$$

This measure was used by Claessens et al. (2012) but they renamed it "slope." With such a measure a comparison of the steepness of expansions versus contractions in the average cycle would involve (due to a negative sign on the amplitude of a contraction)

$$COMP = \frac{\sum_{t=1}^{T} S_t \Delta y_t}{\sum_{t=1}^{T} S_t} + \frac{\sum_{t=1}^{T} (1 - S_t) \Delta y_t}{\sum_{t=1}^{T} (1 - S_t)}$$

$$= \hat{p}_e^{-1} T^{-1} \sum_{t=1}^{T} S_t \Delta y_t + (1 - \hat{p}_e)^{-1} T^{-1} \sum_{t=1}^{T} (1 - S_t) \Delta y_t,$$

where p_e is the proportion of time spent in expansions. Because $S_t(1 - S_t) = 0$ the two elements making up COMP are uncorrelated, and so the variance of COMP will just be the sum of the variances of each component.

It is worth dwelling on the relation of our proposed measure to that of Sichel. Suppose that $S_t = 1(\Delta y_t > 0)$. Then our test would come down to comparing the sample means of the absolute values of the positive and negative values of Δy_t, weighted by $\hat{p}_e^{-1}$ and $(1 - \hat{p}_e)^{-1}$, respectively. Hence it is a test for symmetry in Δy_t. In contrast, while Sichel's test has a similar form, it uses the cubes of Δy_t rather than the Δy_t themselves. The advantage of working with COMP seems to be that it measures and tests the notion of steepness in a direct rather than indirect way. It also generalizes to other ways of forming S_t.

5.5.4 Sharpness

Sharpness was a concept introduced in McQueen and Thorley (1993) which looks at the extent to which peaks and troughs are rounded. The series $(k^{-1} \Delta_k y_t) \wedge_t$ will be the average growth rate for the level of activity for the k quarters leading up to the peak at time t, and $(k^{-1} \Delta_k y_{t+k+1}) \wedge_t$ will be the average growth rate for the k quarters that follow the peak. McQueen and Thorley suggested that one form the difference of the two as a test statistic. As it should be the case that one quantity will always be negative and the other positive, provided the turning points have been dated with NBER-type rules, the absolute values of the growth rates are utilized. This leads to a sharpness index for peaks of (because McQueen and Thorley work with monthly data k is set to 6)

$$SHARP_{peak} = (k)^{-1} \sum_{t=1}^{T} |\Delta_k(y_{t+k+1} + y_t)| \wedge_t .$$

An analogous index $SHARP_{trough}$ can be formed by replacing $\wedge_t$ with $\vee_t$. Then sharpness of peaks and troughs can be compared through $SHARP_{peak} - SHARP_{trough}$.

Although details are not given by McQueen and Thorley, it seems as if their test statistic is based on the assumption that $\Delta_k(y_{t+k} + y_t)\wedge_t$ is *i.i.d.* In fact the use of the operator Δ_k will mean that there is serial correlation to be taken into account. They comment that (348) "the significance at which the null hypothesis of equal turning point sharpness is rejected is surprising given the low test power that results from the small sample size."

5.6 The Diversity of Phases

It is also possible to compute all the characteristics mentioned above for each individual cycle. But this produces a large amount of information that is hard to summarize for comparative purposes. Consequently we seek some parsimonious summaries of the diversity of cycle outcomes to answer the question "Are cycles all alike?" Simple indexes of this type come from coefficients of variation, in particular the ratio of the standard deviation of the durations and amplitudes to their means. Thus, for durations we would have

$$CV_D^E = \frac{\sqrt{(\frac{1}{K} \sum_{i=1}^{K} (D_i^E - \overline{D}^E)^2)}}{\frac{1}{K} \sum_{i=1}^{K} D_i^E}$$

$$CV_D^C = \frac{\sqrt{(\frac{1}{K} \sum_{i=1}^{K} (D_i^C - \overline{D}^C)^2)}}{\frac{1}{K} \sum_{i=1}^{K} D_i^C}.$$

The same quantities can be computed to measure the variability of amplitudes. A high value for the coefficient of variation would say that cycles tend to be very dissimilar.

5.7 Plucking Effects and Recovery Times

Friedman (1993) suggested that there was a plucking phenomenon in the business cycle. He says that "a large contraction in output tends to be followed on the average by a large business expansion; a mild contraction by a mild expansion." This has often been interpreted as implying that there is a strong recovery from contractions, although the reading would seem to suggest that this only happens following a large contraction. The problem with formulating a measure is clearly that no statement is given of what the threshold would be to define a "large contraction." One way of operationalizing it is to look at the correlation of the amplitude of the *ith* expansion with the preceding contraction. A regression of the expansion on the contraction amplitude for postwar cycles in GDP in the United States does give an estimated coefficient of 4.9 with a t-ratio of 2.3, so there seems some weak evidence of the effect. One difficulty is that there are so few expansions and contractions.[3]

One might also want to study events that are not extreme but relate to segments of expansions and contractions. Thus Eckstein and Sinai (1986) focus on the recovery phase, defined as the period of time required for output to return to its previous peak, while Sichel (1994) looks at the magnitude of growth rates four to six quarters into an expansion. Formally the recovery time statistic is the time taken for output to rebound from the trough to the previous peak level. Following the last U.S. recession, a great deal of interest has emerged in this statistic. Prior to that recession recovery times were between one and three quarters, but nine quarters were needed to return to the GDP level of 2007/4 after that

---

[3]There are other variants of the relations between expansion and contraction duration. Diebold (1993) looks at the hypothesis that a long expansion means that the succeeding contraction would be of smaller duration and seems to find some evidence of this.

recession ended. This was not just a U.S. phenomenon. In 2014/1 the euro area GDP had still not recovered to its previous peak. Claessens et al. (2012) looked at the recovery time for various types of cycles and for different economies, describing the period of time until recovery to the previous peak as an 'upturn', whereas a downturn was a complete contraction. In advanced countries the average recovery time for output was 3.1 quarters, and it was 6.4 for emerging markets. Turning to equity prices, recovery to the peak of the previous bull market took much longer, being 5.4 quarters for advanced countries and 15.9 in emerging markets.

5.8 Duration Dependence in Phases

A major theme in the cycle literature has been whether the probability of exiting a phase depends on how long one has spent in it. If it does, there is *duration dependence*. There is quite a lot of empirical work on duration dependence in business and financial cycles, largely motivated by the question of whether it is possible to predict the termination of either an expansion or a bull market. Fisher (1925) was one of the first investigators to consider this question, asking whether the probability of exiting any phase of the cycle was just a constant. Later work by researchers such as Diebold and Rudebusch (1990), who argued that there was evidence of duration dependence in U.S. business cycles, has attracted quite a bit of attention.

Given the S_t corresponding to the cycle, it is possible to construct the durations of time spent in each phase. Therefore, if we divide the T observations into N phases, the duration of time spent in the ith phase will be designated as X_i. Duration dependence has then been investigated by either using the estimated moments of X_i or the estimated density.

Consider a random sample of N observations $(X_1, X_2, \ldots X_N)$ and let the density function of X_i be $f(x)$. Then the hazard rate function is defined as

$$h(x) = f(x)/G(x),$$

where $h(x)$ is the hazard (or failure) rate and $G(x) = P(X \geq x)$ is known as the survival function. For a small $\Delta, h(x)\Delta$ is the probability that the expansion will terminate during the interval $(x, x + \Delta)$, given it has lasted until time x. If there is to be no duration dependence, then the hazard rate must be constant, regardless of the duration of time spent in the phase. Consequently, under duration independence the hazard rate does not depend on x, that is,

$$H_0 : h(x) = P(X = x)/P(X \geq x) = q,$$
$$\text{for some } q > 0 \text{ and all } x > 0.$$

A density for discretely measured data that has a constant hazard function ($h(x) = q$) is the geometric density $P(X = x) = (1 - p)^x p$. Thus the literature has focused on whether the X_i have such a density, either indirectly via the moments of the X_i or directly by estimating the density of the X_i.

5.8.1 Moment-Based Tests

The basic test employed under this heading comes from the moments implied by the geometric density, namely, $E(X) = (1 - p)/p$ and $V(X) = (1 - p)/p^2$. Given those definitions it is possible to test if the sample moments are compatible with those of a geometric density by testing if $\tau = 0$ using the moment condition

$$V(X) - [E(X)]^2 - E(X) - \tau = 0. \tag{5.8}$$

This was done by Mudambi and Taylor (1995) and is called the MT test here. While the MT test statistic is asymptotically centered at zero and can be standardized so that it is asymptotically $N(0,1)$, Mudambi and Taylor (1995) found that its distribution is highly skewed in finite samples and that it was necessary to use simulations to obtain finite-sample critical values. Now a feature of the MT test (once standardized) is that it is asymptotically pivotal, that is, asymptotically it does not depend on unknown parameters. In this case one can bootstrap the critical values and these are generally more accurate than those based on first-order asymptotic theory. Horowitz (2001) provides a highly readable account of why it is generally desirable to use pivotal statistics when bootstrapping.

5.8.2 Distributional Tests

An obvious alternative procedure is to directly compare the empirical density of the durations with the geometric density (the latter constructed by using an estimated value of p). This would then involve a standard chi-square test for the correspondence of these densities. The question arises of how to get a density that adequately describes the duration data. Early work on this, for example Sichel (1991), suggested that one choose a generalized parametric form, while the Weibull density has also been popular. There have been other proposals—Diebold et al. (1993) used a nonlinear exponential density. More recently nonparametric methods have been advocated. Specifically, a nonparametric estimate of the hazard function is made and compared to a constant. The perceived advantage of a distributional test is that it might be expected to be more complete than any tests based on moments. Obviously, one needs larger numbers of observations to perform a distributional test. Nevertheless, it can be a very useful adjunct to the moment-based tests. Indeed, a graphical display of what the data say about duration dependence through a plot of a nonparametric estimate of $h(x)$ can be very informative about why any moment-based test rejects the null hypothesis. The latter information is useful in assessing the appropriate response to any rejection. A more extensive discussion of the issues and some applications is contained in Ohn et al. (2004).

5.8.3 Regression-Based Tests

If there are only a few cycles, the use of distributional tests seems unlikely to be successful. Consequently, Ohn et al. (2004) looked at a regression model of the form

$$S_t = a + bS_{t-1} + fS_{t-1}d_{t-1}, \tag{5.9}$$

where d_{t-1} is the duration of time spent in a phase up to and including time $t-1$. This captures the idea that transiting from one phase to another depends on $\Pr(S_t|S_{t-1})$, and so allowing that probability to depend on the time spent in a phase seems a reasonable specification. They showed that a test of $f = 0$ from the regression (5.9) involves testing if $V(X) - E(X)^2 + E(X) = 0$. At first sight this seems to be inconsistent with the moment implications of a geometric density given above, but the resolution of the difference comes from noting that for the durations constructed from the S_t for business cycles, any expansion or contraction must be at least one period long. Thus it is not possible to get a duration of zero periods when using the S_t, ruling out a geometric density as the description of the durations, since such a random variable can take a zero value. This suggests that it is necessary to check the relationship between the moments when the geometric density is left-censored at unity. In this case the censored probability function will be $P(X = x) = (1 - p)^{x-1}p$ $(1 \leq x < \infty)$, and therefore $E(X) = \frac{1}{p}$, $V(X) = \frac{1-p}{p^2}$. Consequently, in the case where durations must be at least one quarter long but they come from a geometric density, the relation between moments is $V(X) - E(X)^2 + E(X) = 0$, which agrees with the regression-based test of $f = 0$ above.

In fact there is further censoring than this. As pointed out in Chapter 2, algorithms such as MBBQ impose a minimum phase duration of two quarters (for quarterly data). Hence, for analyzing business cycles one would need to modify the various statistics to capture this. Consequently, rather than (5.9) the description of S_t under the null hypothesis (in the quarterly case) would most likely be

$$S_t = a + bS_{t-1} + cS_{t-2} + \gamma S_{t-1}S_{t-2} + e_t \qquad (5.10)$$

where $a + b = 1$ and $c = -a$, and we might consider how to augment (5.10) to capture extra duration dependence. Following the strategy above, one possibility is to add on $S_{t-1}d_{t-1}$. Doing this, the t-statistic for the coefficient will be -1.6, so the evidence for duration dependence in post–World War II data is weak.

An alternative is to allow the coefficients a, b, and c in (5.10) to depend on d_{t-1}. Because there are only two independent coefficients, it is useful to follow Harding (2010a) and write (5.10) as

$$S_t = S_{t-1}(1 - S_{t-2}) + \varphi_1 S_{t-1} S_{t-2} + \varphi_2(1 - S_{t-1})(1 - S_{t-2}) + e_t,$$

where $\varphi_2 = a, \varphi_2 = 1 + \gamma - a$. Then the augmented alternative model to capture duration dependence would have the form

$$S'_t = S_t - S_{t-1}(1 - S_{t-2}) = (\varphi_1 + \delta_1 d_{t-1}) S_{t-1} S_{t-2}$$
$$+ (\varphi_2 + \delta_2 d_{t-1})(1 - S_{t-1})(1 - S_{t-2}) + e_t, \qquad (5.11)$$

After fitting (5.11) a joint test for $\delta_1 = 0, \delta_2 = 0$ can be performed. The F-test is 5.45 with a p-value of .0047, so this test suggests duration dependence. However, it is not clear whether this finding reflects a feature of economic activity or a feature of the procedures used to date business cycles. Harding (2014) shows that the NBER-type business cycle dating procedures induce a duration dependence when the underlying series y_t is a random walk.

5.8.4 Application to Business and Financial Cycles

Cardinale and Taylor (2009) give a comprehensive review. Ohn et al. (2004) first replicated the study of Diebold and Rudebusch (1990) using business-cycle data taken from Diebold and Rudebusch's paper.[4] The data consist of durations of contractions and expansions measured in *months*. To construct p-values for the moment-based test, they generated 10,000 samples of size N from a geometric distribution, with the parametric parameter p fixed at the maximum likelihood estimator. The p-value for a given statistic was then obtained from the 10,000 ordered realized values.

The moment-based test termed the MT statistic above showed that there was evidence for duration dependence in pre–World War II expansions and post–World War II contractions. The distributional tests also pointed in this direction, although they suggest that the pre–World War II contraction durations may not be modeled very well with

---

[4]The results are given in tables 2–5 of Ohn et al. (2004).

a geometric density. This observation came from the fact that the observed frequency that contraction durations lay in the interval of [6,15] months was 12, while the expected frequency was just 6.5. Similarly, the observed frequency for the interval [0,5] is only two, while the expected frequency is six. Thus, relative to a geometric density, there are fewer short-term contractions and more intermediate-length contractions than expected. Diebold and Rudebusch detected only some evidence of duration dependence for contractions when they applied the chi-square distributional test by varying the number of bins from two to five. Their results were strongest for the prewar period, but overall, they concluded that the evidence was weak.

5.9 Conclusion

The chapter began with a discussion of why we would expect to find that the time spent in expansions (bull markets, etc.) would be much greater than the time spent in contractions (bear markets, etc.). By focusing on the probabilities of getting particular outcomes for the binary variables summarizing the recurrent events, we can provide an explanation of this long-observed feature. The remainder of the chapter looked at many proposals for summarizing other features of the recurrent events. These involve well-known quantities such as durations and amplitudes, as well as lesser known ones, such as the sharpness of peaks and troughs.

Chapter 6

Measuring Synchronization of Recurrent Events in Multivariate Data

6.1 Introduction

Because one is often interested in looking at recurrent events in a variety of series, it is necessary to consider how to measure synchronization between them. Moreover, there may be many series that represent economic activity and we might wish to combine these in such a way as to come up with a representative measure. To do the latter effectively, it is necessary to first determine which series move together. If they don't exhibit "comovement" it seems unlikely that there would be a common factor in them. When a single series (say) GDP is selected as the measure of economic activity, it is interesting to examine how (say) the cycles in other series—such as hours, consumption, and investment—relate to the cycle in GDP. For this reason it is of interest to first focus on bivariate measures of synchronization.[1]

We assume that the data available for analysis involve binary time series capturing the recurrent events. The special features of the unconditional densities of binary series recommend the use of moment-based measures of synchronization, and Section 6.2 deals with that. Synchronization focuses attention on the similarity of events but it is not the only way this might be done. Section 6.3 therefore looks at similarity across the events in terms of a range of features, such as

---

[1] Sections 6.2 and 6.7 include, with permission of Elsevier, excerpts from Harding and Pagan (2006).

amplitudes. As an alternative to studying synchronization of events using binary variables coming from prescribed rules, Section 6.4 looks at the situation when model-based rules are used to define them. Finally, Section 6.5 gives an application of the methods to studying the synchronization of cycles in industrial production across countries.

The question often arises of whether there is synchronization of the events across a number of industries, countries, and so on. This involves multivariate synchronization and is studied in Section 6.6. As in previous chapters the recurrent events studied here relate to cycles, although the methods are not specific to that choice. In this context there is interest in understanding the relationship between the synchronization of cycles and the comovement in the continuous variables in which those cycles occur. This relationship is examined in Section 6.7.

6.2 Moment-Based Measures for Studying Synchronization of Bivariate Cycles

It is useful to initiate a discussion of synchronization by concentrating on the relations between the unconditional densities of two cycles S_{xt} and S_{yt} in series x_t and y_t. It seems natural to define *perfect (positive) synchronization (PS)* as the case where these two random variables S_{xt} and S_{yt} are identical. Because of the binary nature of the random variables, necessary and sufficient conditions for this type of synchronization are

$$(a) \ \Pr(S_{yt} = 1, S_{xt} = 0) = 0 \qquad (6.1)$$

$$(b) \ \Pr(S_{yt} = 0, S_{xt} = 1) = 0. \qquad (6.2)$$

We couch our discussion in terms of positive synchronization since it is easy to translate the requisite tests to the other case and, in most instances, it is positive synchronization that is of greatest interest.[2] Cycles that are *nonsynchronized (NS)* might then be regarded as the case where S_{xt} and S_{yt}

---

[2]Negative synchronization would be defined as $\Pr(S_{yt} = 0, S_{xt} = 1) = 1$ and $\Pr(S_{yt} = 1, S_{xt} = 0) = 1$.

are independent, that is, the joint probability function for S_{xt} and S_{yt} factorizes into the product of the marginal probability functions.

Because S_{yt} and S_{xt} are binary indicators, it is easily seen that the probabilities in (6.1) and (6.2) can be expressed as expectations. Thus

$$E(S_{yt}(1 - S_{xt})) = \sum_{i=0}^{1} \sum_{j=0}^{1} \Pr(S_{yt} = i, S_{xt} = j) i(1 - j)$$
$$= \Pr(S_{yt} = 1, S_{xt} = 0),$$

so that the following moment conditions need to hold under the two null hypotheses relating to synchronization mentioned in (6.1) and (6.2)

$$PS\ (a) : E(S_{yt}(1 - S_{xt})) = E(S_{yt}) - E(S_{xt}S_{yt}) = 0 \quad (6.3)$$

$$PS\ (b) : E(S_{xt}(1 - S_{yt})) = E(S_{xt}) - E(S_{xt}S_{yt}) = 0. \quad (6.4)$$

Furthermore, nonsynchronization would require

$$NS : E(S_{xt}S_{yt}) - E(S_{xt})E(S_{yt}) = 0. \quad (6.5)$$

Instead of (6.3) and (6.4), it is useful to form a new set of conditions by subtracting (6.4) from (6.3) to get (6.6) and then associating it with (6.4) (which becomes (6.7)). Consequently, the two conditions for PS can alternatively be written as

$$PS(i): \quad E(S_{yt}) - E(S_{xt}) = 0 \quad (6.6)$$

$$PS(ii): \quad E(S_{xt}) - E(S_{xt}S_{yt}) = 0. \quad (6.7)$$

These are useful since the first implies that the unconditional densities of S_{xt} and S_{yt} are identical, while the second is a property of the conditional density. Indeed, since $E(S_{xt}S_{yt}) = cov(S_{xt}, S_{yt}) - E(S_{xt})E(S_{yt})$, PS(ii) can be expressed as

$$\mu_{S_x} - \sigma_{S_x}\sigma_{S_y}\rho_S + \mu_{S_x}\mu_{S_y} = 0, \quad (6.8)$$

where $\mu_{S_x} = E(S_{xt})$, $\mu_{S_y} = E(S_{yt})$, and ρ_S is the correlation coefficient between S_{xt} and S_{yt}. When PS(i) holds $E(S_{yt}) = E(S_{xt}) = \mu_S$

and $\sigma_{S_x}^2 = E(S_{xt})(1 - E(S_{xt})) = \sigma_{S_y}^2$, so that (6.8) becomes

$$(1 - \rho_S)\mu_S(1 - \mu_S) = 0, \tag{6.9}$$

which implies that $\rho_S = 1$ if PS is to hold. Thus, when testing for perfect synchronization, the two tests $PS(i)$ and $PS(ii)$ come down to testing if $\mu_{S_x} = \mu_{S_y}$ and $\rho_S = 1$. Although it is clear that when $\rho_S = 1$, it has to be the case that $\mu_{S_x} = \mu_{S_y}$, our experience has been that there is value in performing the tests sequentially, since this is more informative about the reasons for any failure of perfect synchronization. When testing (NS) we have $\sigma_{S_x}\sigma_{S_y}\rho_S = 0$ and so $\rho_S = 0$ is required. By concentrating on $\hat{\rho}_S$ we are therefore able to provide a natural measure of the *degree* of synchronization as well as a test for it.

6.2.1 Bivariate Test Statistics

The foregoing discussion leads to the following quantities being the basis of test statistics,

$$PS(i) : \hat{\mu}_{S_x} - \hat{\mu}_{S_y} \tag{6.10}$$

$$PS(ii) : \hat{\rho}_S - 1 \tag{6.11}$$

$$NS : \hat{\rho}_S. \tag{6.12}$$

For later reference it should be noted that perfect synchronization between S_{yt} and S_{xt} only occurs when S_{yt} is identical to S_{xt}, and so one could have derived the moment conditions in (6.6) and (6.7) directly from that equality. This alternative interpretation is useful when looking at multivariate issues.

The test for $PS(i)$ is naturally formulated as a moment-based test and derives from

$$E(S_{yt} - S_{xt}) = 0.$$

This involves testing if two sample means are equal and is easily done. In generalized method of moments (GMM) terms one would test the moment condition by testing if $\tau = 0$, where

$$E(S_{yt} - S_{xt} - \tau) = 0.$$

The GMM estimator of τ can be found using this moment condition and standard methods can then be employed to produce a standard error for $\hat{\tau}$ that is asymptotically robust to any serial correlation and heteroskedasticity that is present in S_{xt} and S_{yt}.

For testing nonsynchronization the correlation between S_{xt} and S_{yt}, ρ_S, is an obvious quantity to examine. To estimate ρ_S we have the moment condition

$$E[\sigma_{S_x}^{-1}(S_{xt} - \mu_{S_x})\sigma_{S_y}^{-1}(S_{yt} - \mu_{S_y}) - \rho_S] = 0, \qquad (6.13)$$

with estimator generating equation of

$$\frac{1}{T}\sum_{t=1}^{T}\hat{\sigma}_{S_x}^{-1}(S_{xt} - \hat{\mu}_{S_x})\hat{\sigma}_{S_y}^{-1}(S_{yt} - \hat{\mu}_{S_y}) - \hat{\rho}_S = 0. \qquad (6.14)$$

Since estimates of the means and variances of S_{xt} and S_{yt} are needed to compute $\hat{\rho}_S$, it is necessary to ask if some allowance has to be made for this when finding the asymptotic distribution of $\hat{\rho}_S$. This can be done by thinking about the joint estimation of means, variances, and ρ_S in the framework of sequential method of moments, to use Newey's (1984) term. The moment condition for estimating ρ_S in (6.13) can be written as

$$E[m_t(\theta, S_{xt}, S_{yt}) - \rho_S] = 0, \qquad (6.15)$$

where $\theta' = [\mu_{Sx}, \sigma_{S_x}, \mu_{Sy}, \sigma_{S_y}]$. Now because $E\{\frac{\partial m_t}{\partial \theta}\} = 0$ under the null hypothesis that $\rho_S = 0$, the fact that θ has been estimated from the data does not impact the asymptotic distribution of $T^{1/2}(\hat{\rho}_S - \rho_S)$.

Testing the second criterion used in judging perfect synchronization (PS(ii)) is a little more complex. When testing PS(ii) with (6.11) it would be expected that $T^{1/2}(\hat{\rho}_S - \rho_S)$ would be asymptotically $N(0, v)$, and so $T^{1/2}\hat{v}^{-1/2}(\hat{\rho}_S - \rho_S)$ would be $N(0, 1)$ asymptotically. However, the proposed PS(ii) test involves a hypothesis test on the boundary of the parameter space $H_0 : \rho_S = 1$, since $|\rho_S| \leq 1$. There is a literature on the distribution of $T^{1/2}\hat{v}^{-1/2}(\hat{\rho}_S - 1)$ in that case. As Chant (1974) and Andrews (2001) point out, it is asymptotically a half normal. Since the series S_{xt} and S_{yt} are serially correlated, the value of v will need to be estimated by using a robust covariance estimator. In this scalar case it is simply a matter of doing a one- rather than two-tail test. Candelon et al. (2009) have argued that it is extremely unlikely one would have perfect synchronization, and they therefore propose testing if ρ equals ρ_0, where ρ_0 is some prespecified value in the range $(-1 < \rho_0 < 1)$. They compute this test statistic for a range of values of ρ_0, finding the value ρ^* that minimizes the test statistic, and presenting that as the evidence relating to synchronization.

Although method of moments is an obvious way to perform estimation and inference about ρ_S, it is often useful to recognize that $\hat{\rho}_S$ can be found from the regression

$$\hat{\sigma}_{S_y}^{-1} S_{yt} = a_1 + \rho_S \hat{\sigma}_{S_x}^{-1} S_{xt} + u_t. \qquad (6.16)$$

This regression also shows the difficulties that can arise with some procedures advocated for testing $H_0 : \rho_S = 0$ in the existing literature. In particular, the critical role played by any implicit or explicit assumption that u_t is $i.i.d.$ Thus the well-known Pearson test of independence in a contingency table embodies that assumption, and it has often been used to study the correlation between S_{xt} and S_{yt}, for example, Artis et al. (1997) advocate a transformed version of ρ_S for this purpose.

As one can see from the regression, when the null $\rho_S = 0$ holds the error term inherits the serial correlation properties of S_{yt}. As has already been seen the S_{yt} are positively serially correlated, and as is well known, positive serial correlation sharply increases the chance of rejecting the null that $\rho_S = 0$ when using conventional test statistics. Consequently, inferences need to be made robust to the serial correlation, as well as to any heteroskedasticity in the errors. This can be easily done within the method of moments framework. Thus in applications below we report the t-ratios for testing if $\rho_S = 0$ using the method of moments estimator in two ways—one makes an allowance for serial correlation and heteroskedasticity and the other doesn't. Notice that an advantage of the method of moments approach over the regression model is that no assumptions are being made about which of S_{yt} and S_{xt} are "exogenous."

The regression interpretation has other uses. One is in defining concepts such as *pro-* and *countercyclical*. Often when researchers have tried to decide which relationship a given series bears to the "aggregate cycle," they have felt the need to compute a correlation between two stationary series. This has led them to the application of filters that removed all the permanent components of the two series under investigation. But the series of states S_t will be stationary even if the underlying series have permanent components, so the sign of the correlation (or regression coefficient) between the S_t relevant to each series is the natural way to decide on the issue of whether there is pro- or countercyclicality. Another use of the regression approach is that it is a natural way of looking at questions about whether the degree of synchronization has changed over time, since it is possible to compute ρ_S recursively and study its evolution over time. For formal testing of parameter stability one can utilize the methods in Sowell (1996).

6.2.2 Measures Based on Phase States for Cycles

Rather than focus directly on turning points, a different way of measuring the degree of synchronization of cycles is to ask what fraction of time the cycles are in the same phase. This *concordance index*, which is the sample analog of $Pr(S_{xt} = S_{yt})$, was advocated in Harding and Pagan (2002) and has the following form (for two series y_t and x_t and a sample size of T)

$$\hat{I} = \frac{1}{T}\left\{\sum_{t=1}^{T} S_{xt}S_{yt} + \sum_{t=1}^{T}(1 - S_{xt})(1 - S_{yt})\right\}. \quad (6.17)$$

There are close connections between this index and those advanced in the meteorological literature for assessing forecast accuracy; see Granger and Pesaran (2000). Artis et al. (1997) use a modified version of $\hat{I}$ that is transformed to lie between 0 and 100.

It useful to rewrite and reparameterize this index in a different way, namely,

$$\hat{I} = 1 + \frac{2}{T} \sum_{t=1}^{T} S_{xt} S_{yt} - \hat{\mu}_{S_x} - \hat{\mu}_{S_y} \qquad (6.18)$$

$$= 1 + 2\hat{\sigma}_{S_x S_y} + 2\hat{\mu}_{S_x}\hat{\mu}_{S_y} - \hat{\mu}_{S_x} - \hat{\mu}_{S_y}, \qquad (6.19)$$

where $\hat{\sigma}_{S_x S_y}$ is the estimated covariance between S_{xt} and S_{yt}. For the discussion that follows it will be convenient to write (6.19) as

$$\hat{I} = 1 + 2\hat{\rho}_S (\hat{\mu}_{S_x}(1 - \hat{\mu}_{S_x}))^{1/2} (\hat{\mu}_{S_y}(1 - \hat{\mu}_{S_y}))^{1/2}$$

$$+ 2\hat{\mu}_{S_x}\hat{\mu}_{S_y} - \hat{\mu}_{S_x} - \hat{\mu}_{S_y}, \qquad (6.20)$$

where $\hat{\rho}_S$ is the estimated correlation coefficient between S_{xt} and S_{yt}. Because of the binary nature of S_{xt} and S_{yt} the estimated standard deviations have the form $\sqrt{(\hat{\mu}_{S_j} - \hat{\mu}_{S_j}^2)}, j = x, y$. Now the concordance index has a maximum value of unity when $S_{xt} = S_{yt}$, and zero when $S_{xt} = (1 - S_{yt})$. Consequently, it is easily shown that when either of these holds, $\hat{\sigma}_{S_x}\hat{\sigma}_{S_y} = \hat{\sigma}_{S_x}^2$, and so the value of $\hat{\rho}_S = 1$ corresponds to a concordance index of one, while $\hat{\rho}_S = -1$ gives a concordance index of zero. Since the concordance index is also monotonic in ρ_S, it is natural to shift attention away from the former to the latter, that is, to focus on the correlation between the two states S_{xt} and S_{yt}. Accordingly, the tests based on $\hat{\rho}_S$ laid out in the previous section will be those employed in the empirical work, although it can sometimes be useful to reinterpret the value of $\hat{\rho}_S$ as a value for $\hat{I}$.

A problem with looking at the value of $\hat{I}$ can be seen when $\rho_S = 0$. Then $E(\hat{I}) = 1 + 2\mu_{S_x}\mu_{S_y} - \mu_{S_x} - \mu_{S_y}$, so that $E(\hat{I}) = .5$ only if $\mu_{S_x} = .5, \mu_{S_y} = .5$. Since μ_{S_x} is the probability of x_t being in an expansion, for the business cycle it is likely that it will be closer to .9 than .5. In that case $E(\hat{I}) \simeq .82$, and so one could easily think that the cycles are synchronized, even though there is no relation between them. Of course a policy maker may not be too concerned with that fact, as they may only be interested in the fraction of time that (say) two economies are in the same phase, and not the reason for it. But the example points to how what might appear to be a high degree of association between cycles (seen in a high concordance index value) can be quite misleading, as it is simply an artifact of expansions lasting for a large fraction of the sample. If one is to use $\hat{I}$ as a test statistic, it is necessary to mean correct it, and that is essentially what happens when one uses $\hat{\rho}_S$.

6.3   Other Approaches to Measuring Synchronization

Camacho et al. (2008) feel that there has been an overuse of synchronization ideas relative to other measures of similarity. They look at statistics on features such as amplitude and durations and ask whether these fall into clusters. Let these statistics be arranged in a vector x_n for each country. Then they think of the density of x_n as being built up from a mixture of G clusters, these having the form $f(x_n) = \sum_{j=1}^{G} \varphi(x_n; \mu_g, \sigma_g)$. With this density it is possible to construct a likelihood and maximize it with an EM algorithm to get around the problem of an unbounded likelihood for mixtures. They also suggest some ways for choosing the number of clusters G.

A different perspective on clustering is to look at what fraction of units (say, countries) have their turning points at the same time. In this instance, if there are M countries, $\psi_t = \frac{1}{M} \sum_{j=1}^{M} S_{jt}(1 - S_{jt+1})$, will give the fraction having a peak at the same time, and there is an analogous definition for troughs. This statistic has been favored by the IMF. Of course one might want to say that turning points are synchronized even if they don't occur at exactly the same point in time, but in a preset window around it. If ψ_t is large then the IMF refers to the phases as being "highly synchronized." When M is large one can obviously determine a standard error to place on this estimated fraction by using normal statistical methods. Indeed, one can think of this as a panel data set in which ψ_t is estimated through having fixed time effects, and that interpretation would enable one to compute standard errors for ψ_t relatively easily.

6.4 Synchronization and Model-Based Rules

Instead of using the states S_t found from prescribed rules, one could compute all the previously mentioned tests for synchronization using the model-based cycle states ζ_{jt} found after fitting some multivariate model. In this vein Cakmakli et al. (2011) proposed a two-equation MS-VAR driven by latent states ξ_{1t} and ξ_{2t} as the model. Rather than extracting and using ζ_{jt}, they argue that there is perfect synchronization if $\xi_{1t} = \xi_{2t}$, and nonsynchronization if ξ_{1t} and ξ_{2t} are independent. In the latter case they comment that the two variables y_{1t} and y_{2t} driven by the MS-VAR would then have "its own idiosyncratic cycle." As has happened before, this confuses the latent variables ξ_{jt} and MS model-defined cycle states ζ_{jt}. To make this point more forcibly, take the simple two-equation MS model (with no VAR terms)

$$\Delta y_{1t} = \mu_{11}\xi_{1t} + \mu_{10}(1 - \xi_{1t}) + \sigma_1\varepsilon_{1t}$$

$$\Delta y_{2t} = \mu_{21}\xi_{2t} + \mu_{20}(1 - \xi_{2t}) + \sigma_2\varepsilon_{2t}.$$

Now letting $\xi_{1t} = \xi_{2t}$ we would get

$$\Delta y_{1t} = \mu_{11}\xi_{1t} + \mu_{10}(1 - \xi_{1t}) + \sigma_1\varepsilon_{1t}$$

$$\Delta y_{2t} = \mu_{21}\xi_{1t} + \mu_{20}(1 - \xi_{1t}) + \sigma_2\varepsilon_{2t}.$$

So the means $E(\Delta y_{jt})$ would be different if $\mu_{11} \neq \mu_{21}, \mu_{10} \neq \mu_{20}$ and the variances of the shocks ε_{jt} would be different if $\sigma_1 \neq \sigma_2$. Hence the prescribed rule cycle states S_{jt} (or the model-based states ζ_{jt}) would point to there being different cycles in the series y_{jt}, that is, the equivalence of the latent states is not enough to ensure equivalence of the cycle states. One needs to determine either ζ_{jt} or S_{jt} and to then test synchronization

6.5 Application to Synchronization of Industrial Production Cycles

Our investigation of synchronization of cycles is with the data on monthly industrial production for 6 of the 12 countries in Artis et al. (1997, table 2). A more comprehensive use of

Table 6.1: Concordance Indexes and Correlations of Cycles in
Industrial Production, Selected Countries

	UK	CAN	GER	US	JAP	FRA
UK	1	.61	.66	.65	.58	.63
CAN	.11	1	.62	.83	.70	.66
GER	.20	.08	1	.74	.84	.83
US	.14	.60	.26	1	.76	.76
JAP	−.04	.22	.55	.20	1	.84
FRA	.05	.11	.50	.13	.43	1
$\widehat{\mu}_S$	.66	.68	.74	.82	.82	.84

this data is in Harding and Pagan (2006). We first focus on
the statistics $\{\widehat{I}, \widehat{\rho}_S, \widehat{\mu}_S\}$ that are presented in Table 6.1. In
this table the concordance statistic $\widehat{I}$ is above the diagonal,
$\widehat{\rho}_S$ is below the diagonal, and $\widehat{\mu}_S$ is in the bottom row of
the table. Reported values of $\widehat{I}$ are large, suggesting that
industrial production in these six countries spends much of
the time in the same cyclical state. However, the pairwise
correlations $\widehat{\rho}_S$ are typically small, which points to the fact that
the high values for $\widehat{\mu}_S$, rather than a strong correlation between
industrial production in different countries, lies behind the
high degree of concordance. This effect is most evident for
the United Kingdom, which shows concordance with other
countries in the range of 0.58 to 0.66, while the correlations
range from −0.04 to 0.20.

As might be expected with the monthly data, there is
extensive serial correlation in the states. For example, the
first-order serial correlation coefficient in $S_{GER,t}$ is .95, so that
there will need to be a serial correlation correction performed
to get the correct t ratio for $\widehat{\rho}_S$. Accordingly, we use a HAC
standard error with Bartlett weights to account for the serial
correlation. The number of lags is set to be the integer part of
$\widehat{\gamma}T^{\frac{1}{3}}$, where $\widehat{\gamma}$ is estimated using the procedures in Newey and
West (1994). Results are in Table 6.2, where the uncorrected
t-statistics are above the diagonal, while those based on
HAC standard errors are below the diagonal. The robust

Table 6.2: Standard and Robust t-Statistics for Null Hypothesis of
No Synchronization of Business Cycles

	UK	CAN	GER	US	JAP	FRA
UK	*	4.0	8.1	6.6	−2.0	2.7
CAN	.6	*	3.3	34.9	10.6	5.3
GER	.9	.4	*	12.3	31.1	28.9
US	.6	6.9	1.1	*	9.7	6.6
JAP	−.2	.9	3.3	.6	*	23.5
FRA	.2	.4	2.8	.7	1.6	*

t-ratios shows that the evidence for the null hypothesis of no association is quite strong; something that was not true of the test performed with the uncorrected t-ratios.

6.6 Multivariate Synchronization

Turning to the general case where there are n series $y_{1t}, \ldots, y_{nt}$, these will have associated specific cycles $S_{jt}, j = 1, \ldots, n$. Then the hypothesis that all pairs $(S_{jt}, S_{kt}) j \neq k$ are strongly nonsynchronized will be referred to as multivariate nonsynchronization (MNS). A test for MNS is therefore available by asking if the correlation matrix of the S_{jt} is diagonal, that is, all the pairwise correlations ρ_S^{ij} $(i \neq j)$ are tested for whether they are zero. For perfect synchronization two conditions must hold – $\mu_{S_i} = \mu_{S_j} \forall i, j = 1 \ldots n$, and all pairwise correlations ρ_S^{ij} $(i \neq j)$ are unity. It is useful when performing these tests to choose a "numeraire" series. In many instances there will be an obvious choice, for example, the United States would often be that for business cycle analysis. If we take the numeraire to be the first series, then the first of the two tests for perfect synchronization would involve $H_0 : \mu_j - \mu_1 = 0, j = 2, \ldots, n$. Notice that the numeraire does not matter for this test as test statistics will be invariant to which series is chosen as the numeraire, since the vector of mean differences with (say) the second series as the numeraire is a nonsingular transformation of that with the first. The situation is less clear for the test that all ρ_S^{ij} are unity. However, if the null hypothesis $H_0 : \rho^{1j} = 1 \forall j$ is accepted (rejected), it implies that S_{it} and S_{jt} are identical (not identical), so that $\rho^{ij} = 1 (\neq 1)$ must hold for all (some) i.

Candelon et al. (2009) point out that the joint test based on $\hat{\rho}^{ij}$ will be unlikely to follow distributions from asymptotic theory if the number of series being investigated for synchronization is large. Instead they recommend that the tests be bootstrapped by resampling the S_{jt}. Even a use of the bootstrap, however, did not seem to correct size distortions when the number of series was large, leading them to conclude that it might be preferable to make a judicious selection of subsets of the series to test. In the case of MNS one possible solution is to test whether $\eta_i = \sum_{j=1}^n \rho_S^{ij} (i \neq j) (i = 1, \ldots, n)$ are jointly zero. The null hypothesis that $E(\eta_i) = 0$ will hold under $H_0 : \rho_S^{ij} = 0, i \neq j$. Consequently, testing if $\eta_1, \ldots, \eta_n$ are jointly zero is likely to be less subject to distributional biases under the null hypothesis of MNS. Of course, the power of the test may be affected.

6.7 Comovement of Cycles

Loosely speaking, if variables have cycles that are synchronized, we would like to say that they possess a common cycle. To be more precise about this concept, it is necessary to examine the determinants of ρ_S in the two-series case. From the definition of ρ_S,

$$\rho_S = \frac{E(S_{xt} S_{yt}) - [E(S_{xt}) E(S_{yt})]}{\sqrt{E(S_{xt})(1 - E(S_{xt}))} \sqrt{E(S_{yt})(1 - E(S_{yt}))}}$$

$$= \frac{\Pr(S_{xt} = 1, S_{yt} = 1) - [\Pr(S_{xt} = 1) \Pr(S_{yt} = 1)]}{\sqrt{\Pr(S_{xt} = 1) \Pr(S_{xt} = 0)} \sqrt{\Pr(S_{yt} = 1) \Pr(S_{yt} = 0)}},$$
(6.21)

it is seen that the degree of synchronization of cycles depends on two items: the characteristics of the specific cycles—which are determined by $\Pr(S_{xt} = 1)$ and $\Pr(S_{yt} = 1)$—and the probability of the event $\{S_{xt} = 1, S_{yt} = 1\}$. The latter event is more likely to occur when the turning points in both cycles are located at the same point in time, that is, when turning points *cluster* around a given date. From the expression for ρ_S it is clear that given individual cycle characteristics summarized by $\Pr(S_{xt} = 1)$ and $\Pr(S_{yt} = 1)$, the higher is ρ_S the greater the probability that turning points will occur together, and so the greater the chance of observing synchronized cycles.

Now the $\Pr(S_{xt} = 1)$ and $\Pr(S_{yt} = 1)$ are characteristics of the marginal densities of S_{xt} and S_{yt}, respectively, and these derive from the marginal densities of x_t and y_t. The joint density of x_t and y_t will be involved in determining $\Pr(S_{xt} = 1, S_{yt} = 1)$. If we keep $\Pr(S_{xt} = 1)$ and $\Pr(S_{yt} = 1)$ unchanged then, as $\Pr(S_{xt} = 1, S_{yt} = 1)$ changes, so will ρ_S. Consider therefore the case when Δx_t and Δy_t are jointly normal with expected values $\mu_x = E(\Delta x_t)$ and $\mu_y = E(\Delta y_t)$; variances σ_x^2 and σ_y^2; and correlation ρ. If the marginal density parameters are held constant, it is clear that $\Pr(S_{xt} = 1, S_{yt} = 1)$ varies directly with ρ, and so ρ_S and ρ are related.

This connection is useful since it shows how our concept of synchronization relates to that of comovement used in the fluctuations literature. The latter has been the focus of attention of RBC researchers. That group studies the correlation among series (z_t) from which the permanent component has been removed through some form of filtering, and so it is effectively studying the growth cycle. Examples of this methodology applied to a single economy include Cooley and Prescott (1995) and Cooley and Hansen (1995), and involves the correlation between variables such as GDP, consumption, investment, employment, unemployment, hours worked, and prices, from which permanent components have been removed. There are also several papers that study correlation between the z_t from different countries, including Backus et al. (1992), Canova and Dellas (1992), Canova (1993), and Artis and Zhang (1997). The autocorrelations and cross-correlations between the z_t of different countries can be used to reconstruct the equivalent quantities for Δz_t, and the latter will be important to the nature and existence of growth cycles. However, the correlation of Δx_t and Δy_t is the appropriate quantity to study synchronization of business cycles. The latter cycle depends on all the second-order moments of Δx_t and Δy_t, although in a very complex way, since ρ_S also depends on what determines the marginal probabilities like $\Pr(S_{xt} = 1)$, as well as the joint probability.[3] Consequently, the moments of the series Δx_t and Δy_t, as well as their covariance, will determine ρ_S. Studying any individual moment, such as the covariance, will not be very informative about synchronization.

6.8 Conclusion

Methods for capturing the synchronization of recurrent events in bivariate and multiple series are presented and applied. The relationship between synchronization of cycles and comovement of the underlying continuous variables is investigated.

---

[3]Of course it is really the joint density of Δy_t and Δx_t which determines the cycle characterictics rather than the second moments per se.

Chapter 7

Accounting for Observed Cycle Features with a Range of Statistical Models

7.1 Introduction

This chapter looks at observed features of the cycle in a variety of time series. Section 7.2 and 7.3 sets out these features for the United States and a number of other countries. Section 7.4 then asks whether these features can be replicated by the use of a particular statistical model—a linear autoregression. For such linear models it is possible to broadly account for the observed features using moments of the series for growth rates, and this strategy is employed in Section 7.2. The emphasis in this chapter contrasts with the next one where interpretations of the features are offered through the use of models that have economic content. Because one of the features—the excess statistic—suggested that some nonlinear structure would be needed, Section 7.5 uses a particular nonlinear statistical model to see if it can match all the features. It is impossible to cover all nonlinear models, so we have chosen one that is a representative of many used in the literature, in that it incorporates regime switching allied with a mechanism to produce the "bounceback" effect thought to be the source of the nonlinearity.

Section 7.6 then looks at two other nonlinear models first dealt with in Chapter 4. It is argued that a useful exercise for validating such models is to see what their cycle properties are when compared to what can be seen in the data using prescribed rules. This involves simulating the models, passing the simulated data through algorithms such as MBBQ, and comparing the outcomes to what was found when doing the same exercise with actual data. In our opinion, simulating fitted models is important to an understanding of their strengths and weaknesses. Despite being a simple task with today's technology, the technique has had remarkably little use. Finally, the chapter concludes with an examination of whether the binary indicators summarizing the recurrent states can be used in the context of standard multivariate methods such as vector autoregressions. This turns out not to be straightforward owing to the nature of the binary variables.

7.2 U.S. Cycles as a Benchmark

It is worth looking at cycles in a number of U.S. series. These will be GDP (y), aggregate consumption (c), aggregate investment (i), monthly industrial production (ip), and the monthly S&P500 index. For y, c, and i the sample period runs from 1947/1 to 2013/1. In contrast those for industrial production and the S&P500 series are 1949.2–2011.1 and 1950.1–2013.1, respectively.[1] The industrial production data is that used in Billio et al. (2012). We apply the MBBQ algorithm to all five series (the monthly version in the case of the monthly series) and the results from this are given in Table 7.1. For the monthly series duration is quoted in months. For the S&P500 we just used the same dating rules as for monthly industrial production, that is, they coincide with those employed in NBER-type work. This ensures comparability, although Pagan and Sossounov (2003) used longer phases for the S&P500 (8 versus 6 months) and a longer complete cycle (16 versus 15 months). They also imposed a quantitative constraint that enabled an override of bear market durations to capture the 1987 stock market crash, which lasted only four months. Although this produces some quantitative differences the results of Table 7.1 are quite similar to what was found in Pagan and Sossounov.

---

[1] It should be remembered that following Chapter 3 we use a / for quarters and a period for months when describing dates.

Table 7.1: U.S. Cycle Characteristics, Various Data Series, and
Samples 1947-2013

	y	c	i	ip	S&P500
Dur con	2.9	3.3	4.9	13.6	14.4
Dur expan	21.1	34.9	9.0	43.5	40.6
Amp con	−2.3	−2.2	−18.2	−8.0	−30.8
Amp expan	20.9	32.6	30.5	22.9	60.6
Excess con	2.0	−12	−11	−9.0	−15.7
Excess expan	11.3	2.1	10	16.2	12.9
CV dur con	.47	.53	.63	.57	.42
CV dur expan	.86	.81	.64	.71	1.15
CV amp con	−.59	−.51	−.73	−.59	−.71
CV amp expan	.74	.85	.58	.53	.85

It is clear that stock market and industrial production expansions are around 13–14 quarters on average, and so are much shorter than that for GDP. Indeed, Maccini and Pagan (2013) looking at the cycle in goods-GDP found it had much the same duration as industrial production, so that the different behavior of industrial production to that for GDP is due to the presence of the service sector in the latter. Following on by looking at the durations of phases, we observe that the amplitudes of industrial cycle contractions and expansions, as well as for the expansions in the S&P500, are very high, although one should note that the latter is for a cycle in the nominal price index rather than in a real index. Nevertheless, deflating by a price index has a relatively small effect on that cycle. It is noticeable from the "excess statistic" that GDP expansions are 11% higher than if growth was a constant over the whole of the expansion. This is also true of investment and the S&P500, but not for consumption. We should also note that the excess statistic is not reliable when there is only a small duration for any phase. This comes about because we are measuring the excess by reference to a triangle, and any two points will determine the hypotenuse. Thus, if there are only two periods in the phases, the excess statistic would always be zero. Because recessions have a duration that is often just three periods long, the excess statistic is essentially being determined by one observation.

One seeks some explanations for these outcomes. Because the turning points are determined by sequences of the signs of Δy_t, it must be that the explanations reside in the characteristics of the DGP of Δy_t. It is therefore useful to consider a simple representation for Δy_t of the form

$$\Delta y_t - \mu = \rho(\Delta y_{t-1} - \mu) + (\sigma_y \sqrt{1 - \rho^2})\varepsilon_t, \qquad (7.1)$$

where ε_t is $n.i.d.(0, 1)$. It is clear that for this process, $E(\Delta y_t) = \mu$, $std(\Delta y_t) = \sigma_y$. The importance of formulating the process in this way is that the mean and variance of Δy_t are invariant to the serial correlation ρ. In the work that follows we set $\mu = .7757$ and $\sigma_y = .9839$ to match the statistics for U.S. GDP growth over 1947/1 to 2013/1.

Now consider raising μ. It would be expected that there would be less chance of getting a negative value of Δy_t, and so a smaller probability of getting a peak. Similarly, a fall in σ_y will mean the same. There is no obvious relationship between the probability of turning points and ρ however, and no analytical results have emerged. Table 7.2 presents some simulations of the process in equation (7.1), with MBBQ being first applied to 66 years of simulated quarterly data followed by an averaging of the cycle features over 500 replications. It suggests that there is a U-shaped relationship between expansion durations and ρ—as positive serial correlation strengthens, expansion duration initially shortens, but at some threshold it begins to rise again. At that point recessions get longer, too. This behavior goes over into the amplitudes of those phases. There is also a strong rise in the variability of recessions. Of course, as ρ rises toward unity the process for Δy_t is moving toward having a unit root, that is, y_t is $I(2)$. Because growth rates in most series have serial correlation below .4, we would expect a limited impact of serial correlation on business cycle features.

Table 7.2: Cycle Characteristics of the AR(1) Linear Model as Serial
Correlation of Growth Varies

	$\rho = 0$	$\rho = .2$	$\rho = .4$	$\rho = .7$	$\rho = .8$
Dur con	2.8	3.0	3.4	4.6	5.5
Dur expan	26.1	21.2	19.1	19.8	22.9
Amp con	−1.4	−1.6	−1.9	−3.0	−3.0
Amp expan	23.8	20.4	19.4	21.0	26.0
Excess con	1.5	.88	.58	.18	.72
Excess expan	.17	.30	.04	.16	.24
CV dur con	.38	.44	.50	.60	.66
CV dur expan	.82	.83	.83	.87	.88
CV amp con	−.61	−.62	−.70	−.90	−.98
CV amp expan	.82	.84	.89	1.02	1.01

Table 7.3: U.S. Series Characteristics

	y	c	i	ip	S&P500
μ	.78	.82	.89	.26	.61
σ_y	.98	.84	5.4	.99	4.2
ρ	.37	.10	.21	.38	.05

It should be observed that on average the excess statistic in
all cases shows little evidence of the phases departing much
from a triangle shape.

Before returning to accounting for the outcomes of
Table 7.1, we need to record the values for μ, σ_y, and ρ for
each of the series in that table. Table 7.3 does this.

It's now easy enough to account for the outcomes in
Table 7.1. For example, while GDP and consumption have
much the same long-run growth rate (μ), the volatility of the

consumption growth rate is much lower than that for GDP, implying that the cycle in consumption is of much longer duration. Moreover, the GDP growth rate series has more serial correlation, and therefore Table 7.2 would point to a shorter cycle as a consequence. As was mentioned in earlier chapters, the ratio of the mean to the standard deviation of the growth rates is important for many cycle outcomes, and this is lower for the consumption series. Turning to investment, we find that the same ratio is very much lower, which accounts for why its phase durations (but not amplitudes) are much shorter. In the same way, the high volatility of the stock market keeps stock market cycles relatively short. These comments illustrate how one needs to have information on both the mean of the growth rate and its volatility to speak effectively about cycles.

The shape of expansions is interesting. It is worth noting that the shapes of expansions in GDP and investment are much the same, suggesting that it is a strong pick-up in investment that drove the "bounceback" feature that is evident in Table 7.1. However, this conclusion needs to be qualified by the fact that the effect has not been constant over time. A typical example of the "fast growth" in the early stages of an expansion would be the 1954–1957 expansion shown in Figure 7.1. This clearly differs from the 1991–2000 expansion in Figure 7.2.

Focusing directly on the growth rates in the expansion phase, Sichel (1994) divided them into three equally long sections, and then looked at the average growth rate over each section. Thus the average quarterly growth rate over his sample period was 1.37% per quarter (first section), 1.29% in the second section, and .83% in the final section of expansions, showing the slowdown in growth as the average expansion proceeds. Using the same technique, Camacho et al. (2011) observed that the expansions of the 1990s and early/late 2000s did not show such a feature, being smaller than the growth rate over the whole expansion. This is certainly true of the first two of these expansions, but using either the graphs of the log of GDP (as in Figures 7.1 and 7.2) or the sectional average growth approach, it seems that the current (incomplete) expansion is a return to the old pattern,

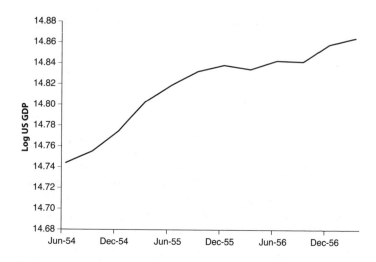

Figure 7.1: The 1954/2–1957/3 U.S. Expansion.

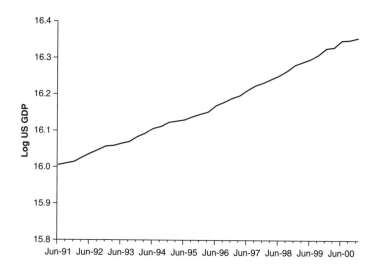

Figure 7.2: The 1991/2–2000/4 U.S. Expansion.

with the first two quarters of growth averaging 2.69% against the average over the period to 2013/1 of 2.07%. To some extent the analysis in Camacho et al. (2011) seems flawed by the fact that they refer to the expansion with peak in 2009/2, which is odd, since the NBER (and GDP levels) place the *end* of the recession in 2009/2. It may be that they were using data that have since been revised.

7.3 The Business Cycle in a Range of Countries

In Table 7.4 we summarize the nature of business cycles in the GDP of a number of countries. The sample period is 1960/1–2013/1 except for the euro area where it is 1970/1–2013/4. It is clear that there is considerable diversity in the nature of cycles across countries. Some of the differences are readily explained. The United Kingdom has lower long-run growth in quarterly GDP than does the United States (.6% versus .8%). It also has higher volatility (.99 versus .85), which accounts for the weaker expansions and stronger recessions. Offsetting this is a larger degree of serial correlation in U.S. growth (.35) than in UK growth (.1). The euro area has smaller mean growth than the United States. (.6% versus .8%), much the same volatility (.87% "versus" .85%), and much the same serial correlation (.36 "versus" .35). So expansions end up being shorter in the euro area.

Perhaps the most interesting feature of Table 7.4 is the lack of any shape effect in UK expansions, although it does seem present in those of the euro area.

7.4 Can U.S. Business Cycles Be Generated by Linear Models?

Can linear statistical models for growth rates in output produce the features of the business cycle that we see above? There are many statements in the literature that one needs some sort of nonlinear structure. Table 7.2 gave simulations of linear models based on U.S. GDP, and two of these (the $\rho = 0$ and the $\rho = .4$ cases) are transferred from it to Table 7.5, along with the actual outcomes for U.S. GDP over 1947/1 to

Table 7.4: Business Cycle Characteristics for Different Countries*

	U.S.	UK	Euro area
Dur con	3.1	4.3	3.9
Dur expan	27.1	22.8	21.1
Amp con	−2.3	−3.4	−2.4
Amp expan	25.2	18.9	18.4
Excess con	5.8	2.5	6.1
Excess expan	9.3	.6	13
CV dur con	.53	.42	.46
CV dur expan	.76	1.1	1.1
CV amp con	−.57	−.77	−.74
CV amp expan	.72	1.1	1.0

*United States/ United Kingdom 1960/1–2013/1; euro area
1970/1–2013/4

2013/1 recorded in Table 7.1 ($\hat{\rho} = .38$ over this period for U.S. GDP growth). It is clear that the match is generally quite good.

In the case $\rho = 0$ one is simulating a random walk with drift and Table 7.5 shows that a cycle is produced with some similarities to that seen in U.S. GDP, but also a few important differences. Although it produces expansions that are much longer than contractions, and the average amplitude is larger, the biggest discrepancy relates to the shapes of expansions. This is also true when Δy_t is an AR(1) with $\rho = .4$, showing that these linear models always predict that the average phases look like triangles. Consequently, to get the typical shape of most U.S. expansions will require either some type of nonlinearity or shocks in a linear model that are not symmetrically distributed.

It is important to observe that the random walk with drift simulation is of a series *that only has a permanent component*. There is no transitory component to y_t, and yet there is a

Table 7.5: Observed U.S. Cycle Characteristics and Those from a
Linear Model

	y	$AR(1)(\rho = .4)$	$AR(\rho = 0)$
Dur con	2.9	3.4	2.8
Dur expan	21.1	19.1	26.1
Amp con	−2.3	−1.9	−1.4
Amp expan	20.9	19.4	23.8
Excess con	2.0	.6	1.5
Excess expan	11.3	.04	.2
CV dur con	.47	.50	.38
CV dur expan	.86	.83	.82
CV amp con	−.59	−.70	−.61
CV amp expan	.74	.89	.82

recognizable cycle. This harkens back to the point made in the second chapter: the permanent component is fundamental to the business cycle and one cannot just focus on transitory components. Eliminating the permanent component from the series, as is done with filters like HP, will produce a radically different cycle. If U.S. data had been generated by a process that was stationary around a long-run trend, then after subtracting it, we would have a series with $\mu = 0$. This series would be used to date the growth rather than business cycle. The number of growth cycles exceeds the number of classical or business cycles. A simple way of understanding why this is so is to look at the calculus rule. With it a growth cycle contraction is entered into whenever $\Delta y_t < \mu$, whereas a business cycle contraction requires $\Delta y_t < 0$. Thus we go into a growth cycle contraction before the business cycle contraction begins and emerge from it after the business cycle contraction is over, that is, a growth cycle contraction is of much longer duration than is true of the business cycle, since it is simply a matter of growth falling below long-run trend (μ) rather than becoming negative.

7.5 What Do Nonlinear Models Add to Linear Models in Replicating Cycles?

In a sense we already know the answer to this question. Since the excess statistic cannot be generated by linear models, some form of nonlinearity is needed. Therefore the real question is what type of model will produce the requisite type of nonlinearity? A number of statistical models have been proposed to account for this task and they were analyzed in Engle et al. (2005). Here we focus on a representative of them—the so-called bounceback model of Morley et al. (MPT) (2013)—which has the form

$$\Delta y_t = 3.35 - 4.44\xi_t + 1.31(1 - \xi_t)\left(\sum_{j=1}^{6} \xi_{t-j}\right) + \sigma\varepsilon_t. \quad (7.2)$$

In (7.2) ξ_t is a latent state following a first-order MS process. So now the process for Δy_t is extended to allow for a bounceback effect, which is captured by the $(1 - \xi_t)(\sum_{j=1}^{6} \xi_{t-j})$ term. Because it is a statistical model that is designed to capture the excess phenomenon one would be surprised if it doesn't do that. Of course this leaves the question open about the economic cause of the effect since statistical models are silent on this. MPT also give a second model that allows the variance of the shocks to differ from the mid-1980s, to capture the effects of the Great Moderation. We refer to these two models as MPT1 and MPT2 respectively.

Table 7.6 gives the business cycle characteristics for the simulated data from the two models (and using their estimation period and data from 1948/4 to 2007/4 to describe the observed outcomes). It is apparent that MPT2 adds little to MPT1. The match to the characteristics looks quite good, although not greatly superior to a linear model. The biggest failure is in relation to the variability in the amplitudes of expansions, where both models have much greater variability than what is in the data.

Table 7.6: Business Cycle Characteristics for the Two MPT Models
and Observed Outcomes over 1948/4-2007/4

	Data	MPT1	MPT2	Linear
Dur con	2.7	3.7	3.7	3.2
Dur expan	24.1	23.6	21.4	21.0
Amp con	-2.3	-2.2	-2.1	-1.7
Amp expan	24.1	22.5	22.7	21.7
Excess con	-.45	-5.3	-2.4	-.75
Excess expan	11.4	8.6	10.7	.11
CV dur con	.38	.55	.55	.45
CV dur expan	.82	.95	.99	.82
CV amp con	-.45	-.66	-.72	-.66
CV amp expan	.65	.93	.91	.87

Because this is an MS model, it is worth doing some experiments with it to reinforce some of the points made earlier. First, there is the question of asymmetry in the business cycle, that is, the duration of expansions being longer than contractions. It is often said that this feature is why a nonlinear model for growth is needed. Indeed, there are endless statements of this ilk in the literature to justify why one needs another nonlinear model for Δy_t. In contrast, we have said previously that it arises largely because of nonzero trend growth ($\mu > 0$). To assess which of these is correct, we remove a trend growth term from the model to focus on what the nonlinear structure provides in the way of cycle asymmetry. The trend growth term removed from MPT1 is that implied by the linear model

$$\Delta y_t = .0055 + .333\Delta y_{t-1} + .0093\varepsilon_t,$$

fitted over the estimation period. This is chosen so that if the nonlinear model implies a different trend growth rate, that would be allowed for. When MPT1 is simulated under these conditions, the average durations of recessions and expansions are 5.8 and 6.3 quarters, that is, the asymmetry produced by the nonlinear model only accounts for a one-quarter difference in the durations.

It has also been said previously that the latent states ξ_t should not be confused with the business cycle states S_t that would be found by MBBQ or NBER-type dating rules. In this case the correlation between S_t and ξ_t is just .59 (using 1000 simulated observations). Part of the reason for this small correlation is that S_t is required to have a minimum duration of two quarters, so there will be a different number of turning points implied by S_t than in the latent states which do not impose such a constraint. It is also interesting to look at $E(\xi_t) = .19$ and $E(R_t = 1 - S_t) = .14$, again making the point that the durations of business cycle states cannot be inferred from the time spent in the latent states.

Finally it is instructive to look at what the implied relations would be for a number of conditional densities. First $E(\Delta y_t | \Delta y_{t-1})$ is estimated from the MPT1 model simulation using a nonparametric kernel estimator (this was done in MATLAB using an Epanechnikov kernel and with the bandwidth chosen by cross-validation to be $1.4N^{-\frac{1}{5}}$). It was necessary to use 1 million simulated data points to obtain an accurate estimate of the conditional mean in the tails of the distribution. Figure 7.3 presents the results and the cloud comprising 1 in every 10 simulated data points. It is clear that across the range of annualized last-quarter growth from -6% to 10%, the relation is essentially linear.

Figure 7.4 compares the nonparametric mean with a cubic fit to the simulated data. This establishes that there is a very mild nonlinearity in the conditional mean which can be well approximated by a cubic over the range -8% to 15%. It is evident that the nonlinearity is not useful in generating predictions of negative growth as even using 1 million simulations the conditional mean is positive for $\Delta y_{t-1} > -11$. As only 121 of the 1 million simulated data points are less than -11% it is evident that even if a large negative growth rate was seen last period, the model would still opt for a positive one in the current period. Things are better on the

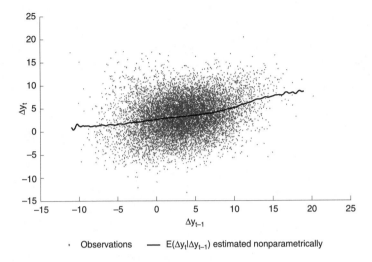

Figure 7.3: Nonparametric Estimate of $E(\Delta y_t | \Delta y_{t-1})$ from the MPT1 Model.

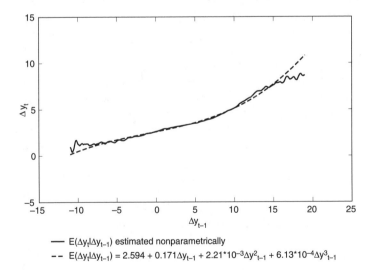

Figure 7.4: Nonparametric and Cubic Estimates of $E(\Delta y_t | \Delta y_{t-1})$ from the MPT1 Model.

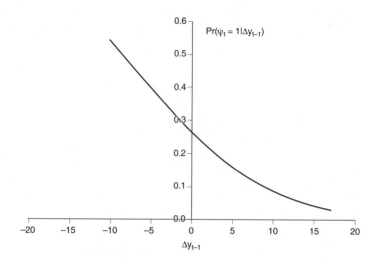

Figure 7.5: Probit Model Estimate of $\Pr(\Psi_t = 1 | \Delta y_{t-1})$ for the MPT1 Model.

right-hand side, where there are 30,991 simulated growth rate observations greater than 11%. It is evident from Figure 7.4 that any nonlinear response shows up as producing a greater positive growth rate at time t—given a large positive growth rate at $t - 1$—than would be predicted by a linear model.

Of course the conditional mean only captures the central tendency, and a better measure of its ability to produce negative growth rates would be to look at $\Pr(\Delta y_t < 0 | \Delta y_{t-1})$. Let the event $\Delta y_t < 0$ be represented by the indicator function $\Psi_t = 1(\Delta y_t < 0)$. Figure 7.5 gives the probability computed from the simulated data assuming that the mapping between Ψ_t and Δy_{t-1} is captured by a probit model. Even with extremely large negative growth rates ($< $-10%) in the previous quarter, the model would only assign a probability of around .55 to getting a negative growth rate. To make this point more starkly, if the previous growth rate was zero, the probability of getting a current period growth rate that is negative would be about .25, compared to the .14 which is the unconditional probability.[2]

---

[2]The probit model may be the wrong functional form, so that $\Pr(\Psi_t = 1 | \Delta y_{t-1})$ was computed nonparametrically. Of course there are so few observations beyond -6% that the results in that region are not trustworthy.

7.6 Two Markov Switching Models

7.6.1 *The Eo and Kim (2015) model*

In Chapter 4 two MS models were discussed that aimed to identify the phases of U.S. business cycles. The model used by Eo and Kim (2012) gave a strong signal for recessions in the 1990s and 2000s, unlike that of the original model proposed by Hamilton, which we estimated in Chapter 4 with a longer sample of data than Hamilton used. It was noted then that some of the moments from the simulated data from the Eo and Kim model did not seem to match those from the actual data, in particular the frequency of getting negative growth. Hence it is time to look at the business cycle characteristics of this model. We note again that there are issues about how to perform the simulations, because there seems to be a unit root for growth in the model, so it is necessary to simulate over the same sample size as was used in estimation. Table 7.7 shows the cycle features from the model and from data over the estimation period of 1947/4–2011/3. For comparison a simple AR(1) model is estimated from the data on GDP growth and then simulated.

It is clear that the model produces recessions of longer durations than in the data and very strong expansions, in both durations and amplitudes. The fit of these features does not seem to be as good as that provided by a linear model. Moreover, this MS model does not match the excess statistic.

7.6.2 *The Billio et al. (2012) Model*

Just as for Eo and Kim, Chapter 4 suggested that the Billio et al. (2012) model gave more negative growth rates then were in the data. So we now consider its cycle properties. The authors look at the log of industrial production (ip_t) but they do not look at the cycle in it. Rather, they fit an MS model to $z_t = (1 - L^3)ip_t$. Because this can be written as $z_t = (1 - L)(1 + L + L^2)ip_t$, we are now looking at turning points

---

Nevertheless, the probit and nonparametric estimates are generally fairly close, and this is particularly true for probabilities when Δy_{t-1} is close to zero (the nonparametric ones are slightly higher).

Table 7.7: Eo and Kim Model 1947Q4–2011Q3

	Model	Data	Linear
Dur con	3.9	3.0	3.2
Dur expan	24.8	20.5	19.9
Amp con	−3.7	−2.5	−1.7
Amp expan	43.4	20.5	20.1
Excess con	−.6	−2.0	.11
Excess expan	1.2	9.6	.13
CV dur con	.54	.47	.47
CV dur expan	.90	.91	.84
CV amp con	−.69	−.49	−.69
CV amp expan	.93	.78	.88

in the moving average $y_t = (ip_t + ip_{t-1} + ip_{t-2})$, rather than ip_t itself. For this reason the cycle characteristics in y_t can be different to those in ip_t, as seen in the last two columns of Table 7.8. Note that the cycle in the moving average of industrial production has an average duration of expansions that is much closer to that of the cycle in GDP (60 months) although the recessions are much longer at 15 months rather than nine. This MS model seems to be producing too many recessions and making them stronger than they should be. This agrees with the tendency of the model to produce too many negative growth rates. We should also note that just like the Eo and Kim model, the nonlinearity introduced by this model fails to capture the excess statistic.

7.7 Using the Binary Indicators in Multivariate Systems

Often one might wish to work with the binary indicators in some system. There are a number of types of systems

Table 7.8: Business Cycle Characteristics Billio et al. Model
1960M1–2011M1

	Model	Linear	*AvIP*	*ip*
Dur con	17.8	17.1	15	13.6
Dur expan	37.9	42	53	43.5
Amp con	−45.1	−17.5	−20.7	−8.0
Amp expan	72.5	58.7	67.7	22.9
Excess con	3.9	−.22	−14.7	−9.0
Excess expan	−.06	2.2	7.4	16.2
CV dur con	.62	.61	.58	.57
CV dur expan	.78	.80	.60	.71
CV amp con	−.91	−.75	−.74	−.59
CV amp expan	.90	.89	.66	.53

that could be considered. The first of these incorporates some observable variables z_t along with the recurrent event indicator S_t. A second option involves working with more than a single set of binary states, for example, if there were two countries or industries. Finally one might have both observable and latent variables as well as a single S_t. Perhaps the best-known example of the latter would be the Qual-VAR model of Dueker (2005). We discuss the issues raised by these systems in separate subsections.

7.7.1 Systems of Observables and S_t

The most likely multivariate system would be a VAR in a set of observable variables z_t as well as the S_t. Two difficulties arise when working with such a set of variables. One of these relates to the fact that the S_t follow a Markov chain of at least second order (under MBBQ) and this is not a linear AR process. A second involves the fact that it may be that

S_{t-1} depends on z_t since it may have been constructed using either one of the variables in z_t or from a variable that is correlated with members of z_t. This means that S_{t-1} would need to be instrumented with higher lags in S_t. Whether this needs to be done depends on the objectives of the exercise. In some cases good estimates of the VAR coefficients are important, for example, in computing impulse responses. For other applications such as prediction this may be of lesser interest, for example, suppose that the data followed an AR(2) but only an AR(1) was fitted. Then the coefficient on the first lagged variable would be an inconsistent estimator of the true coefficient. However, if one just wanted a good predictor, the coefficient value is not as important, and it often pays to work with a misspecified model if that action reduces the number of parameters to be estimated.

7.7.2 Systems of States S_t

The problems with using S_t above are of course magnified if a number of the S_t are used. For example, suppose the system involves S_{yt} and S_{xt}, where these are constructed from two different series y_t and x_t. Each of these has been constructed to follow univariate Markov chains and this would need to be recognized when formulating the system.

7.7.3 Latent and Observed Variables and S_t

One approach that introduces the binary variables S_t into a VAR was the Qual-VAR model of Dueker (2005). In this instance z_t are observable variables and ψ_t is a latent variable. The latent variables Qual-VAR was then assumed to be

$$z_t = a_{zz}z_{t-1} + a_{z\psi}\psi_{t-1} + \varepsilon_t \qquad (7.3)$$

$$\psi_t = a_{\psi z}z_{t-1} + a_{\psi\psi}\psi_{t-1} + \upsilon_t, \qquad (7.4)$$

where the shocks $\varepsilon_t, \upsilon_t$ were taken to be normally and independently distributed with a zero expectation. Deuker completed this system by defining $S_t = 1(\psi_t > 0)$, where the S_t were the NBER business cycle indicators. In the descriptions of his model, the variables in z_t seem to be the levels of variables such as GDP, but in his Qual-VAR code they are growth rates. Hence, following his code, one might think that ψ_t is the growth in economic activity, and then $S_t = 1(\psi_t > 0)$ would be rationalized as a calculus rule applied to finding turning points in the level of economic activity z_t. The problem with that solution is his identification of S_t with the NBER business cycle states, as we know that they do not use a calculus rule.

Harding (2011) has recently looked at some of the problems in the empirical work performed with Deuker's Qual-VAR program. It is clear that to estimate the system it is necessary to set $var(v_t) = 1$, since the only information on ψ_t is $S_t = 1(\psi_t > 0)$ and, just as for the probit model, one cannot identify the variance of the latent variable from this. Because Deuker uses a Gibbs sampler to get the joint posterior of the VAR coefficients and variances, and this involves draws from an unrestricted VAR, it is not clear that he actually imposed such a constraint in the Qual-VAR program. The other difficulty is that of imposing stability on the VAR. One would expect that this would be done by making the eigenvalues of the system less than unity, but Dueker allows them to be larger. These two issues seem to have a major impact on the estimates obtained and markedly affect at least one of the applications, namely prediction of the U.S. 2001 recession.

It would be more appropriate to adjoin the equations (7.3) and (7.4) with $S_t = 1(\psi_t > 0)$. These equations could then be jointly estimated. The simplest approach would be to use an indirect estimation procedure in which a VAR in z_t and S_t is taken to be the auxiliary model. This approach preserves what is known about how the NBER states are found. A quick approximation to it is to set up a VAR composed of the observables and with S_t replacing the latent variable. The logic of this is that since $S_t = 1(\psi_t > 0)$, we know from Kedem (1980) that the autocovariance function of S_t would be a function of that for ψ_t. Hence this suggests that the effects of a latent variable might be captured (to a linear approximation) by estimating the proposed observables-VAR. Of course it may be that a much higher order VAR is needed if only observables are used. But the method has the advantage of enabling one to exploit many of the features of VARs.

7.8 Conclusion

The chapter has applied many of the measures of cycle features to data from a number of countries and sectors. This data cover both aggregate economic activity as well as asset prices. Of course there are many other series that exhibit recurrent events and which are now being modeled, for example, interest rates, credit, economic sentiment. Our methods can be applied to all such series. As well as summarizing the recurrent events in an informative way, the measures are useful for evaluating the utility of various statistical models, and this is illustrated by using a number of nonlinear models. Finally, a brief account was provided of how one might use the binary indicators which define the recurrent events. This research is far less complete than in many of the other areas that the book covers, and our summary suggests that further work on these issues is needed.

Chapter 8

Using the Recurrent Event Binary States to Examine Economic Modeling Issues

8.1 Introduction

This chapter looks at using the binary states describing the recurrent events to help in either constructing economic models of time series or evaluating the fit of such models. Section 8.2 provides a general discussion of the issues that come up when using the binary states in regressions. Some of these have already been encountered, for example, when getting standard errors for the concordance statistic in Chapter 6. Because the S_t are binary, it has been a temptation to assume that their relationships with other variables can be handled with models such as probit and logit. However, the S_t are not like the binary variables found in microeconometrics— they are *constructed* from continuous variables and do not occur naturally as a consequence of some decision. This fact is important in determining how they are to be used when looking at relationships. Section 8.2 provides a perspective on this by constructing a simple example that showcases some of the issues that arise in their use.

Section 8.3 then turns to the analysis of complete economic models. In these it is very common to see variance decompositions computed and used to draw conclusions about which shocks are responsible for the recurrent events. We show that this methodology is flawed when it comes to shedding light on what causes the business cycle. What can be done is the subject of Section 8.4, which illustrates how to determine which shocks are important to a matching of the business cycle features discussed in Chapter 5.

Section 8.5 moves on to some economic models that have been constructed in the wake of the global financial crisis and which aim to highlight the role of financial shocks. These models emphasize the financial accelerator, the role of collateral, and the impact of shocks to the financial intermediation sector. Generally the success of these modeling strategies is judged by how the impulse responses change as a result of the financial constraints. One difficulty with such an exercise is that the design of many of these models means that output must be fully explained by the model shocks, and therefore there is no residual term. Consequently, it is always unclear when using such decompositions whether a shock accords with its label or simply represents a residual. We view our methodology of focusing directly on the business cycle characteristics as a useful complement to such analyses. The characteristics we look at are standard business cycle features such as duration and amplitude, but we also consider whether the models produce a substantial probability of a recession when negative financial factors are in play and how long the recession lasts. Such an investigation aims to provide a response to the Claessens et al. (2012, 190) criticism that

> as discussions following the financial crisis have clearly shown, it is critical to have a better understanding of the amplitude and duration of business and financial cycles and their interactions, not just of their second moments. Most models with financial frictions are evaluated in terms of their ability to replicate the standard second moments, such as volatility, of key macroeconomic and financial aggregates. The performance of these models has, however, not been assessed against aggregate empirical regularities associated with different phases of business and financial cycles.

8.2 Estimating Univariate Models with Constructed Binary Data

8.2.1 S_t as an Independent Regressor

Consider the case where there is a regression of the form

$$y_t = a + bx_t + cS_t + dx_tS_t + e_t, \qquad (8.1)$$

where e_t is $i.i.d.(0, \sigma^2)$. In (8.1) the effect of x_t on y_t may change according to the outcome of the constructed binary variable S_t. An example would be when y_t is output, x_t is an interest rate, and S_t describes the phases of the cycle. In such a configuration interest rates have different impacts during expansions and contractions. Such possibilities are often mentioned. In particular there have been tests for the asymmetric effects of monetary policy, for example, Cover (1992), but in the past these tests have been done through a definition of S_t such as $1(z_t > 0)$, where z_t has mostly been e_t. Clearly such tests do not effectively address the question of whether the impact of monetary policy is different in different phases of the cycle, unless the S_t match published business cycle phases. Another difficulty is that if one used the S_t that comes from passing some variable z_t through a dating program such as MBBQ, it is problematic that S_t could be used as a regressor, since it is a function of current and future information in the form of Δz_{t+j} ($j = 0, \ldots, 2$). In the event that z_t and y_t are part of the same system, then S_t will most likely be correlated with e_t. In such cases it would be necessary to use S_{t-3} as an instrument for S_t.

8.2.2 S_t as the Dependent Variable in a Regression

A different situation would be if S_t is the dependent variable in a regression

$$S_t = a + bx_t + e_t,$$

and it is desired to test if $H_0 : b = 0$. Then, under the null hypothesis, the error term will inherit the properties of S_t. Apart from the situation when a calculus rule is employed for dating yearly data (y_t), and y_t follows a pure random walk with no conditional heteroskedasticity, there will almost always be some serial correlation in the S_t. Hence t ratios for the test of $b = 0$ need to be made robust to serial correlation and heteroskedasticity. If this is not done, very misleading inferences can be made, as was seen when testing for a lack of synchronization in Chapter 6.

8.2.3 Using S_t in Probit/Logit and Other Models

Because the S_t are binary, they are often related to some observable variables x_t by using models such as probit and logit. Designating a latent variable as ψ_t it is assumed that $\psi_t = x_t'\beta + e_t$, where x_t is observable and e_t is $n.i.d.(0, 1)$. If S_t is then constructed as $S_t = 1(\psi_t > 0)$ this would imply that $\Pr(S_t = 1|x_t'\beta) = \Phi(-x_t'\beta)$, and so produces a probit functional form. After this it is asserted that the log likelihood for the model would be $\sum_{t=1}^{T}\{S_t \log[\Phi(-x_t'\beta)] + (1 - S_t)\log[1-\Phi(-x_t'\beta)]\}$ —see, for example, Kauppi and Saikkonen (2008). But this is only the correct log likelihood if S_t is $i.d.$ When S_t is serially correlated then the likelihood has to reflect such dependence. Now the fact that S_t are not $i.d.$ has been recognized in empirical work, but the solution has been to make the probit form $\Phi(-x_t'\beta - S_{t-1}\delta)$, which has been termed a dynamic probit model by Dueker (1997), Kauppi and Saikkonen (2008), and Candelon et al. (2014). Because many applications have been made of this model, we will want to see if it is a correct formulation.

In practice the S_t that are used in these dynamic probit models are those associated with MBBQ-type methods of dating cycles. Accordingly, it is known from Chapter 2 that they are at least a second-order Markov chain, simply because of the censoring constraints that are applied in their construction. Because of that S_t has a form like (8.2)

$$S_t = a + bS_{t-1} + cS_{t-2} + cS_{t-1}S_{t-2} + \eta_t. \qquad (8.2)$$

In light of this it would be expected that the probit model would require both S_{t-1} and S_{t-2} to be present in the single index defining it. Omitting S_{t-2} will mean it is subsumed into the error term of the probit model, and, as S_{t-1} and S_{t-2} are correlated, S_{t-1} cannot be treated as a predetermined variable. However, the latter assumption is required when estimating the dynamic probit model. This correlation between S_{t-1} and e_t will result in inconsistent estimators of β and δ.

To see this effect we set up a simple simulation from the model

$$\Delta y_t = .0055 - .6(z_t - .03) + .005e_{1t} \qquad (8.3)$$

$$z_t = .03 + .01e_{2t}, \qquad (8.4)$$

where e_{jt} are $n.i.d(0, 1)$ and uncorrelated with each other. The simulation is designed so that the average duration of contractions and expansions from the simulated data would be 3 and 20 quarters, while the fraction of time spent in recession is .13. These are close to U.S. cycle outcomes. One might think of z_t as the interest rate spread since this is a variable often related to cycle outcomes. Notice that in this formulation $\psi_t = \Delta y_t$ is $n.i.d.$, so if $I_t = 1(\Delta y_t > 0)$, I_t would be i.d., and the probit model would be a correct description of $E(I_t|x_t'\beta)$. However, when S_t is found by applying MBBQ to y_t, it will be serially correlated, owing to the use of censoring and alternation constraints. The dependence can be seen by fitting the second-order Markov chain process in (8.2) to the S_t that would result by applying MBBQ to 1000 simulated observations from (8.3)–(8.4). This gives

$$S_t = .49S_{t-1} + .51S_{t-2} - .49S_{t-2} + .44S_{t-1}S_{t-2} + \eta_t.$$
$$(8.7) \qquad (9.1) \qquad (-8.7) \qquad (7.7)$$

Using the simulated data we find that the correlation between S_{t-1} and e_{1t} is -.15, so that using S_{t-1} in a probit regression will give inconsistent estimators of the single index parameters.

To assess this further, four probit models with different {dependent/independent} variables are fitted. These are $\{I_t/z_t\}, \{S_t/z_t\}, \{S_t/z_t, S_{t-1}\}$, and $\{S_t|z_t, S_{t-1}(S_{t-3})\}$, where $S_{t-1}(S_{t-3})$ means that S_{t-3} is used as an instrument for S_{t-1}. The latter should be a valid instrument. The correlation between S_{t-1} and S_{t-3} is .25 so it is not a weak instrument. To compare these models we evaluate the marginal effect on S_t of a change in z_t. This is done at the mean of z_t and, for those models where S_{t-1} is present, setting $S_{t-1} = 1$. For the third model above the marginal effect has the form $\varphi(\bar{z}\beta + \delta)\beta$, where $\varphi(\cdot)$ is the p.d.f. of an $N(0, 1)$ random variable. The marginal effects from the four models are then estimated as -27.1, -10.2, -4.0, and -1.7. To understand why the first two of these differ we note that for the first model, only a single value $\Delta y_t > 0$ is involved in defining I_t, while for the second model, the definition of S_t requires a sequence of Δy_t having the correct signs, and this reduces the impact of a change in z_t. Looking at the third and fourth models, the difference is that the last produces a consistent estimate of the marginal effect and so the marginal effect estimator from the third model has an upward bias. We also observe that setting $S_{t-1} = 1$ in the dynamic probit model when evaluating the marginal effect is important, since it would increase the likelihood that further S_t are unity, and that is why any negative effect of a change in z_t will be smaller.

Leaving aside the fact that S_{t-1} may not be predetermined, but taking cognizance of the fact that S_t is at least a second-order Markov process, one might think about including both S_{t-1} and S_{t-2} in the single index of the probit form. Harding and Pagan (2011) noted that one cannot do this with NBER quarterly business cycle data since the sequences $\{S_{t-1} = 1, S_{t-2} = 0\}$ and $\{S_{t-1} = 0, S_{t-2} = 1\}$ must result in $S_t = 1$ and $S_t = 0$, respectively, and these events have *known probability of unity*, because phases must be at least two quarters long. Accordingly, the probit model will exhibit a singularity when this happens. Consider however computing the two unknown probabilities $P_1 = \Pr(S_t = 0 | S_{t-1} = 1, S_{t-2} = 1, z_t)$ and $P_2 = \Pr(S_t = 1 | S_{t-1} = 0, S_{t-2} = 0, z_t)$. These describe the probabilities of a peak at $t - 1$ and a trough at $t - 1$, respectively. To estimate P_1 we could therefore compute $\Pr(\Lambda_{t-1} = 1 | S_{t-1} = 1, S_{t-2} = 1, z_t)$, and this equals $E(\Lambda_{t-1} | S_{t-1} = 1, S_{t-2} = 1, z_t)$. If one thought about doing a nonparametric estimator of P_1 we might just compute $E(\Lambda_{t-1} | z_t)$ for those observations where $\{S_{t-1} = 1, S_{t-2} = 1\}$, that is, it will involve using a subset of the complete data. It would also be possible to fit a probit model to the Λ_{t-1} and z_t using such a restricted data set. Now because $E(S_t | S_{t-1} = 1, S_{t-2} = 1, z_t) = 1 - P_1$ we can derive the expectation of S_t. This quantity was not available from applying the probit model directly to data on $\{S_t, S_{t-1}, S_{t-2}, z_t\}$ due to the singularity mentioned above. Essentially this was what was done in Harding and Pagan (2011), where $z_t = sp_{t-2}$ was the two-period lagged yield spread and Λ_t came from the peaks in activity recorded by the NBER.

The method would be expected to work quite well if one knows exactly how S_t is formed. If not, then one needs to be flexible in describing the S_t process. To see the issue about the order of the Markov process generating S_t when there is censoring, we use NBER statistics on monthly business cycle outcomes over 1854.12–2003.11 Because it is already known that censoring would be expected to make S_t a sixth-order Markov chain, there would be 64 parameters to estimate (at a minimum). There are singularities if one tries to fit such a process to the NBER data, because some of the regressors are identical over the sample period. There are restrictions that can be applied to reduce the number of parameters being estimated, but even these are not enough to eliminate the singularity.[1] However the simplified model in (8.5), which retains the sixth-order character of S_t, has a good fit ($R^2 = .87$) and many terms such as $S_{t-1}S_{t-2}$ are insignificant when added to the equation. The terms in brackets are HAC standard errors, although they don't differ much from OLS. As well, terms such as S_{t-7} and S_{t-8} are insignificant, suggesting that no more than a sixth-order Markov chain is needed. We note that an implication of the above is that augmenting the probit model with just S_{t-1} to produce a dynamic probit model is not likely to be successful with monthly data as much higher lags of S_t are needed.

$$S_t = .08 + .91S_{t-1} - .08S_{t-6} - .41S_{t-1}S_{t-6} + .5\prod_{j=1}^{6} S_{t-j}$$

$$(6.2)(62.3) \quad (-5.8) \quad (-15.2) \quad (22.6) \quad (8.5)$$

---

[1] As seen in Chapter 2 censoring meant that restrictions $a + b = 1$ and $a = -c$ would apply to (8.2). The equivalent restrictions for a sixth-order Markov chain are linear but complicated to write down, although it is possible to derive a recursive algorithm that would implement them.

In general the S_t will follow Markov chains and these involve products of different lags of S_t as well as the lags themselves. Because these Markov chains are effectively nonlinear autoregressions, they can approximate processes such as Startz's (2008) (non-Markov) binary ARMA (BARMA) model to an arbitrary degree of accuracy, provided they are of sufficiently high order. Just as VARs are mostly preferred to VARMA processes in empirical work due to their ease of implementation, we feel that Markov chains should be the workhorse when modelling constructed binary time series.

8.3 What Do Variance Decompositions Tell Us About the Cycle?

Models that incorporate items such as financial frictions not only change the structure of the model relative to those without them but often introduce "financial" shocks to capture exogenous changes to credit supply, and so on. Consequently, one may be interested in both how the financial frictions change the importance of the existing shocks and the role of these new financial shocks. A common way to assess the impact or relative importance of different shocks is to observe that if there are as many shocks as variables in the model, then one can exhaustively decompose the behavior of any variable y_t into the contributions from the shocks using

$$y_t = y_0 + \sum_{i=1}^{K} y_i' = y_0 + \sum_{i=1}^{K} \sum_{j=0}^{t-1} C_{ii}(j)\varepsilon_{i(t-j)}.$$

Here ε_{it} are K uncorrelated (structural) shocks, $C_{ii}(j)$ is the impulse responses of y_t to a unit rise in ε_{it-j} and y_i' is the contribution to y_t of the ith shock. Many researchers have used this device to gain an impression of which shocks have been important for contractions and expansions in economic activity.

An alternative that is also widely used has been to look at contributions to the forecast variance of $y_{t+L} - y_t$. This can be written in terms of the sums of the products of C_{ij}^2 with the variance of the ith shock, and consequently the fraction of the variance of $y_{t+L} - y_t$ explained by each of the shocks can be determined. The forecast variance decomposition technique is widely used in VAR work with L being set to the business cycle horizon, after which the dominant contributor to the variance of $y_{t+L} - y_t$ is regarded as the "cause" of the business cycle. There is no consensus on what L should be, and choices have often ranged between $L = 10$ and $L = 25$ quarters.

One often finds that the information from a forecast error variance decomposition differs from that seen by looking at the historical contributions (y_i'). An example is Galí (1992). Using quarterly data, he estimated a four equation SVECM intended to represent an IS/LM model augmented with a Phillips curve. By plotting y_i' he concluded that demand shocks were important for recessions. However, his variance decomposition analysis showed that when predicting variables 10 quarters out, 92% of the variance of the forecast error was explained by supply-side shocks, while only 3% was accounted for by demand shocks. This led him to comment (1992, 722), "The results here seem less akin to a traditional Keynesian view of economic fluctuations."

What does this variance decomposition have to do with the business cycle? Although it is often said that the decomposition tells about which shocks cause the cycle, the connection is more one of assertion than coming from any analysis.[2] The reason variance decompositions at long horizons tell us little about business cycle determinants is simply that the turning points in the series y_t are found from the *DGP* of Δy_t, as the latter is the indicator of whether y_t is still rising (falling) or has started to fall (rise), and *not that of a long difference* $\Delta_L y_t = y_t - y_{t-L}$.

It is informative to look at the definition of a recession to clarify this further. As Chapter 2 showed, conditional on being in an expansion in $t - 1$, recessions involve the occurrence of the event $\{\Delta y_t < 0, \Delta_2 y_{t+1} < 0\}$, where $\Delta_2 y_{t+1} \equiv y_{t+1} - y_{t-1}$. So the probability of a recession is the probability that $\{\Delta y_t < 0, \Delta_2 y_{t+1} < 0\}$. If Δy_t and $\Delta_2 y_{t+1}$ are multivariate normal,

---

[2]The following material comes from Pagan and Robinson (2014), with permission from Elsevier the following material comes from Pagan and Robinson (2014).

then their covariance matrix depends on the $var(\Delta y_t)$ and the first *two* serial correlation coefficients of Δy_t. Therefore, the probability of a recession depends on these quantities (along with the mean and variance of Δy_t). This can be contrasted with a variance decomposition at horizon $L = 10$ (Gali's choice), which depends on the $var(\Delta y_t)$ and the first 10 serial correlation coefficients. It follows that it is the variance decomposition at the horizon $L = 2$ which uses some of the same moment information as the event $\{\Delta y_t < 0, \Delta_2 y_{t+1} < 0\}$, that is, one should look at *short horizon* variance decompositions, *not long horizon* ones when assessing contributions to business cycles. Gali does not give a variance decomposition for $L = 2$ but, when $L = 1$, his work shows that 31% of the variance is due to demand shocks, in contrast to the 3% at $L = 10$, that is, recessions are strongly dependent on demand shocks. Of course the probability of the event $\{\Delta y_t < 0, \Delta_2 y_{t+1} < 0\}$ depends also on the mean growth rate in economic activity, and not just the moments involved in a variance decomposition.

8.4 The Role of Structural Shocks in Determining Cycle Features

In the previous section we saw that when properly applied, the variance decomposition indicated that demand shocks play an important role in determining the probability of recession. It is often of interest to establish the relative importance of demand, supply, and monetary shocks. The new Keynesian model estimated by Cho and Moreno (2006) on U.S. data is useful for illustrating this application of our techniques. The model has the form

$$\pi_t = \delta E_t(\pi_{t+1}) + (1 - \delta)\pi_{t-1} + \lambda x_t + \varepsilon_{AS,t}$$
$$x_t = \mu E_t(x_{t+1}) + (1 - \mu)x_{t-1} - \phi(r_t - E_t\pi_{t+1}) + \varepsilon_{IS,t}$$
$$r_t = \rho r_{t-1} + (1 - \rho)[\beta E_t\pi_{t+1} + \gamma x_t] + \varepsilon_{MP,t},$$

where π_t is the GDP deflator, y_t is an output gap, and r_t is the Federal Funds rate. Three shocks appear in the model—an aggregate supply shock $(\varepsilon_{AS,t})$, an IS (demand) shock $(\varepsilon_{IS,t})$, and

Table 8.1: U.S. Business Cycle Characteristics New Keynesian
Model: 1947/1–2002/2

	All shocks	$\varepsilon_{AS} = 0, \varepsilon_{MP} = 0$	$\varepsilon_{MP} = 0$
Dur con	2.4	3.7	2.4
Dur expan	47.6	11.5	48.4
Amp con	−.8	−3.7	−.8
Amp expan	38.4	15.1	39.0
Cum con	−1.42	−10.0	−1.4
Cum expan	1492	137.5	1539
CV dur con	.203	.517	.206
CV dur expan	.765	.738	.764
CV amp con	−.659	−.597	−.590
CV amp expan	.735	.664	.764

a monetary policy shock ($\varepsilon_{MP,t}$). These shocks are assumed to
be uncorrelated. The equations are estimated over the period
1980/4–2001/1. Parameter estimates are given in their table
for three measures of the output gap. We choose the first,
which involves deducting a linear trend from the log of GDP.
Consequently, we add back the linear trend to get a series for
the log of GDP that can be subject to business cycle analysis.

Because their estimation period is 1980/4–2001/1 we
would expect that the business cycles implied by their model
would tend to be longer than seen in data over the complete
postwar period. Table 8.1 gives the cycle characteristics using
simulated observations from the complete model, the model
when the AS and MP shocks are suppressed, and the cycles
when the MP shock alone is suppressed.

The expansions predicted by the model are around 12 years
long. Of course over this period they averaged around 9 years,
so although this is an overestimate, it is compatible with the
evidence. It is also clear that *monetary shocks* play little role
in the business cycle, as seen by the fact that eliminating
these shocks only has minor effects on cycle characteristics (of
course this is different from *monetary policy* as the component

of it that is the feedback part of the interest rate rule has been ignored). In contrast it is clear that demand and supply shocks have a big influence. If the supply and monetary shocks are removed from the system, a cycle of about 3.5 years is obtained. This is roughly what one would get with a growth cycle when all permanent components have been removed, so it is consistent with the supply-side shocks being very persistent and a major influence on the length of the business cycle.

8.5 Financial Effects and the Business Cycle

Since the global financial crisis (GFC) there has been an explosion of models that aim to elucidate the role of financial shocks in causing recessions. Examples of models with financial/real interactions are Christensen and Dib (2008), Gilchrist et al. (2009), Liu et al. (2009), Gertler and Kiyotaki (2015), Gertler and Karadi (2011), and Iacoviello and Neri (2010). These papers deal with a number of issues such as credit availability and collateral, and their implications for the real economy. The success of the models is generally judged by whether impulse responses are changed when financial effects are present. This is a useful test to apply when considering model performance, but given that many of these models came about as a consequence of the Great Recession that accompanied the GFC, it is also important to assess whether they can produce recessions of that severity. Pagan and Robinson (2014) considered this question. As well as looking at baseline business cycle characteristics, they looked at two other well-documented effects of financial stress on cycles. These are

1. The probability of a recession increases with a financial crisis.
2. Recessions that are accompanied by a financial crisis are expected to last longer than those without (IMF 2009, 126). A reasonable rule of thumb from a wide variety of evidence mentioned in Pagan and Robinson is that the duration of a recession is likely to double in the presence of a crisis.

8.5.1 Evaluating a Financial Accelerator Model

The first model Pagan and Robinson (2014) look at involves the financial accelerator of Bernanke et al. (1999), which is presented in the form of a model due to Gilchrist et al. (2009). The second revolved around the role of collateral, and is fundamental to the model of Iacoviello and Neri (2010). Each of these models has parameters estimated from the data. In this chapter we consider only the outcomes for the first of these models. The Gilchrist et al. model is driven by the fact that asymmetric information exists between borrowers and lenders about the realized return on capital, and so the interest rate charged by a lender includes a premium above the risk-free rate. This is known as the external finance premium, and it depends on the leverage (or net worth) of the borrower. Consequently, shocks that, say, decrease the net worth of the borrower also increase the interest rate, and this constitutes the financial accelerator mechanism. Gilchrist et al. (2009) added this feature to a standard macroeconometric model set out by Smets and Wouters (2007) (SW).

To assess the business cycle properties of the Gilchrist et al. model, data were simulated from it (15,000 observations) and the MBBQ cycle-dating procedure was applied. A large sample size was selected so as to obtain population characteristics, that is, to ensure that the standard errors of the simulated quantities are small. As the real variables in the Gilchrist et al. model are log deviations from a constant growth path, it was necessary to add back a deterministic trend growth term to the simulated data to get a series on the level of GDP. That can then be used to determine the business cycle characteristics of the model. We use the trend growth rate for GDP assumed by Gilchrist et al. in their model. The model shows a good match to basic business cycle characteristics. Expansions have durations of 14.8 quarters (13.3 in the data) with amplitudes of 9.9% (9.2% in the data). Contractions are 4.2 quarters (versus 4.2) and −1.6% (versus −2.8%).[3]

---

[3]The cycle is in per capita GDP and so cycles are shorter than those in the level of GDP.

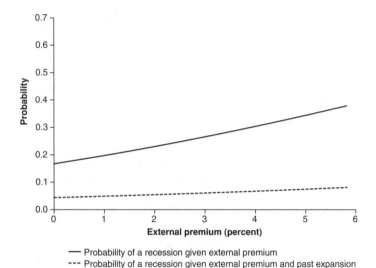

Figure 8.1: Probability of Recession Given External Finance Premium.

To investigate the dependence of recessions on financial factors consider using the binary recession indicator $R_t = 1 - S_t$. Then we are interested in $\Pr(R_t = 1|s_{t-j})$, where $j \geq 0$. A lagged value for s_t might be expected to provide a higher probability since it would take some periods for the higher spreads to have their impact on real variables. One could compute this either nonparametrically or by some parametric method, for example, by probit. Of course there is nothing which guarantees that the probit form is a good representation of the functional form for the probability, so it is always useful to check it against a nonparametric estimate. As discussed earlier $\Pr(R_t = 1|s_{t-j}) = E(R_t|s_{t-j})$, so that the conditional probability can be found by applying standard non-parametric methods to the simulated data. The nonparametric estimator's limitations are that there may be few observations on extreme values of s_{t-j}, and the estimated functional form may not be monotonic.

Figure 8.1 fits $\Pr(R_t = 1|s_t)$ using the probit function and simulated data on R_t and s_t from the Gilchrist et al. model.[4]

---

[4]Setting $j = 0$ yields the best fit.

The probit and nonparametric estimates agreed quite well—the nonparametric estimates are slightly smaller but show the same pattern as s_t changes. Note that the unconditional probability of an NBER-defined recession over 1953/2–2009/4 (the sample period used for parameter estimation) was approximately 0.16. Thus, while the rise in the external premium does increase the probability of a recession, it never gets to a standard critical value of .5 often used in calling them. The value for the external finance premium during the GFC is that at the end of the x-axis in Figure 8.1.

Instead of looking at the probability of *being in a recession*, we might ask what is the probability of *going into a recession*, that is, of there being a peak at $t - 1$. This is given in (8.6),

$$Pr(\wedge_{t-1} = 1 | s_t) = Pr(R_t = 1 | R_{t-1} = 0, R_{t-2} = 0, s_t) \quad (8.6)$$
$$= E(\wedge_{t-1} | s_t), \quad (8.7)$$

and, as indicated earlier, this can be estimated by applying probit or non-parametric estimation methods to the subset of the sample for which $R_{t-1} = 0, R_{t-2} = 0$. Figure 8.1 shows this for a probit form. There is clearly a big difference between it and $Pr(R_t = 1 | s_t)$. Even for large values of the external finance premium $Pr(\wedge_{t-1} = 1 | s_t)$ is low. This result suggests that the external finance premium will not be useful for predicting peaks, that is, the onset of a recession.

The next question involves the second of the empirical regularities given at the beginning of this section, namely, whether the duration of recessions depends on the magnitude of the external finance premium. There are two ways this might be done. One is to relate the durations of recessions directly to the external finance premium. To do this we regressed the computed durations of recessions from the simulated data against the external finance premium at the beginning of each recession. While this showed a positive relationship, the connection was very weak—even large changes in the premium only caused the duration to increase by a fraction of a quarter. Pagan and Robinson give another measure which involves computing $Pr(\vee_{t+m} = 1 | \wedge_t = 1, s_{t-j})$, that is, the probability that conditional on the external finance premium and a peak at t, in m periods time the economy will be at a trough.

With this measure m can be regarded as the duration of the recession. They find that there is a weak dependence of this probability on the external finance premium and this agrees with the earlier conclusion.

8.5.2 Evaluating The Gertler and Karadi (2011) Model of Financial Intermediaries

Kashyap (in Sniderman 2010) commented that he believed that the impact of financial stress would be most felt through a decline in the supply of credit by intermediaries. This comes about because of the funding problems they would experience. Gertler and Karadi (2011) made a first step to formally modeling this phenomenon. They begin with a standard financial accelerator model. This has an implicit financial intermediary who imposes a risk premium on loans. Shocks to the system can change this premium. Gertler and Karadi propose augmenting the basic financial accelerator (FA) system so that there is a shock to the quality of the assets of the financial intermediation sector. This shock is exogenous and might be interpreted as a loss of confidence in asset values. It is assumed to take place when a crisis emerges and then decay as an AR(1) process with parameter .66, that is, after about 6 quarters the shock has largely dissipated. They comment that the crisis should happen infrequently, but when it does occur, it will result in higher risk premia and a severe decline in asset values. During the crisis the Taylor rule that describes monetary policy also changes. Specifically it is assumed that the monetary authorities don't have any inertial responses in their decisions—they react immediately to the state of the economy rather than slowly. Gertler and Karadi show that the impulse responses for their base FA model and their model augmented by the shock to the "quality" of assets are different.

Unlike the other models mentioned in the previous subsection, the parameters of the Gertler and Karadi model are not estimated from data. Instead, they are either set to standard values or are chosen to replicate statistics such as the leverage ratio and the actual decline in asset values during the 2006–2009 period. So this is an experiment in which we will be utilizing the business cycle measures to examine the cyclical properties of the model per se, rather than using them to see if the model can match the data.

To study the business cycle implications, it is necessary to note that if there are no asset quality shocks, the model would reduce to a VAR in its variables of the form

$$y_t = A^{FA}y_{t-1} + B^{FA}\varepsilon_t.$$

Just as in the Gilchrist et al. model, the shocks ε_t are net worth, technology, and monetary. When the crisis happens a new shock comes into the system: ε_t^Q. It follows the AR(1) process

$$\varepsilon_t^Q = .66\varepsilon_{t-1}^Q - v_t,$$

where v_t is a once-off deterministic shock that affects asset quality. During the crisis the variables are generated by a new VAR of the form

$$y_t = A^c y_{t-1} + B^c \varepsilon_t + D\varepsilon_t^Q.$$

These differing VARs will mean that there are different impulse responses during a crisis compared to when it is not present.

We took the Gertler-Karadi Dynare program from the The Macroeconomic Model Data Base, Version 1.2 described in Wieland et al. (2011). This can be used to generate the VARs for both the financial accelerator and crisis models. To simulate the model some mechanism is needed whereby a crisis is generated and to determine how long it lasts. Gertler and Karadi suggested crises should happen infrequently, so we defined a binary random variable η_t that took the value one with probability .025 and zero otherwise. When there is a draw of unity for η_t, a crisis is initiated, and the VAR for the crisis economy generates the data on y_t. Otherwise y_t is found using the VAR for their base financial accelerator model. As noted, the crisis is assumed to last for six quarters, in line with the AR(1) process describing the way in which the crisis dissipates.

First it should be said that the economy with crises does produce a higher volatility for per capita output growth: .014 versus .011. The mean growth rate in both economies is

Table 8.2: Business Cycle Features for FA+Crisis and FA Models

	FA	FA+Crises
Duration: contractions	4.4	4.2
Duration: expansions	10.7	9.6
Amplitude: contractions	−3.1	−3.4
Amplitude: expansions	10.9	10.5
CV: contraction durations	.53	.50
CV: expansion durations	.62	.67
CV: contraction amplitudes	−.68	−.67
CV: expansion amplitudes	.64	.64

set to .0052 to agree with U.S. quarterly per capita data. Table 8.2 then gives some business cycle features. It is clear that there are quite small differences between the model with crises and without. The most significant would seem to be that the duration of the average cycle is about one quarter shorter when crises occur. To summarize the impact of financial stress the probability of being in a recession was related to the asset price q_t, as the latter declines in a crisis. But the $\Pr(R_t = 1|q_t)$ reached .51 only for the largest possible decline in asset values, so this yields much the same conclusion as found for the Gilchrist et al. model.[5]

Inspection of when the crises occurred does not reveal that the recessions at that point in time are of longer duration. In passing it should be observed that if one just looks at impulse responses (as done by Gertler and Karadi) one is effectively shutting off the other shocks in the model when studying the impact of the shock to quality v_t, whereas in our business cycle measurements, all the wealth, monetary, and technology shocks are arriving in each period. Perhaps

---

[5]This also happened for the Iacoviello and Neri (2010) collateral model. It should be noted that the latter model allows for nonlinearities, sometimes thought to be important during financial crises. However Pagan and Robinson (2014) found that it provided a poorer fit to business cycle characterictics than was available from the financial accelerator model.

it might be thought that the asset quality shock is too small, but it is set to be some 10 times what the technology shock is (based on values used by Gertler and Karadi where the shock is deterministic). It may also be that crises should last longer than six periods, but that would involve changing the degree of persistence from that assigned by Gertler and Karadi. There are many questions like this that can be raised and addressed, but the essential point of this investigation has been the weak cyclical effect of current models that have financial effects introduced either through the financial accelerator or variations in asset quality from crises. Perhaps the latter just reflects the fact that crises occur so infrequently.

8.6 Conclusion

This chapter has looked at how one uses the recurrent event information to address interesting questions about their cause. Initially, we looked at single-equation methods to do this and discussed the econometric problems that arise from them. At the end we turned our attention to what complete models can tell us about such connections by analyzing some models that emphasize financial effects. The key to all this work is the ability to simulate data from the models and thereby extract their business cycle implications. It was shown that the information gathered from this exercise is sometimes very striking, as it suggests that many of the models developed to deal with the GFC have little ability to explain the Great Recession that emerged from it. One does not learn this by simply looking at how the impulse responses change with the introduction of financial effects. In many ways the best way to view the approach proposed here is as providing a different cut of the data to that provided by impulse responses, and so on, but one that is particularly informative when the focus is on the ability of models to generate realistic business cycles. The cut we perform involves constructing statistics that measure the duration and amplitude of business cycle phases, as well as the probability of a recession given some factors. As shown in previous chapters the former effectively combine together the moments of the growth rate in economic activity, viz. its mean, variance, and serial correlations. Mostly these quantities are all computed separately, but the way they are combined produces the statistics which directly relate to some characteristics of the business cycle. Thus we view the use of recurrent event statistics as an important complement to many traditional techniques for analyzing model outcomes.

Chapter 9

Predicting Turning Points and Recessions

9.1 Introduction

The fact that the global financial crisis and the Great Recession it ushered in were largely unforeseen has led to the common opinion that macroeconomic modeling and analysis is deficient in some way. Of course it has probably always been true that businessmen, journalists, and politicians have agreed on the proposition that economists can't forecast recessions. Yet we see an enormous published literature that presents results which suggest it is possible to do so, either with some new model or some new estimation method, for example, Kaufmann (2010), Galvao (2006), Dueker (2005), and Wright (2006). Moreover, there seems to be no shortage of papers still emerging that make claims along these lines. So a question that naturally arises is how one is to reconcile the existence of an expanding literature on predicting recessions with the skepticism noted above?

Many reasons have been given for why one might not be able to predict recessions. One is that the economy is complex. However, the systems involved in producing weather events are also complex, yet the record of meteorologists seems quite good. Another is that there are too few recessions, so one is faced with a small number of events. Now there are more bear markets for equity prices than recessions, yet the extra observations available on these do not seem to have produced a more successful prediction record of stock market crashes. Clearly, the answer must lie elsewhere.

In this chapter we argue that the problems in predicting recessions stem from the nature of the definition of a recession. Much of the literature that claims success does not predict recessions as such. Rather it focuses on either whether one can predict growth in economic activity or whether one can identify the *current status* of the economy—what is often referred to as "nowcasting" rather than forecasting. Other papers focus on the ability to predict what we will call a "recession-derived event," not a recession per se.

Accordingly, the chapter seeks to provide a review of the literature on predicting recessions. The review leads to the conclusion that there are good reasons it is extremely difficult to predict recessions. Understanding these leads to an appreciation of the barriers to be faced in the task, and also suggests that many of the claims made about how the forecasting record can be improved should be treated with skepticism. This is not to deny that some of these suggestions might be able to improve our understanding of business cycle issues, even if they do not improve the forecasting capacity. Moreover, being aware of the limits to forecasting suggests that we should focus our research on questions that we might have a better chance of addressing, for example, whether it is possible to predict how long a recession will last once it is initiated.

The chapter will concentrate on quarterly data. It can be extended to monthly series, although there is little to be gained to doing that for an understanding of the prediction issues. Our aim is to look at whether recessions can be predicted utilizing currently available data sets, but here we need to be careful to define what event it is we are trying to forecast when we use the term "recession." Section 9.2 begins by recalling the distinction made in the preceding chapter between the probability of *going into* a recession versus that of *being in* a recession. The former is the probability of a turning point, in this case in the form of a peak. The distinction is important when it comes to looking at how these probabilities vary with the type of information F_t available when making a prediction. Much of the literature focuses on the probability of being in a recession, whereas the concerns raised in the introduction are about the probability of going into a recession.[1]

Section 9.2 then goes on to show that an upper bound to the probability of a peak occurring at t is to be had from the probability of getting negative growth in economic activity at $t + 1$. Because a recession gets initiated with a period of negative growth, if the latter event cannot be predicted then one cannot predict the "peak" event, since previous chapters showed that such an event involves the consideration of the signs of a number of *future* periods of growth. Consequently, it is often useful to concentrate on looking at the simpler event of a negative growth rate in GDP, since that avoids difficulties in defining exactly what a recession is, because all existing definitions involve an initial negative growth rate. Moreover, it points to the fact that the ability to predict peaks (and even being in a recession) is bound up with the possibility of predicting *future shocks* to the economy.

Section 9.3 looks at a number of variables that have been proposed to predict recessions. It has been known for quite a while that the past history of growth in GDP provides very little in the way of predictive success, but we use it to illustrate the essential issues. There is a growing literature on the utility of wider information sets, some of which claim success for variables such as the yield spread, various leading indicators, and variables constructed from micro-economic surveys of households and businesses. We look at the evidence for the effectiveness of a few of these. Often the variables used are treated as exogenous and their influence on either $\wedge_t$ or R_t is found simply by running a regression. But there are also models that recombine variables in a prior step with weights stemming from economic or statistical models that work with

---

[1] Hamilton (2011) looks at what he calls "calling a recession." This is not about predicting a peak but has some connection with prediction of "being in a recession." Given a peak occurs at time t Hamilton seeks to find at what point in time $t + j$ ($j \geq 0$) we would know that a peak had happened at t. The motivation for this is that the NBER committee dates the times of peaks and troughs well after they occur, and so it would be useful if we had a method for settling on these dates much earlier.

multivariate data. We look at the predictive success of two of these—the financial accelerator model of Gilchrist et al. (2009) mentioned in the previous chapter, and the Qual-VAR structure proposed by Dueker (2005). Section 9.3 looks briefly at a literature that attempts to improve predictive success either by averaging forecasts from a number of models or utilizing big data.

Section 9.4 is devoted to papers that work with a "recession-derivative indicator" (RDI) (e.g., Wright 2006), rather than a recession. These claim to have an impressive record of predicting recessions, whereas they are actually predicting the RDI. We show that there are two effects of switching to an RDI perspective. First, the unconditional probability of encountering an RDI event is much higher than that of entering into a recession – often twice as high – and what may look like predictive success is simply an artifact of the definition. Second, the timing of the origin of an RDI event is very different to that of a recession. Mostly the event happens before a recession, so it may look as if one has managed to predict recessions in advance, particularly if only graphical evidence is tendered. Again, this is an artifact of the definition. Section 9.5 concludes.

9.2 Bounding the Probability of the Occurrence of a Peak

From previous chapters it is known that $R_t = 1 - S_t$ follows a process such as

$$R_{t+1} = 1 - (1 - R_t)R_{t-1} - (1 - R_t)(1 - R_{t-1})(1 - \wedge_t)$$
$$- R_t R_{t-1} \vee_t, \tag{9.1}$$

where $R_t = 1$ if a recession holds at time t and zero otherwise. As mentioned in the introduction, the literature has often concentrated on evaluating $\Pr(R_{t+1} = 1 | F_t)$. However, while the discussion that surrounds these analyses seems to implicitly assume that $R_t = 0, R_{t-1} = 0$, that is, prediction is for a turning point, the conditioning information on R_t, R_{t-1} does not seem to be explicitly used. Unless this information is used in the computation of the probability, the computed expectation will involve the possibility that $R_t = 1$. But the latter event would mean that one is asking whether the recession *is to continue*. Imposing the fact that interest is in whether a recession will occur at $t + 1$ given that an expansion is running in R_t means that one needs to evaluate $\Pr(R_{t+1} = 1 | R_t = 0, R_{t-1} = 0, F_t) = \Pr(\wedge_t | F_t)$, that is, whether F_t affects the probability of a peak. Evaluation of this event is not found from an *unconditional* relationship between R_{t+1} and F_t. To see more clearly why this is so, let I_{ij} be the data sets for which $S_t = i, S_{t-1} = j$ $(i = 0, 1; j = 0, 1)$. Then $\Pr(R_{t+1} = 1 | F_t) = E(R_{t+1} | F_t)$ is

$$\Pr(R_{t+1} = 1 | F_t) = \sum_{i=0}^{1} \sum_{j=0}^{1} w_{ij} \Pr(R_{t+1} = 1 | I_{ij}, F_t),$$

where w_{ij} are probability weights reflecting the occurrence of I_{ij}. Because the probability of a peak at t is $\Pr(R_{t+1} = 1 | I_{11}, F_t)$ it is clear that what is generally computed, namely, $\Pr(R_{t+1} = 1 | F_t)$, differs from this. It is not entirely clear how different $\Pr(R_{t+1} = 1 | F_t)$ and $\Pr(R_{t+1} = 1 | I_{11}, F_t)$ are. One can get some feel for this by comparing a regression of R_{t+1} on some regressor x_t over the whole sample with the same regression over the smaller data set that conditions on $S_t = 1, S_{t-1} = 1$.[2] The second of these regressions would give an estimated coefficient of

$$\hat{\beta}_P = \frac{\sum_{t=1}^{T} S_t S_{t-1} x_t R_{t+1}}{\sum_{t=1}^{T} S_t S_{t-1} x_t^2}$$

$$= \frac{\sum_{t=1}^{T} S_t S_{t-1} x_t (1 - S_{t+1})}{\sum_{t=1}^{T} S_t S_{t-1} x_t^2}$$

$$= \frac{\sum_{t=1}^{T} S_{t-1} x_t \wedge_t}{\sum_{t=1}^{T} S_t S_{t-1} x_t^2},$$

---

[2]Of course we would have a constant in the regression, but for the point we want to make, it is simplest to omit it.

while the first will be

$$\hat{\beta}_R = \frac{\sum_{t=1}^{T} x_t R_{t+1}}{\sum_{t=1}^{T} x_t^2}.$$

It is clear that the denominator of $\hat{\beta}_R$ exceeds that of $\hat{\beta}_P$, and the numerator of $\hat{\beta}_P$ is less than that of $\hat{\beta}_R$, so we cannot be sure of their relative magnitudes. It seems likely that the difference in the numerators will dominate, so that $\hat{\beta}_R$ will exceed $\hat{\beta}_P$, and therefore the estimated probability $x_t\hat{\beta}_R$ will exceed the probability of a peak $x_t\hat{\beta}_P$. This is certainly true with U.S. data.

So we really want to compute $\Pr(\wedge_t = 1 | I_{11}, F_t)$ and not $\Pr(R_{t+1} = 1 | F_t)$. Sometimes it is useful to use the definition of a peak so as to decompose $\Pr(\wedge_t = 1 | I_{11}, F_t)$ into

$$\Pr(\wedge_t = 1 | I_{11}, F_t)$$
$$= \Pr[1\,(\Delta y_{t+1} \le 0)\,1\,(\Delta_2 y_{t+2} \le 0)\,|I_{11}, F_t] \quad (9.2)$$

$$\le \Pr[1\,(\Delta y_{t+1} \le 0)\,|I_{11}, F_t]. \quad (9.3)$$

The last expression shows that an upper bound on the probability of a peak in equation (9.2) is available from $\Pr[1\,(\Delta y_{t+1} \le 0)\,|I_{11}, F_t]$. In turn this can be bounded by $\Pr[1\,(\Delta y_{t+1} \le 0)\,|F_t]$. Accordingly, it is often simpler to initially compute this last measure and compute the more precise measures later. Such a strategy will often be used in what follows. However, it should always be kept in mind that the joint event in equation (9.2) will be harder to predict than the single future period of negative growth.

9.3 Predicting Recessions with a Range of Variables

This section asks whether recessions can be predicted by a range of variables. The examples are a selection of those given in Harding and Pagan (2010).

9.3.1 Using Univariate Growth History for Prediction

Now for two reasons $\Pr[1(\Delta y_{t+1} \le 0)|F_t] = E(1(\Delta y_{t+1} \le 0)|F_t)$ will be a non-linear function of the information, F_t, used for prediction at time t. One is that the conditional expectation will be nonlinear in F_t, as it must lie between zero and unity. A second is that Δy_{t+1} may depend in a nonlinear way on F_t. In most instances the nonlinear function underlying the expectation will not be analytically derivable. If the number of elements in F_t is limited, then one can use nonparametric methods to estimate it, as in Harding and Pagan (2011). Because we are estimating a probability it might be desirable to take account of the first source of nonlinearity by making the function monotonic, and Harding (2010b) shows how one can adjust the nonparametric estimates to impose monotonicity in a reasonably simple way.

Suppose Δy_t followed an $AR(1)$ process of the form

$$\Delta y_{t+1} = \mu + \rho \Delta y_t + \sigma \varepsilon_t, \qquad \varepsilon_t \sim n.i.d.\,(0, 1)\,, \qquad (9.4)$$

and $F_t = \Delta y_t$. Then we need to compute $\Pr(\Delta y_{t+1} < 0|\Delta y_t)$. This equals $E\{1(\Delta y_{t+1} < 0)|\Delta y_t)\}$ and, given the normality assumption, this would be $\Phi(-\frac{\mu}{\sigma} - \frac{\rho}{\sigma}\Delta y_t)$, where $\Phi(\cdot)$ is the c.d.f. for the standard normal. In this case a probit model fitted to $1(\Delta y_{t+1} < 0)$ and Δy_t would give the estimated probability. If ε_t was not normal then Harding and Pagan (2011) argued that there is a strong case for a nonparametric fit. However, here we use the probit form for simplicity, since the nonparametric estimate of $E(1(\Delta y_{t+1} < 0)|\Delta y_t)$ was much the same as that from a probit model when using our data sets. With other conditioning variables this might not be true.

Figure 9.1 then looks at the ability to predict $1(\Delta y_{t+1} < 0)$ when information Δy_t—in the form of GDP growth—is available for the euro area. This is a rolling prediction, that is, at point t in the sample it computes $1(\Delta y_{t+1} < 0)$ using the information on Δy_t. The gray shaded areas are euro area recessions. Table 9.1 shows what happens to this probability as we move from a period before the recession through the recession. The first prediction should be related to that for a peak, while the predictions following that are about whether one can predict a negative growth rate within a recession.

It is worth looking more closely at the probabilities as one moves through the 1992–93 recession, and this is given in Table 9.1 along with the outcomes for growth. This is a

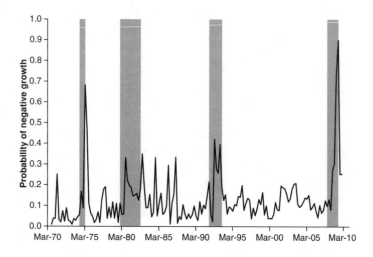

Figure 9.1: Probability of Negative Growth Given Lagged Growth for the Euro Area (Recession Periods Overlayed in gray).

Table 9.1: Probabilities of Predicting One Period of Negative Growth, Euro Area 1992–93 Recession

Prediction at t / For $t+1$	$Pr((\Delta y_{t+1} < 0)\|\Delta y_t)$	$1(\Delta y_{t+1} < 0)$
1992 : 1/1992 : 2	.02	1
1992 : 2/1992 : 3	.42	1
1992 : 3/1992 : 4	.28	1
1992 : 4/1993 : 1	.26	1

typical pattern; the peak is predicted with very low probability, but then the probability of being in a recession rises as the recession gets under way. This is because the one-period-ahead prediction is a rolling one and as the recession goes on, Δy_t will become negative. As Δy_t becomes more negative, we would expect to see that $Pr(\Delta y_{t+1} < 0|\Delta y_t)$ rises. Because the highest negative growth rate is found early in the recession, it will be the case that the probability peaks early in the recession and then begins to decline. This behavior is evident in Table 9.1.

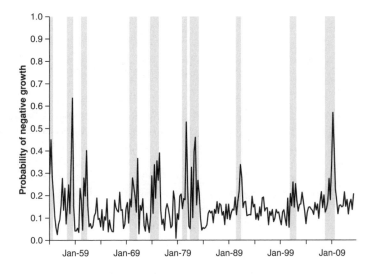

Figure 9.2: Probability of Negative Growth Given Lagged Growth and Recession Periods for the United States.

In all the euro area recessions, the $\Pr(\Delta y_{t+1} < 0|\Delta y_t)$ are .09 (1974/4), .06 (1980/2), .02 (1992/2), and .08 (2008/2). If we think that a critical value here is .5 (a fairly common choice) then none of the five peaks would have been predicted. In practice it is highly unlikely that Δy_t would be available, unless there is a very precise nowcasting method being used by forecasters. To put these numbers into context, since 11.6% of the time was spent in recession, if you just allocated a value of .116 every period you would be doing better than trying to exploit the information available in growth rates.[3] A similar result holds for the United States, with the upper bound for probabilities of a peak varying between .1 and .28 for the recessions since 1953—this is shown in Figure 9.2. In this case the unconditional probability of a recession over the period 1953/2 to 2009/3 in the United States is .16. As a comparison one might compute the exact probability $Pr(\wedge_t = 1|\Delta y_t)$, which will be lower than $Pr(\Delta y_{t+1} < 0|\Delta y_t)$. This can be

---

[3]Using $\Delta y_{t-1}, \Delta y_{t-2}$ and Δy_{t-3} as regressors does not change this conclusion.

done by fitting a probit model to the binary variable $\wedge_t$. These probabilities are never greater than .08 for the United States.

Why is the predictive performance for a peak so poor? An examination of $\Pr(\Delta y_{t+1} \le 0 | \Delta y_t)$ is useful. The fact that there is positive serial correlation in GDP growth in the euro area (and the United States) militates against successfully predicting $\Delta y_{t+1} < 0$, since a positive growth in the previous period points toward it being positive again. Indeed, the correlation of $\psi_t = 1(\Delta y_{t+1} < 0)$ with ψ_{t-1} is .33. Hence, it is very difficult to predict negative growth coming out of an expansion, and only after the recession has arrived will the dependence make the probability of $\Delta y_{t+1} < 0$ substantial. Using the euro area data it is possible to compute a nonparametric estimate of the $\Pr(\Delta y_{t+1} < 0 | \Delta y_t)$ and, for a small value of Δy_t close to zero, the probability is .16—only a little bigger than the unconditional probability. The same is true for the United States.

Now these results point to one difficulty with the literature— graphs such as Figure 9.2 are often presented and interpreted as if they suggest that there is a much higher probability for predicting a peak than anything we have found. The reason is that the eye gets drawn to the large probabilities in the gray-shaded areas. But these are *during the recession.* An upper bound to the probability of predicting a peak is right at the *beginning of the gray-shaded areas,* and close examination shows these are almost always low. The event in the gray-shaded area essentially asks what the probability is of *the continuation of a recession* given it has already been entered.

9.3.2 Predicting Negative Growth: Can Nonlinear Models of GDP Growth Help?

The previous section drew attention to studying $\Pr(\Delta y_{t+1} < 0 | F_t)$ as a first test of the ability to predict a recession. So far little mention has been made of the relationship between current and past growth, but implicitly this has been taken to be linear. One way of introducing nonlinearity is to allow F_t to depend on the state of the economy at (say) S_{t-1} (since S_t would generally not be known), and this is often mentioned as a possibility. Of course, since S_{t-1} depends on Δy_t, it is still the case that the relationship is between the current and past growth rates. Fitting a probit model to $1(\Delta y_{t+1} < 0)$ for the euro area, with explanatory variables Δy_t and S_{t-1}, suggests that the probabilities are much the same as if one had just used Δy_t. This is also true of the United States if one uses the S_{t-1} determined by NBER.

An alternative modification is to allow for GDP growth to depend in a nonlinear way on its past history. Many nonlinear models for Δy_t have been proposed, and one often sees comments that these produce better forecasts of GDP growth than linear models. A popular one that is used in a lot of the business cycle literature is that of a Markov switching (MS) model. A simple version of this was described in Chapter 1 and is

$$\Delta y_t = \mu_t + \beta \Delta y_{t-1} + \sigma \varepsilon_t \tag{9.5}$$

$$\mu_t = \mu_1 \xi_t + (1 - \xi_t)\mu_0 \tag{9.6}$$

$$p_{ij} = \Pr(\xi_t = i | \xi_{t-1} = j), \tag{9.7}$$

where ξ_t is a binary random variable that follows a first-order Markov process with transition probabilities p_{ij} and ε_t is $n.i.d(0, 1)$. Fitting this model to U.S. data shows that $E(1(\Delta y_{t+1} < 0)|\Delta y_t)$ would be around .13 when growth Δy_t was around zero, that is, it is still highly unlikely that one can predict a negative growth in activity with this nonlinear model. More complicated models are available, but we doubt that these would improve on the turning point predictions. As evidence of this contention, we observe that Chapter 7 analyzed a more complex MS model for U.S. growth—the bounceback model of Morley et al. (2013) (MPT). At that time it was observed that the model implied that $\Pr(\Delta y_t < 0|\Delta y_{t-1})$ was not large, even when Δy_{t-1} was close to negative, and it only became larger when Δy_{t-1} became very negative.

9.3.3 Predicting with Spreads

It has often been suggested that the spread between the 10-year bond rate and the 3-month bill rate is informative for anticipating recessions. Indeed, there are hundreds of articles looking at this for a variety of countries. Here we consider how useful it is for predicting a peak. In what follows we

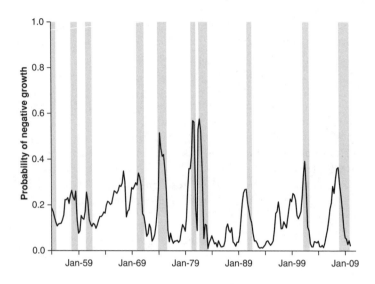

Figure 9.3: Probability of Negative Growth Given Interest Rate Spread for the United States.

look at the U.S. case, as the predictive efficacy of spreads for that country's recessions has been a constant theme in the literature. As before, focusing on predicting a peak, we look at the probabilities of getting a negative growth for the first period into a recession. During the nine recessions between 1954/2 and 2008/4 one obtains .23, .22, .34, .52, .56, .53, .18, .39, and .24. The information used in this prediction was the spread lagged two periods (the best for predicting R_t according to Estrella and Mishkin 1998). The estimated probit model shows a probability of negative growth of .31 when there is a zero spread, rising to .51 when the spread is -100 basis points. The latter is a very rare occurrence in U.S. history. In fact, with the exception of 1973/3, the only other time the term structure inverted to such an extent was during the "Volcker experiment" over 1979–1982, when the Fed targeted money supply. In only the 1974–75 and double-dip recessions of the early 1980s would the spread have managed to indicate a negative growth rate. Figure 9.3 shows a plot of $\Pr(\Delta y_t < 0 | sp_{t-2})$ from 1953/2 until 2009/2.

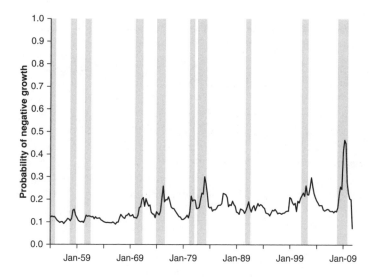

Figure 9.4: Probability of Negative Growth Given Baa Spread in the United States.

Now because the upper bound to the probability of a peak found from using $Pr(\Delta y_{t+1} < 0|F_t)$ is quite high for the United States, it is worth doing a direct computation of the probability of a peak. A probit model was therefore fitted to $\wedge_t$ and the second lag of the spread. With the exception of the recession beginning in 1981, it is always less than .15. In this double-dip recession it reaches .42, so that seems the only period of time in which a peak could be predicted. Of course it has sometimes been argued that the double-dip recession might be better regarded as a single recession and that seems consistent with what has just been found.

Another spread that has been mentioned as a possible indicator is that between the yield on Baa bonds and the 10-year bond rate, for example, Gilchrist et al. (2009). As Figure 9.4 reveals, with the exception of the last recession, this spread does not have much predictive success. Even for that recession the probability of a peak at the beginning of it is quite low.

9.3.4 Assessing the Possibility of Predicting a Peak with an Economic Model

Suppose that we had a model which implied that Δy_{t+1} is normally distributed around $E(\Delta y_{t+1}|z_t) = z_t'\beta_1$ with variance σ^2. Then $E(1(\Delta y_{t+1} < 0)|z_t) = \Phi(-z_t'\beta_1/\sigma)$, where Φ is the cumulative standard normal c.d.f. Similarly, if $E(\Delta_2 y_{t+2}|z_t) = z_t'\beta_2$ we could find $E(1(\Delta y_{t+1} < 0)|z_t'\beta_1)$ and $E(1(\Delta_2 y_{t+2} < 0)|z_t'\beta_2)$ from a bivariate normal with mean zero and covariance matrix given by the covariance of the errors for $\Delta_2 y_{t+2}$ and Δy_{t+1}. These expectations are the ingredients for prediction of peaks given information z_t. The need to compute $E(1(\Delta y_{t+1} < 0)|z_t'\beta_1)$ and $E(1(\Delta_2 y_{t+2} < 0)|z_t'\beta_2)$ have the implication that if the information z_t is to be useful in predicting recessions, it must be correlated with future shocks.

A quick check on whether a model would be able to predict such quantities is available by asking how important the unpredictable part of future shocks are to these growth outcomes? Here we need to be precise about what we mean by "unpredictable part" of shocks. Shocks, such as technology, often have an autoregressive structure, so some part of them is predictable. To illustrate this, make the shock ξ_t follow an AR(1), $\xi_t = \rho\xi_{t-1} + e_t$, where e_t is white noise. Then $\xi_t^- = \rho\xi_{t-1}$ is the predictable part of the shock and e_t the unpredictable part. It is the latter innovation whose impact on the business cycle we wish to determine. We therefore simulate the Gilchrist et al. (GOZ) model discussed in the preceding chapter while turning off the contemporaneous innovations. That is, the model is run with the current innovations at t set to zero, but reset to their actual values in later periods, as by then they are known.

Table 9.2 shows business cycle characteristics from the GOZ model with current innovations present (equivalent to basing the computation on ξ_t) and with them suppressed (equivalent to using just ξ_t^-, and hence designated GOZ^-). It is clear that the innovations have a substantial effect on the average cycle characteristics. Without these innovations, expansions become very long, and so there are fewer recessions. Because these innovations are so important, and they are what makes Δy_{t+1} differ from $E(\Delta y_{t+1}|z_t)$, we can see why

Table 9.2: Impact of Current Shocks on Business Cycles in
GOZ Model

	GOZ		GOZ⁻	
Durations (quarters)				
Expansions	14	8	33	9
Contractions	4	2	4	2
Amplitude (%)				
Expansions	9	0	15	9
Contractions	−1	6	−0	8
Cumulative amplitude (%)				
Expansions	107	9	461	8
Contractions	−5	2	−2	8

the GOZ model would have limited success when it comes to predicting recessions (on average). Thus this simple strategy of rerunning a model with the innovations removed is a good way to assess the likelihood of successful recession prediction with it.

In summary, the issue of good prediction of recessions is always whether a model or an indicator can capture the unknown future shocks coming into the system. It means that any series we think will be useful for predicting recessions has to capture likely future innovations in some way. Because it is very hard to find such series, it is very difficult to forecast recessions.

9.3.5 Predicting Using a Qual-VAR

In Chapter 7 we mentioned that the Qual-VAR model of Dueker (2005) has been proposed as a way of generating recession forecasts. As mentioned there, one possibility would be simply to use an observables-VAR that included both continuous observed variables and the constructed variables S_t. Over the period of the 2001 U.S. recession, the highest probability of a recession found from such an observables-VAR would be .32, which is well below the probability of

.57 that Dueker (2005) gives as coming from his Qual-VAR. Consequently, we turn to a closer examination of that model.

As mentioned in previous chapters the Qual-VAR model involves observable variables z_t and a latent variable ψ_t. A Qual-VAR(1) would be

$$z_t = a_{zz}z_{t-1} + a_{z\psi}\psi_{t-1} + \varepsilon_t \tag{9.8}$$

$$\psi_t = a_{\psi z}z_{t-1} + a_{\psi\psi}\psi_{t-1} + \upsilon_t \tag{9.9}$$

$$S_t = 1(\psi_t > 0), \tag{9.10}$$

where the shocks ε_t, υ_t are taken to be normally and independently distributed with a zero expectation. Dueker made S_t the NBER business cycle indicators. To estimate the parameters of the model he used Bayesian methods in the form of a Gibbs sampler. It is worth noting that (9.8)–(9.10) is a state space form (SSF) with (9.8)–(9.9) being the state dynamics and (9.10) being the observation equation (of course z_t is observable, so we have neglected to include it in the observation equation). The difference from a standard SSF is the nonlinearity in the observation equation and the fact that S_t is a binary random variable.

Now an important point to note is that in Dueker's estimation procedure it must be the case that the final parameter values exactly replicate S_t. Rather than follow what he does, one might approach the estimation problem by first computing $\hat{\psi}_t = E(\psi_t|F_T)$ from (9.8)–(9.9) using the Kalman smoother, and then finding parameters a_{jk} that match the NBER S_t and the resulting model implied $1(\hat{\psi}_t > 0)$ as closely as possible. The matching could be done by minimizing $\sum_{t=1}^{T}(S_t - 1(\hat{\psi}_t > 0))^2$. In this solution $\hat{\psi}_t$ would be a function of all observations on z_t, because the Kalman smoother is applied to past and future values of z_t with the weights produced by the smoother. But the solution also depends on S_t, because they will be a product of the optimization that generates a match of $1(\hat{\psi}_t > 0)$ with S_t.

It is interesting that there are a number of methods for computing output gaps through an SSF which involve weighting the same variables as Dueker had in z_t (the growth rate in GDP, inflation, an interest rate spread, and the Federal Funds rate) (e.g., see Benes et al. 2010). So this might suggest that in the Qual-VAR technique ψ_t represents an output gap. However the weights found by the standard approaches to computing an output gap would rarely reproduce S_t exactly.[4] The reason is that an output gap can be negative even when an economy is growing. Gaps fall below zero when GDP growth is less than potential GDP growth, whereas in a recession there must be negative growth.

Dueker estimated the model using data from 1968/1 to 2000/3. After estimation the task was to forecast $R_t = 1 - S_t$ for 2000/4-2003/3. He assumed that R_t is known up to and including 2000/3, but this simply provides an initial value for ψ_t at 2000/3. The equations (9.8)-(9.10) imply that the process for ψ_t will be an ARMA process—see Wallis (1977) and Zellner and Palm (1974). So one is essentially forecasting from either the ARMA model for ψ_t (which can be derived once the VAR parameters are available) or from the VAR, in which case $\tilde{\psi}_{T+j} = a_{\psi z}\tilde{z}_{T+j-1} + a_{\psi\psi}\tilde{\psi}_{T+j-1}$. Turning to the predictions, Dueker finds that for 2000/4-2001/4 the probabilities of a recession from Qual-VAR would be .032, .169, .488, .568, and .541, respectively. Since the NBER-defined recession had a peak in 2001/1 and a trough in 2001/4, we see that the probability of a peak is just .169. It is only after the recession was under way that the probability of being in a recession rose to a value that exceeded .5.[5]

The probability of .57 found in 2001/3 is a very high probability, given that it is such a weak recession. Indeed, it is a result that is even more puzzling because Dueker notes that the Qual-VAR forecast of GDP growth never becomes negative. It is therefore worth noting that Chauvet and Potter (2005) use the same type of model for predicting this recession, except that z_t is a scalar (the yield spread), their data are monthly, and they forecast the probability of a recession from

---

[4]In fact, let ψ_t be an output gap (expressed as a percentage) found by using a Hodrick-Prescott filter on the log of U.S. GDP. Then, defining $\tau_t = 1(\psi_t > \delta)$, we would need $\delta = -1.4\%$ to match up τ_t with the NBER-defined binary business cycle states. A value of $\delta = 0$ would fail to provide a match.

[5]Chauvet and Hamilton (2005) suggest to declare a recession when the smoothed probability exceeds .65, and that the recession ends when the probability falls below 0.35. We have discussed this choice in Chapter 4.

2000/4 for all of 2001. They have a number of models, one of the distinguishing features being whether $a_{\psi\psi}$ is zero. From their results the probability of a peak is at best around .2 for any model, while that of a recession rises to just over .4 during 2001 for the model with $a_{\psi\psi} = 0$. Once they allow $a_{\psi\psi}$ to be nonzero, the probability of a peak is very small and the recession probability never gets above .35.

Consequently, it appears that the VAR structure is important in getting Dueker's results. To understand why that might be so, we set $\psi_t = 0$ and fitted a VAR(5) to z_t (the same order as chosen by Dueker). Forecasts for z_t from this system are then made from 2000/4 onward. It is found that the forecasts of the spreads are negative, with values of -38, -34, and -2 basis points, and this will certainly push up the probability of a recession. Actually, there were no observed negative spreads in the forecast period. So it seems as if one is getting a large probability of a recession simply due to an incorrect forecast of the spread over the forecast period.

Related to this is an interesting problem with the Qual-VAR results in that a probability of a recession in 2003/3 of .29 is found, well away from the average of .15 in the data. This suggests that the model may have a tendency to assign a high probability to a recession (in 2003/3 of course the economy was in an expansion). Because $R_t = 1(\psi_t < 0)$ it must be the case that $E(R_t) = \Pr(\psi_t < 0)$, and so it should be the case that simulating for long horizons from the Qual-VAR will produce an unconditional forecast of the probability of a recession of around .15 (the mean of R_t over the sample period) and not the .39 that eventuates.[6] In a sense this is a specification test of the Qual-VAR since the forecast should

[6]In an econbrowser blog (http://www.econbrowser.com/archives/2008/02/how_to_balance.html) Dueker reports what seem to be probabilties of R_{t+1} in the 2001 recession of around .42 and not .57. It is now the case that at the end of his 12-period horizon forecast, there is a probability of a recession of .17, and this is close to the unconditional probability. There is no explanation of how the Qual-VAR has been adjusted to produce such different results from that given in Dueker (2005). We also note that in the Internet piece Dueker takes .35 to be the critical value that one compares the predicted probability to when deciding if a recession is to be declared.

return to the unconditional mean in a stationary context, and S_t should be a stationary random variable. It would appear that there could be a bias in the Qual-VAR predictions (at least the 2005 variant) of up to .26, and hence the corrected forecast probability would be closer to .32 than to .57, which agrees with what one would get simply using an observables-VAR, which incorporated the constructed binary variables for forecasts.

9.3.6 Improving Recession Prediction via Model Averaging and Big Data

There are other suggestions for improving the prediction of recessions. These either work by combining different models for Δy_t or by choosing some method to decide on a set of variables that are likely to influence Δy_t, and hence R_t. Billio et al. (2012) is an example of the former. They combined together two models for industrial production growth—an AR and an MS model. In Chapter 4 we argued that their MS model had a tendency to predict recessions too often. Chauvet and Potter (2005) showed that the performance of any one of the models they fitted for predicting recessions could vary at different points in time, so it seems reasonable that combining the predictions made by a variety of models might be useful. It has to be said that the prediction of a peak by any of Chauvet and Potter's models (in-sample) was not good—it is only after recessions had begun that the probability of a recession became large.

Ng (2014) looked at the issue of using a large number of variables to "boost" predictive success. She used "boosting" techniques from statistics to narrow down a set of 1500 potentially relevant predictors to just 10. Thinking of the choice of variables as being a different model it was found that the best set of variables (and hence models) changed with the forecast horizon, and also with whether one was predicting before and after the mid-1980s. In her work it is spreads that turn out to be generally the most useful variables when predicting recessions, although measures of employment replace spreads for the last two recessions in the United States. Again one might want to combine models with some time varying weights, as is done in the model averaging literature. In relation to predicting peaks she says, (28) "Overall, the models seem to give elevated probability estimates around but not always ahead of the actual recession dates."

9.4 Changing the Event Defining Recessions and Turning Points

There are two ways that this can happen. In one approach a variety of series might be combined to measure the level of economic activity. Many suggestions have been made along these lines, for example, the level of unemployment as well as industrial production. Indeed, the NBER S_t involve an analysis of the turning points of a number of series, and this information is then combined in an unknown way by the NBER Dating Committee to produce the final recession and expansion dates. Coincident indexes generally combine together a number of series with fixed weights, while many factor models aim to extract a common factor from a variety of series using a set of weights that may be varying. Chapter 3 discussed these issues. Obviously, it cannot be any easier to predict an indicator based on a variety of series than a single one, since one now has to forecast the sign of future growth in many series to find their turning points.

A different approach is to redefine the recession event. We refer to these as a recession-derivative indicator, RDI. A number of papers that suggest high probabilities of predicting a recession have used RDIs. One example that is often cited is Wright (2006). Wright has an RDI (RW_t) taking the value one if an NBER defined recession happens in the next four quarters and zero otherwise. To see how this affects outcomes, take the following series for S_t–{1, 1, 1, 1, 1, 0, 0, 0, 1, 1, 1, 1}–which produces $R_t = 1 - S_t = \{0, 0, 0, 0, 0, 1, 1, 1, 0, 0, 0, 0\}$. The binary numbers here correspond to when the NBER define expansions and recessions. The RDI used by Wright is then $RW_t = 1(\{R_{t+j} = 1\}_{j=1}^{4})$ and, for the S_t above, it will be $RW_t = \{0, 1, 1, 1, 1, 1, 1, 0, ?, ?, ?, ?\}$, where ? indicates that a decision can't be made because not enough future information is available. It is clear from this that the mean of RW_t is different from that for R_t, that is, the unconditional probability that $R_t = 1$ is much lower than the probability that $RW_t = 1$ (for the United States it is .15 versus .28 over the period 1953/2–2008/4). If one then describes a high $\Pr(RW_t = 1|F_t)$ as "predicting a recession," it can look as if there is much greater predictive success, but it is an artifact of the redefinition of the event being predicted.

Note that the rise in probability comes because expansions are not treated symmetrically with recessions. Thus, for the seventh observation in the R_t sequence, the following four values for R_t are $\{1, 0, 0, 0\}$, and RW_7 was taken to be unity because of the fact that $R_8 = 1$. But given that the quadruple $\{R_8, R_9, R_{10}, R_{11}\} = \{1, 0, 0, 0\}$ largely consists of expansion periods, it might seem more appropriate that $RW_7 = 0$. Except for the instances in which ties occur, wherein RW might be either one or zero, for example, with the quadruple $\{0,0,1,1\}$, treating expansions and contractions symmetrically would just mean that $RW_j = \{R_{j-4}\}$. In this instance the probabilities of $R_t = 1$ and the resulting (symmetric) RDI, $RW_t = 1$, would be the same. Another important effect of moving to RW_t is that there is a timing change. In the example above, consider predicting whether $RW_7 = 1$. Because this is effectively the second period into a recession, comparing it with the R_t outcomes will make it look as if one has managed to predict the recession in advance, but again it is an artifact of changing the event being predicted.

One can see these effects in a number of ways. First suppose we fit the same model to R_t. Then $\{\Pr(R_{t+1} = 1|sp_{t-2}), P(RW_{t+1} = 1|sp_{t-2})\}$ for the recessions between 1954 and 2009 would be

$$\{.22, .45\}, \{.21, .41\}, \{.33, .66\}, \{.49, .89\}, \{.54, .93\}$$
$$\{.50, .89\}, \{.17, .31\}, \{.37, .75\}, \{.24, .47\}.$$

So the move from explaining recessions to an RDI has essentially doubled the probabilities, as noted above. The switch in timing also mentioned can be seen in Figure 9.5.

Another RDI used by Fair (1993), Anderson and Vahid (2001), and Galvao (2006) is similar, except that it defines a

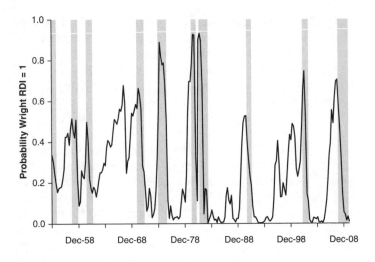

Figure 9.5: Predicting a Recession-Derived Indicator with the Interest Rate Spread.

recession starting at t if the five quarters starting at t have two successive periods of negative growth. One can see that the RDI formed in this way will be $R_t^* = \{1, 1, 0, 0, 0, 0, 0, 1, ?.?, ?, ?\}$. Again the timing has been changed and the unconditional probability of the recession defined event will likely be higher than for that describing recessions, R_t.

Canova and Ciccarelli (2004) look at turning points, but they define a peak and trough in the *growth rates* and so are looking at a *growth rate cycle*. Of course this means that one is interested in whether $\Delta^2 y_t$ and so on are negative, not Δy_t. Thus predictability of a turning point in the series of growth rates would involve a "first-period test" of $\Pr(\Delta y_{t+1} - \Delta y_t < 0 | F_t)$. Suppose $F_t = \Delta y_t$. Now if Δy_t had a unit root, then Δy_t would have no predictive power for the event $1(\Delta y_{t+1} - \Delta y_t < 0)$, but if it was white noise, then there is quite a bit. For the US regressing $1(\Delta y_{t+1} - \Delta y_t < 0)$ against Δy_t gives an R^2 of .24.

9.5 Conclusion

In response to the widespread criticism that macroeconomists failed to predict the global recession coming from the global financial crisis, we look at whether recessions can be predicted. An emerging literature suggests that there are variables that would have enabled one to do so. It is argued in the chapter that one needs to distinguish between predicting the onset of a recession and predicting being in a recession, and that the literature is concentrating on the latter. Looking at whether it is possible to predict the onset of a recession is the same as predicting a peak in activity, and we show that this can be bounded by the probability of getting a negative growth rate in activity for the first period of the recession. Using this as a vehicle of analysis, simple linear and nonlinear models are found to fail to capture the negative growth. The results suggest that it will be very hard to predict a recession before it happens. Moreover, the analysis of the chapter shows that prediction of a turning point requires the prediction of *future* shocks to the economy, and that will be a difficult task. A method is given for assessing whether fitted macromodels can do this. Finally, we looked at some proposals in the literature that involved the prediction of what is termed a recession-derived indicator. Prediction of this event seems to be much more successful, but the increased probability is an artifact of how the indicators are formed.

References

AHKING, F. W. (2013) "Measuring U.S. Business Cycles: A Comparison of Two Methods and Two Indicators of Economic Activities," *Working Paper 2013-10*, Dept. of Economics, University of Connecticut.

ANDERSON, H. M. AND VAHID, F. (2001) "Predicting the Probability of a Recession with Non-linear Autoregressive Leading Indicator Models," *Macroeconomic Dynamics*, 59, 482-505.

ANDERSON, T. W. AND RUBIN, H. (1949) "Estimation of the Parameters of a Single Equation in a Complete System of Stochastic Equations," *Annals of Mathematical Statistics*, 20, 46-63.

ANDREWS, D. (2001) "Testing When a Parameter Is on the Boundary of the Maintained Hypothesis," *Econometrica*, 69, 683-734.

ARNOLD, L. G. (2002) *Business Cycle Theory*, Oxford University Press, Oxford.

ARTIS, M. J., KONTOLEMIS, Z. G., AND OSBORN, D. R. (1997) "Business Cycles for G7 and European Countries." *Journal of Business*, 70, 249-79.

ARTIS, M. J. AND ZHANG, W. (1997) "International Business Cycles and the ERM," *International Journal of Finance and Economics*, 2(1), 1-16.

ARTIS, M. J., MARCELLINO, M. G., AND PROIETTI, T. (2004) "Dating the Euro Area Business Cycle: A Methodological Contribution with an Application to the Euro Area," *Oxford Bulletin of Economics and Statistics*, 66, 537-65.

ARTIS, M. J., KROLZIG, H.-M., AND TORO, J. (2004) "The European Business Cycle," *Oxford Economic Papers*, 56, 1-44.

BACKUS, D. K., KEHOE, P. J., AND KYDLAND, F. (1992) "International Real Business Cycles," *Journal of Political Economy*, 100, 745-75.

BENES, J., CLINTON, K., GARCIA-SALTOS, R., JOHNSON, M., LAXTON, D., MANCHEV, P., AND MATHESON, T. (2010) "Estimating Potential Output with a Multivariate Filter," *IMF Working Paper* 10/285.

BENGOECHEA, P., CAMACHO, M., AND PEREZ-QUIROS, G. (2006) "A Useful Tool to Identify Recessions in the Euro Area," *International Journal of Forecasting*, 22, 735-49.

BERNANKE, B. S., GERTLER, M., AND GILCHRIST, S. (1999) "The Financial Accelerator in a Quantitative Business Cycle Framework," in J.B. Taylor and M. Woodford, (eds.) *Handbook of Macroeconomics*, vol 1, Elsevier Science, Amsterdam, 1341-93.

BIERENS, H. J. (2001) "Complex Unit Roots and Business Cycles: Are They Real?," *Econometric Theory*, 17, 962-83.

BILLIO, M. AND CASARIN, R. (2010) "Beta Autoregressive Transition Markov-Switching Models for Business Cycle Analysis," *6th Colloquium on Modern Tools for Business Cycle Analysis: The Lessons from Global Economic Crisis*, Eurostat, Luxembourg.

BILLIO, M., CASARINA, R., RAVAZZOLO, F., AND VAN DIJK, H. K. (2012) "Combination Schemes for Turning Point Predictions," *Quarterly Review of Economics and Finance*, 52, 402-12.

BILLIO, M., FERRARA, L., GUÉGAN, D., AND MAZZI, G. L. (2013) "Evaluation of Regime Switching Models for Real-Time Business Cycle Analysis of the Euro Area," *Journal of Forecasting*, 32, 577–86.

BLANCHARD, O. J. AND FISCHER, S. (1989) *Lectures on Macroeconomics*, MIT Press, Cambridge, MA.

BLOOM, N. (2009) "The Impact of Uncertainty Shocks," *Econometrica*, 77(3), 623–85.

BOEHM, E. AND MOORE, G. H. (1984) "New Economic Indicators for Australia, 1949–84," *Australian Economic Review*, 4th quarter, 34–56.

BOSCH, A. AND RUCH, F. (2012) "An Alternative Business Cycle Dating Procedure for South Africa," *Working Papers 267*, Economic Research Southern Africa.

BORDO, M. D. AND WHEELOCK, D. C. (2006) "When Do Stock Market Booms Occur? The Macroeconomic and Policy Environments of 20th Century Booms," *Federal Reserve Bank of St Louis Working Paper* 2006–051A.

BORDO, M. D. AND WHEELOCK, D. C. (2007) "Stock Market Booms and Monetary Policy in the Twentieth Centrury," *Federal Reserve Bank of St Louis Review*, 89, 1191–22

BREUNIG, R., NAJARIAN, S., AND PAGAN, A. R. (2003) "Specification Testing of Markov Switching Models," *Oxford Bulletin of Economics and Statistics*, 65, 703–25.

BRY, G. AND BOSCHAN, C. (1971) *Cyclical Analysis of Time Series: Selected Procedures and Computer Programs*, NBER, New York.

BURNS, A. F. AND MITCHELL, W. C. (1946) *Measuring Business Cycles*, NBER, New York.

BURNSIDE, C. (1998) "Detrending and Business Cycle Facts," *Journal of Monetary Economics*, 41, 513–32.

CAGGIANO G., CASTELNUOVO, E., AND NODARI, G. (2014) "Uncertainty and Monetary Policy in Good and Bad Times," "Marco Fanno" Working Papers 0188, Università Degli Studi Di Padova.

CAKMAKLI, C., PAAP, R., AND VAN DIJK, D. (2011) "Modelling and Estimation of Synchronization in Multi-State Markov-Switching Models," Tinbergen Institute Discussion Papers 11-002/4.

CAMACHO, M., PEREZ-QUIRÓS, G., AND SAIZ, L. (2008) "Do European Business Cycles Look Like One?," Journal of Economic Dynamics and Control, 32, 2165-90.

CAMACHO, M., PÉREZ-QUIRÓS, G., AND MENDIZÁBAL, H. R. (2011) "High-Growth Recoveries, Inventories and the Great Moderation," Journal of Economic Dynamics and Control, 35, 1322-39.

CANDELON, B., PIPLACK, J., AND STRAETMANS, S. (2008) "On Measuring Synchronization of Bulls and Bears: The Case of East Asia," Journal of Banking and Finance, 32, 1022-35.

CANDELON, B., PIPLACK, J., AND STRAETMANS, S. (2009) "Multivariate Business Cycle Synchronization in Small Samples," Oxford Bulletin of Economics and Statistics, 71, 715-37.

CANDELON, B., DUMITRESCU, E. I., AND HURLIN, C. (2012) "How to Evaluate an Early-Warning System: Toward a Unified Statistical Framework for Assessing Financial Crises Forecasting Methods," IMF Economic Review, 60, 75-113.

CANDELON, B., DUMITRESCU, E. I., AND HURLIN, C. (2014) "Currency Crisis Early Warning Systems: Why They Should Be Dynamic," International Journal of Forecasting, 30, 1016-29.

CANOVA, F. (1993) "Detrending and Turning Points," European Economic Review, 38, 614-23.

CANOVA, F. AND DELLAS, H. (1992) "Trade Interdependence and the International Business Cycle," *Journal of International Economics*, 34, 23–47.

CANOVA, F. AND CICCARELLI, M. (2004) "Forecasting and Turning Point Predictions in a Bayesian Panel VAR Model," *Journal of Econometrics*, 120, 327–59

CARDINALE, J. AND TAYLOR, L. W. (2009) "Economic Cycles: Asymmetries, Persistence, and Synchronization," in T. Mills and K. Patterson (eds.), *Palgrave Handbook of Econometrics: Applied Econometrics*, Palgrave Macmillan, London, vol 2, 308–48.

CASHIN, P. AND MCDERMOTT, C. J. (2002) "Riding on the Sheep's Back: Examining Australia's Dependence on Wool Exports," *Economic Record*, 78, 249–63.

CHANT, D. (1974) "On Asymptotic Tests of Composite Hypotheses in Nonstandard Situations," *Biometrika*, 61, 291–98.

CHAUVET, M. (1998) "An Econometric Characterization of Business Cycle Dynamics with Factor Structure and Regime Switches," *International Economic Review*, 39, 969–96.

CHAUVET, M. AND HAMILTON, J. D. (2005) "Dating Business Cycle Turning Points," *NBER Working Papers 11422*, National Bureau of Economics Research.

CHAUVET, M. AND MORAIS, I. (2010) "Predicting Recessions in Brazil," *6th Colloquium on Modern Tools for Business Cycle Analysis: The Lessons from Global Economic Crisis*, Eurostat, Luxembourg.

CHAUVET, M. AND PIGER, J. M. (2003) "Identifying Business Cycle Turning Points in Real Time," *Federal Reserve Bank of St Louis Review*, March/April, 47–62.

CHAUVET, M. AND POTTER, S. (2005) "Forecasting Recessions Using the Yield Curve," *Journal of Forecasting*, 24, 77–103.

CHEN, S-S. (2005) "Does Monetary Policy Have Asymmetric Effects on Stock Returns," *Journal of Money, Credit and Banking*, 39, 667–88.

CHIB, S. (1996) "Calculating Posterior Distributions and Modal Estimates in Markov Mixture Models", *Journal of Econometrics*, 75, 79–97.

CHO, S. AND MORENO, A. (2006) "A Small-Sample Study of the New Keynesian Macro Model," *Journal of Money, Credit and Banking*, 38, 1461–81.

CHRISTENSEN, I. AND DIB, A. (2008) "The Financial Accelerator in an Estimated New Keynesian Model," *Review of Economic Dynamics* 11(1), 155–78.

CHRISTIANO, L., COSMIN, I., MOTTO, R., AND ROSTAGNO, M. (2011) "Monetary Policy and Stock Market Booms," *Proceedings of the Jackson Hole Economic Policy Symposium*, Federal Reserve Bank of Kansas.

CLAESSENS, S., KOSE, M. A., AND TERRONES, M. E. (2011) "Financial Cycles: What, How, When?," *IMF Working Paper* 11/76.

CLAESSENS, S., KOSE, M. A., AND TERRONES, M. E. (2012) "How Do Business and Financial Cycles Interact?," *Journal of International Economics*, 87, 178–90.

CLEMENTS, F. E. (1923) "Report on a Conference on Cycles," *Geographical Review*, 13, 657–59.

CLEMENTS, M. P. AND KROLZIG, H-M. (2003) "Business Cycle Asymmetries: Characterization and Testing Based on Markov-Switching Autoregressions," *Journal of Business & Economic Statistics*, 21, 196–211.

COMIN, D. AND GERTLER, M. (2006) "Medium-Term Business Cycles," *American Economic Review*, 96, 523–51

COOLEY, T. F. AND HANSEN, G. D. (1995) "Money and the Business Cycle," in T. F. Cooley (ed.), *Frontiers of Business Cycle Research*, Princeton University Press, Princeton, NJ, 175–216

COOLEY, T. F. AND PRESCOTT E. C. (1995) "Economic Growth and Business Cycles," in T. F. Cooley (ed.), *Frontiers of Business Cycle Research*, Princeton University Press, Princeton, NJ, 1–38.

COVER, J. P. (1992) "Asymmetric Effects of Positive and Negative Money-Supply Shocks," *Quarterly Journal of Economics*, 107, 1261–82.

DARNE, O. AND FERRARA, L. (2011) "Identification of Slowdowns and Accelerations for the Euro Area Economy," *Oxford Bulletin of Economics and Statistics*, 73, 335–64.

DESCHAMPS, P. J. (2008) "Comparing Smooth Transition and Markov Switching Autoregressive Models of US Unemployment," *Journal of Applied Econometrics*, 23, 435–62.

DIEBOLD, F. X. (1993) "Are Long Expansions Followed by Short Contractions?," *Business Review, Federal Reserve Bank of Philadelphia*, July, 3–11.

DIEBOLD, F. X. AND RUDEBUSCH, G. D. (1990) "A Nonparametric Investigation of Duration Dependence in the American Business Cycle," *Journal of Political Economy*, 98, 596–616.

DIEBOLD, F. X. AND RUDEBUSCH, G. D. (1996) "Measuring Business Cycles: A Modern Perspective," *Review of Economics and Statistics*, 78, 67–77.

DIEBOLD, F. X., RUDEBUSCH, G. D., AND SICHEL, D. (1993) "Further Evidence on Business-Cycle Duration Dependence," in J. H. Stock and M. W. Watson (eds.), *Business Cycles, Indicators and Forecasting*, NBER, New York, 255–84.

DIEBOLD, F. X., LEE, J.-H., AND WEINBACH, G. (1994) "Regime Switching with Time-Varying Transition Probabilities," in

C. Hargreaves (ed.), *Nonstationary Time Series Analysis and Cointegration*, Oxford University Press, Oxford, 283–302.

DUEKER, M. (1997) "Strengthening the Case for the Yield Curve as a Predictor of U.S. Recessions," *Federal Reserve Bank of St Louis Review*, 79, 41–51.

DUEKER, M. (2005) "Dynamic Forecasts of Qualitative Variables: A Qual VAR Model of U.S. Recessions," *Journal of Business and Economic Statistics*, 23, 96–104.

DURLAND, J. M. AND McCURDY, T. H. (1994) "Duration-Dependent Transitions in a Markov Model of U.S. GNP Growth," *Journal of Business and Economic Statistics* 12(3), 279–88.

ECKSTEIN, O. AND SINAI, A. (1986) "The Mechanisms of the Business Cycle in the Post-War Era," in R. J. Gordon (ed.), *The American Business Cycle, Continuity and Change*, NBER, New York, 39–120.

EICHENGREEN, B., WATSON, M., AND GROSSMAN, R. S. (1985) "Bank Rate Policy Under the Interwar Gold Standard: A Dynamic Probit Model," *Economic Journal*, 95, 725–45.

ENGEL, J., HAUGH, D., AND PAGAN, A. (2005) "Some Methods for Assessing the Need for Non-Linear Models in Business Cycles," *International Journal of Forecasting*, 21, 651–62.

EO, Y. AND KIM, C-J. (2015) "Markov-Switching Models with Evolving Regime-Specific Parameters: Are Post-War Booms or Recessions All Alike?," *Review of Economics and Statistics* (forthcoming).

ESTRELLA, A. AND MISHKIN, F. S. (1998) "Predicting US Recessions: Financial Variables as Leading Indicators," *Review of Economics and Statistics*, 80, 28–61.

FAIR, R. C. (1993) "Estimating Event Probabilities from Macroeconometric Models Using Stochastic Simulation," in

J. H. Stock and M. W. Watson (eds.), *Business Cycles, Indicators and Forecasting*, NBER, University of Chicago Press, Chicago 157–78.

FILARDO, A. J. (1994) "Business Cycle Phases and Their Transitional Dynamics," *Journal of Business and Economic Statistics*, 12, 299–308.

FISHER, I. (1925) "Our Unstable Dollar and the So-Called Business Cycle," *Journal of the American Statistical Association*, 20, 179–202.

FORNI, M., HALLIN, M., LIPPI, M., AND REICHLIN, L. (2001) "Coincident and Leading Indicators for the EURO Area," *Economic Journal*, 101, 62–85.

FRIEDMAN, M. (1993) "The 'Plucking Model' of Business Fluctuations Revisited," *Economic Inquiry* 31, 171–77.

FRISCH, R. (1933) "Propogation and Impulse Problems in Dynamic Economics," in *Economic Essays in Honour of Gustav Cassel* Allen and Unwin, London, 171–205.

FRÜHWIRTH-SCHNATTER, S. (2001) "Markov Chain Monte Carlo Estimation of Classical and Dynamic Switching and Mixture Models," *Journal of the American Statistical Association*, 96, 194–209.

GALÍ, J. (1992) "How Well Does the ISLM Model Fit Postwar U.S. Data?," *Quarterly Journal of Economics*, 107, 709–35.

GALVAO, A. B. C. (2006) "Structural Break Threshold VARs for Predicting US Recessions Using the Spread," *Journal of Applied Econometrics*, 21, 463–87.

GERTLER, M. AND KARADI, P. (2011) "A Model of Unconventional Monetary Policy," *Journal of Monetary Economics*, 58, 17–34.

GERTLER, M. AND KIYOTAKI, N. (2015) "Financial Intermediation and Credit Policy in Business Cycle Analysis."

in B. M. Friedman and M. Woodford (eds.), *Handbook of Monetary Economics, Volume 3*, Elsevier, Amsterdam, 547–99.

GILCHRIST, S., ORTIZ, A., AND ZAKRAJSEK, E. (2009) "Credit Risk and the Macroeconomy: Evidence from an Estimated DSGE Model," Reserve Bank of Australia Research Workshop "Monetary Policy in Open Economies", Sydney (available at http://www.federalreserve.gov/events/conferences/fmmp 2009/papers/Gilchrist-Ortiz-Zakrajsek.pdf).

GRANGER, C. W. J. AND PESARAN, M. H. (2000) "Economic and Statistical Measures of Forecast Accuracy," *Journal of Forecasting*, 19, 537–60.

HAMILTON, J. D. (1989) "A New Approach to the Economic Analysis of Non Stationary Time Series and the Business Cycle," *Econometrica*, 57, 357–84.

HAMILTON, J. D. (1990) "Analysis of Time Series Subject to Changes in Regime," *Journal of Econometrics*, 45, 39–70.

HAMILTON, J. D. (2011) "Calling Recessions in Real Time," *International Journal of Forecasting*, 27, 1006–26.

HARDING, D. (2004) "Non-parametric Turning Point Detection, Dating Rules and the Construction of the Euro-zone Chronology," in G. L. Mazzi and G. Savio (eds.), *Monographs of Official Statistics: Statistical Methods and Business Cycle Analysis of the Euro Zone*, Eurostat, 122–46.

HARDING, D. (2010a) "Detecting and Forecasting Business Cycle Turning Points," *6th Colloquium on Modern Tools for Business Cycle Analysis: The Lessons from Global Economic Crisis*, Eurostat, Luxembourg.

HARDING, D. (2010b) "Imposing and Testing Monotonicity in Generalized Dynamic Categorical Models of the Business Cycle," presented at the 15th Australasian Macroeconomics Workshop, Wellington, New Zealand.

HARDING, D. (2011) "The Specification and Estimation of Qual-VARS," seminar, La Trobe University, July.

HARDING, D. (2014) "The Econometric Analysis of Recurrent Events Identified by Algorithms", presented at Tinbergen Workshop on the Econometric Analysis of Recurrent Events in Maroeconomics and Finance, Erasmus University, June 13.

HARDING, D. AND PAGAN, A. R. (2002) "Dissecting the Cycle: A Methodological Investigation," *Journal of Monetary Economics*, 49, 365–81.

HARDING, D. AND PAGAN, A. R. (2003) "A Comparison of Two Business Cycle Dating Methods," *Journal of Economic Dynamics and Control*, 27, 1681–90.

HARDING, D. AND PAGAN, A. R. (2006) "Synchronization of Cycles," *Journal of Econometrics*, 132, 59–79.

HARDING, D. AND PAGAN, A. R. (2010) "Can We Predict Recessions?," *6th Colloquium on Modern Tools for Business Cycle Analysis*: The Lessons from Global Economic Crisis, Eurostat, Luxembourg, September.

HARDING, D. AND PAGAN, A. R. (2011) "An Econometric Analysis of Some Models of Constructed Binary Random Variables," *Journal of Business and Economic Statistics*, 29, 86–95.

HARVEY, A. C. AND JAEGER, A. (1993) "Detrending, Stylized Facts and the Business Cycle," *Journal of Applied Econometrics*, 8, 231–47.

HODRICK, R. AND PRESCOTT, E. C. (1997) "Postwar U.S. Business Cycles: An Empirical Investigation," *Journal of Money, Credit and Banking*, 29, 1–16.

HOROWITZ, J. (2001) "The Bootstrap in Econometrics," in J. J. Heckman and E. E. Leamer (eds.), *Handbook of Econometrics*, volume 5, North-Holland-Elsevier, Amsterdam, 3159–228.

IBBOTSON, R. G. AND JAFFEE, J. J. (1975) "'Hot Issue' Markets," *Journal of Finance*, 30, 1027–42.

IACOVIELLO, M. AND NERI, S. (2010) "Housing Market Spillovers: Evidence from an Estimated DSGE Model," *American Economic Journal: Macroeconomics*, 2, 125–64.

IIBOSHI, H. (2007) "Duration Dependence of the Business Cycle in Japan: A Bayesian Analysis of Extended Markov Switching Model," *Japan and the World Economy*, 19, 86–111.

International Monetary Fund (2009) "World Economic Outlook—Crisis and Recovery," *World Economic and Financial Surveys*. IMF, Washington DC.

KAISER, R. AND MARAVALL, A. (2001) "Measuring Business Cycles in Economic Time Series," *Lecture Notes in Statistics 154*, Springer, New York.

KAUFMANN, S. (2010) "Dating and Forecasting Turning Points by Bayesian Clustering with Dynamic Structure: A Suggestion with an Application to Austrian Data," *Journal of Applied Econometrics*, 23, 309–44.

KAUPPI, H. AND SAIKKONEN, P. (2008) "Predicting US Recessions with Dynamic Binary Response Variables," *Review of Economics and Statistics*, 90, 777–91.

KEDEM, B. (1980) *Binary Time Series*, Marcel Dekker, New York.

KIEFER, N. M. (1978) "Discrete Parameter Variation: Efficient Estimation of a Switching Regression Model," *Econometrica*, 46, 427–34.

KILIAN, L. (1998) "Small Sample Confidence Intervals for Impulse Response Functions," *Review of Economics and Statistics*, 80, 218–30.

KIM, C-J. AND NELSON, C. R. (1998) "Business Cycle Turning Points, a New Coincident Index, AND Tests of Duration Dependence Based on a Dynamic Factor Model With Regime Switching," *Review of Economics and Statistics*, 80, 188–201.

KROLZIG, H-M. AND TORO, J. (2004) "Classical and Modern Business Cycle Measurement: The European Case", *Spanish Economic Review*, 1–21.

LIU, Z., WANG, P., AND ZHA, T. (2009) "Do Credit Constraints Amplify Macroeconomic Fluctuations?," *Reserve Bank of Australia Research Workshop on Monetary Policy in Open Economies*, Sydney.

LIU, Z., WAGGONER, D. F., AND ZHA, T. (2011) "Sources of Macroeconomic Fluctuations: A Regime-Switching DSGE Approach," *Quantitative Economics*, 2, 251–301.

LUNDE, A. AND TIMMERMANN, A. (2004) "Duration Dependence in Stock Prices: An Analysis of Bull and Bear Markets," *Journal of Business and Economic Statistics*, 22, 253–73.

MACCINI, L. AND PAGAN, A. R. (2013) "Inventories, Fluctuations and the Goods Sector Cycle," *Macro-economic Dynamics*, 17, 89–122.

MAHEU, J. AND McCURDY, T. (2000) "Identifying Bull and Bear Markets," *Journal of Business and Economic Statistics*, 18, 100–112.

MAZUREK, J. AND MIELCOVÁ, E. (2013) "The Evaluation of Economic Recession Magnitude: Introduction and Application," *Prague Economic Papers*, 2, 185–205.

McQUEEN, G. AND THORLEY, S. (1993) "Asymmetric Business Cycle Turning Points," *Journal of Monetary Economics*, 31, 341–62.

MINTZ, I. (1969) "Dating Post-War Business Cycles: Methods and their Application to Western Germany 1950-1967." *NBER Occasional Paper* 107.

MITCHELL, W. C. (1913) *Business Cycles*, University of California Press, Berkeley.

MITCHELL, W. C. (1927) *Business Cycles: The Problem and the Setting*, National Bureau of Economic Research, New York.

MORLEY, J., PIGER, J., AND TIEN P-L. (2013) "Are Non-Linear Dynamics a Proxy for Multivariate Information?," *Studies in Non-linear Dynamics and Econometrics*, 17, 483-98.

MUDAMBI, R. AND TAYLOR, L. W. (1995) "Some Nonparametric Tests for Duration Dependence," *Journal of Applied Statistics*, 22, 163-77.

NEFTCI, S. N. (1984) "Are Economic Times Series Asymmetric over the Business Cycle," *Journal of Political Economy*, 92, 307-28.

NEWEY, W. K. (1984) "A Method of Moments Interpretation of Sequential Estimators," *Economics Letters*, 14, 201-6.

NEWEY, W. K. AND WEST, K. (1994) "Automatic Lag Selection in Covariance Matrix Estimation," *Review of Economic Studies*, 61, 631-53.

NG, S. (2014) "Viewpoint: Boosting Recessions," *Canadian Journal of Economics*, 47, 1-34.

OHN, J. L., TAYLOR, L. W., AND PAGAN, A. (2004) "Testing for Duration Dependence in Economic Cycles," *Econometrics Journal*, 7, 528-49.

PAGAN, A. R. AND SOSSOUNOV, K. (2003) "A Simple Framework for Analyzing Bull and Bear Markets," *Journal of Applied Econometrics*, 18, 23-46.

PAGAN, A. R. AND ROBINSON, T. (2014) "Methods for Assessing the Impact of Financial Effects on Business Cycles in Macroeconometric Models," *Journal of Macroeconomics*, 41, 94–106.

PERLIN, M. (2012) "MS_Regress—A Package for Markov Regime Switching Models in Matlab", MATLAB Central, http://www.mathworks.com/matlabcentral/fileexchange/authors/21596.

REINHART, C. M. AND ROGOFF, K. S. (2014) "This Time is Different: A Panoramic View of Eight Centuries of Financial Crises," *Annals of Economics and Finance*, 15, 1065–88.

SARGENT, T. J. (1979) *Macroeconomic Theory* Academic Press, New York.

SICHEL, D. (1991) "Business Cycle Duration Dependence: A Parametric Approach," *Review of Economics and Statistics*, 73, 254–60.

SICHEL, D. E. (1993) "Business Cycle Asymmetry," *Economic Inquiry*, 31, 224–36.

SICHEL, D. E. (1994) "Inventories and the Three Phases of the Business Cycle," *Journal of Business and Economic Statistics*, 12, 269–78.

SILIVERSTOVS, B. (2013) "Dating Business Cycles in Historical Perspective: Evidence for Switzerland," *Jahrbücher für Nationalö konomie und Statistik*, 233(5), 661–79.

SMETS, F. AND WOUTERS, R. (2007) "Shocks and Frictions in US Business Cycles: A Bayesian DSGE Approach," *American Economic Review*, 97, 586–606.

SMITH, P. A. AND SUMMERS, P. M. (2004) "Identification and Normalization in Markov Switching Models of 'Business Cycles,'" *Research Working Paper 04-09* Federal Reserve Bank of Kansas City.

SNIDERMAN, M. S. (2010) "Interview with Anil K Kashyap," *Forefront-Federal Reserve Bank of Cleveland.*

SOWELL, F. (1996) "Optimal Tests for Parameter Instability in the Generalized Method of Moments Framework," *Econometrica*, 64, 1085–108.

STARTZ, R. (2008) "Binomial Autoregressive Moving Average Processes with an Application to U.S. Recessions," *Journal of Business and Economic Statistics*, 26, 1–8.

STEPHENS, M. (2000) "Dealing with Label Switching in Mixture Models," *Journal of the Royal Statistical Society*, Series B, 62, 795–809.

STOCK, J. H. AND WATSON, M. W. (1991) "A Probability Model of the Coincident Economic Indicators," in K. Lahiri and G. H. Moore (eds.), *Leading Economic Indicators: New Approaches and Forecasting Records*, Cambridge University Press, Cambridge, 63–90.

STOCK, J. H. AND WATSON, M. W. (1999) "Business Cycle Fluctuations in US Macroeconomic Time Series," in J. B. Taylor and M. Woodford (eds.), *Handbook of Macroeconomics, Volume 1*, Elsevier Science, Amsterdam, 3–64.

STOCK, J. H. AND WATSON, M. W. (2010) "Indicators for Dating Business Cycles: Cross-History Selection and Comparisons," *American Economic Review*, Papers and Proceedings, 100, 16–19.

STOCK, J. H. AND WATSON, M. W. (2014) "Estimating Turning Points Using Large Data Sets," *Journal of Econometrics*, 178, 368–81.

THORP, W. (1926) *Business Annals*, National Bureau of Economic Research, New York.

VAN DIJK D. AND FRANSES, P. H. (1999) "Modelling Multiple Regimes in the Business Cycle," *Macroeconomic Dynamics*, 3, 311–40.

WALLIS, K. F. (1977) "Multiple Time Series and the Final Form of Econometric Models," *Econometrica*, 45, 1481–97.

WIELAND, V., CWIK, T., MÜLLER, G. J., SCHMIDT, S., AND WOLTERS, M. (2012) "A New Comparative Approach to Macroeconomic Modeling and Policy Analysis," *Journal of Economic Behavior and Organization*, 83, 523–41.

WRIGHT, J. H. (2006) "The Yield Curve and Predicting Recessions," *Finance and Economics Discussion Paper 2006-7* Board of Governors of the Federal Reserve.

ZARNOWITZ, V. AND OZYILDIRIM, A. (2006) "Time Series Decomposition and Measurement of Business Cycles, Trends and Growth Cycles," *Journal of Monetary Economics*, 53, 1717–39.

ZELLNER, A. AND PALM, F. (1974) "Time Series Analysis and Simultaneous Equation Econometric Models," *Journal of Econometrics*, 2, 17–54.

Index